THE · COMPLETE · HOME
DECORATOR

THE · COMPLETE · HOME
DECORATOR

Caroline Clifton-Mogg, Jane Lott, Gilly Love,
Lorrie Mack, Jeremy Myerson, Andrea Spencer

FOREWORD BY ROBIN GUILD

Conran Octopus

First published in 1991 by
Conran Octopus Limited
37 Shelton Street
London WC2H 9HN

This paperback edition published in 1993 by Conran Octopus Limited
Reprinted in 1995, 1996

British Library Cataloguing in Publication Data
The complete home decorator.
1. Residences. Interiors. Decorating
I. Clifton-Mogg, Caroline
643.7
ISBN 1-85029-823-8

Typeset by SX Composing Limited

Printed and bound in Hong Kong

CONTENTS

FOREWORD

Every room should reflect, either directly or obliquely, the kind of person you are. There aren't any rules when it comes to individuality – except that it's important to be honest; if you create an artificial 'personality' for a room, you will feel an uncomfortable fraud every time you enter it.

After more than twenty-five years of working in all fields of interior design, I have come to believe that an interior designer should provide you with the environment you want by stimulating *you* to form personal decorating ideas.

The best ideas – the ideas that matter most, the ideas you cherish – are always the ideas you have yourself.

The Complete Home Decorator addresses itself to the designer in you. It is intended to set in motion the wheels of that exciting, intuitive process of self-discovery. It's the first link in a chain of thought which will end in many creative ideas.

That's why this is not a book of answers – it's a book of suggestions and possible solutions. It will provoke you to ask yourself questions. It is about your home, not about glossy homes that others live in. It is inspirational and informative. It is also practical, with chapters on hard-wearing flooring, clever storage, soft furnishings, inspirational paint finishes and lighting to change your focus of attention.

This is a book about ideas. The best ideas are yet to come. They are the ones you are about to have.

Paint is used creatively and with a sense of humour in this highly individual kitchen/dining room. The blue and red triangular edges of the table lead the eye up to the yellow inverted triangular edges of the folding screen via the mock dado rail. Running along all the walls and painted in the same colours as the table edges, the rail serves to lower the height of the ceiling and allows the walls either side to be painted in different shades – the lower section in a gloss buttermilk, the upper colour-washed in a citrus yellow. The theme of blue and yellow is continued through into the hallway, where the stairs are painted with a marbled finish. A seal of varnish protects them against wear and tear. The whole effect is one of individuality and light, and illustrates that paint is much more than just a cheap and easy way to decorate your home.

POWERFUL PAINT AND WALLPAPER

Paint comes in a huge range of quality and price. Always opt for the best you can afford: cheap paint is a false economy, for it covers badly and you will end up needing more than you originally budgeted for.

Types of paint

Most domestic paint consists of particles of pigment dispersed in a medium. The medium, which can be either oil or water, gives the paint certain fundamental characteristics, determining how it is thinned, its ease of application and drying time. Never mix the two types when wet – they are incompatible.

Oil-based: These paints are marginally more expensive than their water-based counterparts. They have a pungent odour, are relatively slow-drying and splashes may be difficult to remove. The solvent is white spirit. They can be applied over any painted surface that is dry, clean and grease-free. It is advisable to sand eggshell or gloss finishes lightly to provide a key for the next coat of paint.

Water-based: Commonly known as emulsion, water-based paints are popular for home decoration. Quick-drying, the solvent is water, which also makes clearing up easier. Ideally, they should be applied over water-based ground coats. If they are used over oil-based grounds, the surface must be clean, dry and grease-free.

Texture

Both main types of paint are available in a variety of finishes: matt, mid-sheen and gloss. Matt is best for large, flat areas, although if the surface is free of imperfections, mid-sheen can give a lustrous look. Gloss has traditionally been a popular choice for woodwork but it can look sticky and overstated; mid-sheen is a more elegant treatment.

Thinning

As a rule two thin coats are better than one thick one, especially if the first coat is sanded down. Never thin non-drip paints. The thinner the paint, the faster it will dry – and the further it will go – but opacity will be sacrificed. When thinning opaque paints, it is important to follow the manufacturer's instructions. Thinning is one of the ways you create glazes and washes, which are central to most special paint techniques; in this case the paint is diluted to a considerable extent.

Tinting

Although modern colour ranges are fairly extensive, tinting may be the only way to get the exact shade you require. Tinters, either oil-based artist's oils or water-based artist's gouache, come in a vast range of colours which can be mixed or used on their own.

First, dissolve the tinter in a small amount of the appropriate solvent. Then, stirring continuously, add the tinter little by little to a base of white paint, or to a coloured paint if that is nearer to the shade you are trying to achieve. (Never use non-drip paints.) Experiment with different tints and amounts – but remember to note which you used and the quantities when you finally get the result you want.

Tints can be used on their own, suitably thinned, to pick out detail in plasterwork, woodwork or furniture. When thinned to transparency they can be used as colour washes.

Colour has been used to unusual and pleasing effect in this hallway. The vividly painted trompe l'oeil jukebox cupboard, recessed under the stairs, is an unexpected and exciting contrast to the warm and tranquil yellows and browns of the hall and staircase.

GLAZES AND WASHES

To accomplish broken colour techniques it is necessary to have a fundamental grasp of the formulation and application of glazes and washes. To avoid confusing terminology, all oil-based paints thinned to transparency will be referred to as 'glazes', all water-based paints thinned to transparency will be referred to as 'washes'. Colour washing (pages 12-15) does present an exception to this rule. Colour washing can be accomplished by using either oil- or water-based paints, hence it is possible to have an oil-based 'wash'.

Types of glaze
A glaze is a semi-transparent film of oil-based colour applied over an opaque ground. There are two main ways of creating a glaze.

Transparent oil glaze is a product available from most paint suppliers, either clear or tinted. It comes in matt, mid-sheen or gloss textures. It can be applied neat but tends to form a skin which prevents the glaze from drying out. It is best thinned in the ratio one part glaze to one part white spirit. The degree of transparency is a measure of its quality. Quality glazes can be very expensive.

Thinned oil paint glaze: White undercoat, flat oil, or eggshell is thinned with white spirit to achieve the required transparency. A thinning ratio of one part paint to three parts white spirit should be satisfactory.

Other possibilities are a home-made glaze formulated by mixing linseed oil and turpentine in the ratio of one to three; and paint glaze. Paint glaze is produced by mixing either undercoat or flat oil paint with transparent oil glaze in the ratio of one to one, then thinning this mixture with an equal quantity of white spirit.

All glazes can be tinted with artist's oil colours, available from paint suppliers or art shops.

Types of wash
A wash is a semi-transparent film of water-based colour applied over an opaque ground. Washes are made by thinning matt or mid-sheen vinyl emulsions with water, in the ratio one part paint to three parts water, depending on the degree of transparency required. As with all glazes and washes, there is no substitute for experimentation.

All washes can be tinted with artist's gouache colours to produce the required tones.

Textural qualities of glazes and washes
Glazes can be prepared in matt, mid-sheen or gloss textures; washes only in matt or mid-sheen. Gloss tends to be rather obvious and revealing, and is often limited to floors and small areas such as furniture or woodwork. It can produce a truly gorgeous effect, such as that of lacquer, and its boldness should be exploited. Where bold patterns are struck, for example in rag-rolling or combing, gloss or mid-sheen finishes can be used to good effect; but the latter should be avoided when attempting fine techniques such as stippling or dragging, where reflection tends to obscure the delicacy of the surface patterning. Matt textures have the widest application and are the safest bet for the novice.

It must be remembered that the texture of the ground coat is as important as the glaze or wash, since it also contributes to the overall surface finish. Matt and mid-sheen textures tend to be the least obtrusive when used as a ground coat. The most satisfactory and successful combination, in fact the choice of the professional, is to use a mid-sheen textured base with a matt textured glaze or wash.

Suitable base coats for glazes and washes
Before you begin, prepare and undercoat your surface, and mask out surrounding areas (see pages 42-3). For the best results, you should apply sufficient coats of your base colour to achieve an even colour. Remember that two thin coats are better than one thick one. Provided a surface is clean, dry and free of oil and grease, a glaze can be applied to base coats of matt or mid-sheen emulsion, undercoat, flat oil or eggshell.

A wash can also be applied over matt or mid-sheen emulsion, or, in situations where a subtractive technique is employed and it is necessary to keep the wash alive, over an oil-based ground of undercoat or flat oil paint. The drying time of the wash will be considerably extended.

Sealing the surface

Certain surfaces that may be liable to heavy wear – such as doors, window frames, or walls in kitchens or bathrooms – will need a final protective coat to seal them and make them washable. Polyurethane varnish is a versatile modern product available in matt, mid-sheen or gloss. When thinned it provides an adequate protective layer that can enhance the underlying decorative treatment. One to two coats should be applied, waiting five to six hours between coats.

Varnish will alter the colouring of a decorative finish, making it noticeably yellower. A varnished finish will also respond differently to light, and this could have unfortunate consequences in a room hung with pictures, where areas of wall remain unexposed. You can to some extent avoid these problems by using matt varnish only, or you may prefer not to varnish the walls at all in, for example, bedrooms and sitting rooms, where the surfaces are not subject to particularly heavy wear.

Altering the drying rate

The drying rate of paint may need to be altered if the room is very cold and damp or very hot, or if a subtractive technique is used which demands that the surface remain workable for some time. In general, the thinner the paint the quicker it will dry. Water-based paints dry much faster than oil-based paints – so quickly that they are unsuitable for some subtractive techniques.

The drying rate of oil-based paint can be accelerated by adding liquid dryer (1 teaspoon dryer to ½ litre thinned paint). To slow drying down, add boiled linseed oil (1 teaspoon to ½ litre thinned paint), but bear in mind that this will alter the final colours of your finish, making them yellower, as well as giving the surface a sheen.

In the case of water-based paints, adding a small quantity of glycerine can retard the drying time (1 tablespoon glycerine to 1 litre thinned paint). The drying time of a wash can also be extended by applying it to a mid-sheen textured base coat, especially an oil-based one. Matt textured oil paints, such as undercoat or flat oil paint, will have a similar effect.

Broken colour techniques

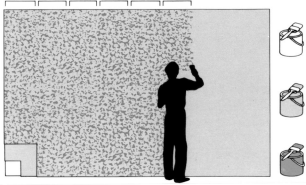

Basic additive technique

Prepare the wall and apply undercoat. When dry, apply a white or coloured opaque ground. Allow to dry. Then prepare a glaze or wash and apply in a broken film so that some of the ground is left uncovered. Where the base coat is covered, it will also be subtly modified.

Basic subtractive technique

This method is best done by two people. Prepare and undercoat the surface, and apply the base coat. Working in vertical strips 60 cm (2 ft) wide, one person applies the glaze or wash while the other distresses it, stopping short 15 cm (6 in.) from the leading, wet, edge.

COLOUR WASHING

Colour washing consists of applying an extremely dilute wash or glaze in a continuous film over a ground colour. This is not true broken colour since the surface is not distressed, but successive washes do progressively modify the base coat, giving a depth and brilliance of colour.

Highly effective in both country-style and town house interiors, colour washing creates a soft, pretty background that lifts a room but does not dominate. Because the paint is so dilute, quite strong shades can be used without running the risk of making the room look too dark. It's also a good way to modify a background colour – a thin, red wash or glaze for example, will add a touch of warmth to a yellow base.

You can use water-based washes or oil-based glazes for this technique, and there is a wide variety of effects you can achieve. Either type of paint, depending on its colour and the degree to which it is thinned, can create a room that is luminous and airy, or rich and sophisticated. The main difference is that oil-based paint is more hard-wearing than water-based, and for this technique probably easier to use. For the purist, a wash or glaze consisting almost entirely of diluted artist's oils or gouache gives a particularly transparent effect. A variation on this technique is to create a series of washes by adding artist's colours to the paint used for the base coat. Start with a neutral colour, add artist's colour to tint and thin with solvent, then wash over the wall. Add another colour and repeat the process. The result will be subtly unified and harmonious. As another adaptation of the colour washing effect, you could also re-create the soft-textured look of distemper (see page 14).

Although in all cases the paint is too insubstantial to be suitable for distressing, water-based washes have an inherently distressed finish, since they always display the marks of the tool used to apply them. This random patterning adds to the general impression of rustic charm.

Oil-based colour washes

For colour washing, dilute the paint (flat oil or undercoat) in the ratio 1:8 or 1:9 paint to white spirit. Drying rates will vary according to temperature and humidity, so if the paint

threatens to be too 'wet', reduce the proportion of white spirit and use the paintbrush itself to move the paint around. If it is impossible to keep a wet edge, decrease the drying rate by adding linseed oil, but remember that this has a yellowing effect on the colour of the glaze.

The application of glazes is a messy business and it is essential to protect against spilling and splashing. It is also advisable to have plenty of clean cloths to hand. These can be used instead of a brush to dab the glaze on to the wall. The glaze must then be brushed out in the direction of natural light. As a rule, thinned paint glaze is messier and more difficult to handle than transparent oil glaze.

The glaze will dry in 24 hours. After this time another coat can be applied, either in the same colour or in a different shade, which can give a rich and lustrous finish.

Water-based colour washes

Dilute matt emulsion in the ratio of 1:9 paint to water. If the day is very hot and the paint is drying too quickly, a small amount of glycerine can be added to slow the drying rate down.

Prepare and paint the surface with your chosen ground colour, and ensure it is clean and grease-free. Avoid drip marks and 'tide lines' by applying the wash with swift, vigorous brush strokes. This will also ensure that you don't linger on one spot too long and begin to dissolve the underlying colour. The wash dries so quickly that brush marks are inevitable, but this fresh, unrefined look can be very pleasing.

After half an hour the wash will be dry and another coat can be applied. It takes at least two coats for the wall really to come to life, and sometimes four or five for the full effect. If you intend to varnish the surface, wait three to four days and then apply two coats of matt clear varnish: this will protect the finish and give a degree of depth.

Pure colour washes

A highly transparent finish can be created by diluting artist's gouache or artist's oils with water or white spirit respectively and applying this over a pale ground. In the case of gouache, a small amount of emulsion should be added to the wash to give it body; in the case of oils, a transparent 'gel' can be added for body.

The colour will richen and deepen with successive applications. Brush the wash on to a dry surface, with quick strokes so that the underlying paint is not removed.

Distemper
Now out of production, distemper was an extremely cheap household paint that could cover a variety of surfaces without too much preparation. Its soft, textured finish made it popular for surfaces that were not perfectly even, or where a quick result was required.

A similar effect today can be achieved by purchasing the ingredients from a trade supplier and mixing them up at home. Although making your own distemper is a protracted business, some people think the effort is worthwhile. (A similar effect can be obtained by applying a wash of flat oil over a trade eggshell base coat.)

Recipe for Distemper

3 kg (1 ⅓ lb) bag whiting, decorator's glue, powder paint

Make the glue according to the manufacturer's instructions, dissolving it in hot water – it should contain alum, a substance which prevents the formation of mould. Leave the glue to cool and set to a jelly. When you are ready to use it, reheat it until it becomes runny.

Half-fill a small bucket with cold water and pour in the whiting until it rises above the surface. Allow to soak for one hour and then stir.

Dissolve the powder colour in cold water and add it a little at a time to the whiting until you like the shade.

Add the warm, runny glue to the dissolved whiting, stirring thoroughly. If it stiffens, reheat gently. This mixture can now be used as a base coat. For a wash, dilute with water to a milky consistency. Distemper will only keep for two days.

Colour washing

 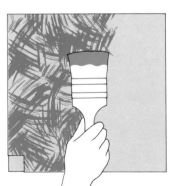

1. Cover a suitably prepared surface with a base colour and allow to dry overnight. Prepare a very dilute glaze or wash in the required colour.

2. Brush on the glaze or wash, working quite quickly to avoid drips; you can go over it with a dry brush. Apply several coats to achieve a rich, deep finish.

Left: The mirrors in this hallway do much to give an illusion of space, and the paint techniques also play their part well, suggesting the effect of stone. The lower half of the walls are colour washed: each successive wash was created by adding solvent and artists' oils in greys and greens to the original, grey, base colour. Above, grey was ragged on.

Below: Walls the intensity and richness of silk were created here by washing oil-based red glaze over a base coat of pink. The brush strokes are clearly evident, and give depth and texture to the effect. To give a sheen to the surface, a transparent glaze was used as the final coat. It is an extravagantly bold finish, deceptively easy to achieve.

SPONGING

Sponging is the easiest and most adaptable of the true broken colour techniques. It can be either an additive technique – 'sponging on' – or a subtractive one – 'sponging off'. As the term implies, it involves the use of a sponge, either to dab on a broken layer of colour or to distress a wet surface.

Either oil-based or water-based paint can be used. Emulsion will give a soft effect; oil is crisper and cleaner. Texture and transparency can be varied too; the sponge wash or glaze can be shiny or matt, opaque or translucent, depending on the type of paint and the degree of dilution.

All of these variables add up to a highly versatile finish. Sponging can range from the subtle and sophisticated to the outrageously obvious; sponging off gives the softest effect. The coherence of sponging techniques means that they are useful for camouflaging unsightly features such as radiators and pipes or for softening unfortunate proportions. But they can also be used in a purely decorative way on vases, cabinets and tables – in fact on any suitably prepared surface.

Experiment with different colour combinations before you begin. Lining paper provides a cheap medium for investigating colours and textures and for practising sponging techniques. Just two colours can be very effective; more than three can become confused and muddy without careful handling. Where more than two colours are used, the lighter shades should be applied last and the darker ones used sparingly.

Which colours you use will depend on your decorative scheme but, in general, the closer the colours are in tone and in shade, the more subtle and sophisticated the effect will be. But don't be afraid to try something more daring. A dilute glaze or wash of a bright colour over white can look very fresh without being brash; for a bolder look, try mixing primaries or accenting two closer shades with a complementary colour.

Sponging on
Apply two coats of the base colour on top of a suitably prepared surface. Allow to dry overnight.

Prepare the sponge by wetting it with water and wringing it out thoroughly. Place the glaze in a sloping tray and dip the

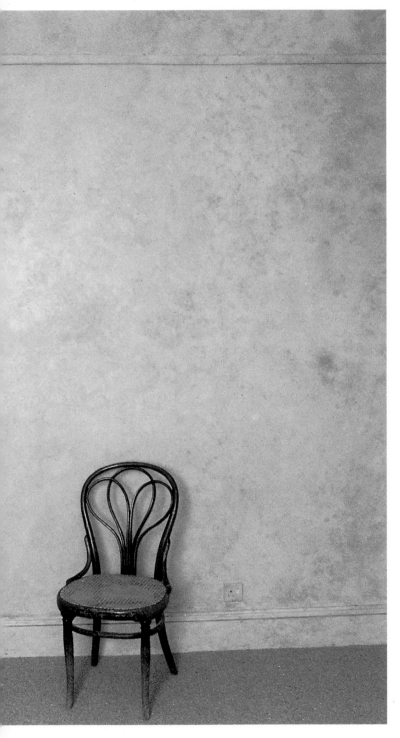

Left: Sponging on can be a very positive treatment, as this example shows. The technique makes good camouflage for pipes and electrical sockets, and for imperfections in the plaster.

Top: A jardiniere is stencilled over an evenly sponged wall to make a focus for a turn in the stairs. The sponging was in two coats over white emulsion, the second lighter than the first.

Below: Paint effects can exist harmoniously alongside wallpaper. Here a radiator has been camouflaged by sponging on three different colours to match the speckled paper.

sponge into it, removing the excess on the side of the tray. Dab the sponge on to paper until you achieve the right sort of print. The sponge should be almost dry so that the print shows a distinct texture. If the sponge is too wet, the texture will be blurry and the paint will tend to run down the wall.

Work quickly and systematically over the surface, trying for a consistent density. Wring the sponge out from time to time to prevent a build-up of colour obscuring the texture. If you are going to apply two glazes or washes, allow more of the ground colour to show through when applying the first coat. Leave the first glaze or wash to dry overnight before applying the second.

Sponging off

In the same way as for sponging on, a coloured ground is prepared and allowed to dry, then a coloured glaze is applied all over the surface. While it is still wet and workable, the surface is distressed with a wet or dry sponge to remove patches of glaze.

The main problem with this technique is the drying time of the glaze or wash. If you use water-based paints, you will need a friend to help you – it's often a race against time, with one person applying the wash and the other distressing the surface. The drying time can be slowed down by adding linseed oil to oil-based paint or glycerine to water-based paint. If the ground coat is mid-sheen, the glaze or wash is also easier to sponge off. Using water-based paint over an oil-based undercoat will also extend the drying time and enable a more consistent pattern to be achieved.

Work in vertical strips about 60 cm (2 feet) wide, distressing all but 15 cm (6 in.) of the leading edge so that the next section can be blended in without losing continuity of pattern. While one person is distressing, the next strip of glaze can be applied by the other. If you get a build-up of colour on the sponge, wait until you reach a corner before washing it out in solvent, and then brush a little paint on to the sponge before starting again: you want to avoid getting a new 'print' in the middle of a wall.

Sponging on

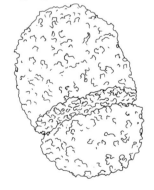 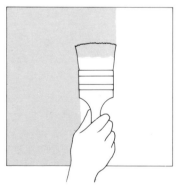  

It is preferable to use a marine or 'natural' sponge rather than a synthetic one. Cut off a section, or use all the sponge: choose an interesting plane.

1. Cover a suitably prepared surface with two coats of base colour. Allow to dry overnight. Prepare the glaze or wash by tinting and diluting.

2. Soak sponge in water and wring dry. Dip it into paint, testing print on paper. Sponge quickly and evenly, and clean the sponge only at a corner.

3. For more than one colour, make the first application fairly sparse. Overlap the second glaze or wash. Use a different sponge for each colour.

Used creatively, colour contributes immeasurably to the richness of a sponged surface. Here shades of pale blue and cream have been sponged over a pale basecoat to give the room a light, fresh and airy feel. The blues and creams on the walls provide just the right backdrop for the striking silhouette of flowers.

Sponging off

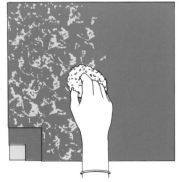

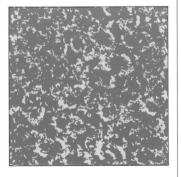

1. Cover a prepared surface with two coats of base colour. Since this technique involves working a wet glaze or wash, enlist a friend's help.

2. Prepare the glaze or wash. One person applies this in a continuous film with a brush, working in strips about 60 cm (2 ft) wide.

3. While the glaze is still wet, the other person distresses it with a sponge, working up to 15 cm (6 in.) of the leading, wet, edge.

4. Wring out sponge regularly to prevent build-up of paint on the sponge. Use a different sponge for each colour to avoid mixing shades.

RAGGING

Ragging is the general term for a whole family of techniques in which a rag or cloth is used to distress the surface. 'Ragging on' is an additive method where the colour is dabbed on; 'ragging off' is a subtractive method where the colour is dabbed off. The texture of the cloth and the type of dabbing action together produce a distinctive pattern.

The most dramatic type of ragging, however, is a version known as 'rag-rolling'. Here a bunched rag is rolled down over the surface, either adding or lifting off patches of glaze to create a dense texture remarkably similar in appearance to crushed velvet. Whereas the other ragging methods are quite static in effect, rag-rolling displays not so much the texture of the cloth as a sense of movement.

Ragging is a good way of camouflaging unsightly pipes or radiators or covering up imperfections in a surface. The technique is also versatile enough for decorating on a much smaller scale, for accentuating furniture, woodwork, vases and fireplaces. It is not a good idea, however, to rag everything in sight – the effect can easily become overpowering, so err on the side of restraint. Ragging on is probably the best way of decorating objects. Since the physical action of rolling demands a flat expanse, rag-rolling is unsuitable for surfaces with tight contours.

Choice of cloth adds greatly to the scope of these techniques. There are no hard and fast rules, but in general the crisper the fabric, the more defined the pattern. For a subtle, more evocative look, use a soft cloth with a close weave. Hessian, chamois, net, dishcloths and even vests all produce interesting textures – experiment with a range of rags to identify the effect you're seeking. When using the rag to remove the glaze or wash, the texture will also vary according to whether the cloth is used dry or wetted with water. Dry cloths produce a clearer pattern.

Whichever cloth you use, however, the overall effect can easily become oppressive if colours are not restrained. It's best to play safe and opt for pastel or neutral shades, fairly close in tone, especially if you're ragging a large area. Even off-white ragged over a white ground can be striking, for the patterning is itself emphatic enough.

Far left: Ragging can produce a very uniform effect, which many find overpowering on a large area. One answer is to apply the glaze in patches, as in this hallway. Blue has been ragged over white, but not consistently over the entire surface. The result successfully avoids monotony.

Left: Another answer to the same problem is to contain ragging within panels. Here the front room of a town house has been transformed into a sophisticated, elegant drawing room by painting the walls with trompe l'oeil panelling, achieved with the dragging technique (pages 24-7). Inside the panels a yellow glaze has been ragged off with a very wet rag, which produces this soft, rather diffused effect.

Using the cloth

For ragging on or off, a rhythmic, systematic dabbing action is used to achieve uniform coverage. To prevent the finish from becoming mechanical and repetitive, adjust the cloth regularly and vary the wrist action.

For rag-rolling, it is crucial to vary the rolling action to prevent the surface becoming too insistent. Rearrange the cloth, apply different amounts of pressure and change the rolling direction.

Cloths should be abandoned once they have become sodden with glaze, so ensure you have a plentiful supply before you begin. It is not advisable to change the texture of the cloth half-way through. All cloths should be clean, lint-free and dye-fixed. It is essential to dispose of used rags carefully because of the fire hazard.

Types of paint

Ragging can be successfully achieved using either oil- or water-based paints, depending on the look you want to obtain. For subtractive techniques, oil-based paints are preferable since the surface will remain workable for longer. Rolling off, however, is relatively quick to do so the drying time is less critical.

The drying time of water-based paints can be extended by adding a small amount of glycerine to the paint, by not thinning the paint or by applying it over a silk or mid-sheen base coat.

Another method is, contrary to normal procedure, to apply water-based paint over an oil-based ground – undercoat or flat oil, for example. This base coat must be clean, dry and degreased. Experiment to arrive at the right consistency for the top coat – if it is too thin it will run off.

Ragging or rolling on

Over a prepared surface, apply a base coat in the required shade with a roller or brush. Thin the glaze or wash to the required consistency.

Dip the cloth in the tray, removing the excess on the side, and test on paper until you get the print you want. For ragging

Ragging on

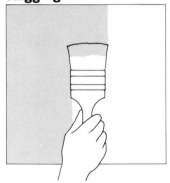

1. Paint on a base coat. Thin glaze or wash to required consistency. Dip cloth in paint and test print on paper.

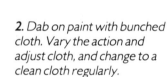

2. Dab on paint with bunched cloth. Vary the action and adjust cloth, and change to a clean cloth regularly.

Ragging off

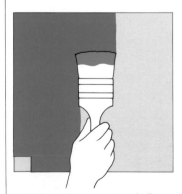

1. Paint on base coat and allow to dry overnight. One person then applies the glaze or wash, working in vertical strips about 60cm (2ft) wide.

2. While the paint is still wet, the other person distresses it with a wet or dry cloth, stopping short 15 cm (6 in.) from the edge.

Rag-rolling on

1. Apply base coat. Prepare glaze or wash. Roll cloth into a sausage shape and soak in glaze or wash.

2. Roll the cloth down over the surface. To avoid a mechanical texture, change direction and adjust cloth.

Rag-rolling off

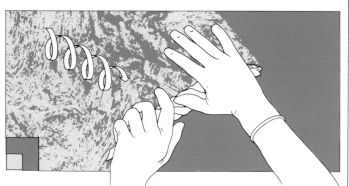

1. Apply a base coat and allow to dry overnight. Then one person applies a glaze or wash with a brush, working in vertical strips.

2. While the paint is still wet, the other person rolls the cloth down over the surface to lift off patches of paint. Avoid a mechanical texture.

on, dab the cloth systematically over the surface, adjusting the motion and rebunching the cloth regularly to avoid repetitive patterning. For rag-rolling, roll the cloth up loosely in a sausage shape and roll over the surface slowly and steadily to prevent smudging. Vary the direction and pressure. Change cloths regularly.

Ragging or rolling off

Prepare the ground coat, and apply the glaze or wash in a single film in vertical strips 60 cm (2 feet) wide. Use the cloth, either dry or dipped in solvent if you want a softer effect, to distress the surface, stopping short 15 cm (6 in.) from the leading edge. This margin is distressed when the next strip of top coat is applied. Change cloths regularly.

Exploit the emphatic qualities of rag-rolling to create a rhythmic signature. This sideboard has white rolled over a blue ground:

the vase has blue ragged on to white. In the background the wall is sponged, blue over white, and the skirting dragged.

DRAGGING AND COMBING

Dragging

An elegant, formal treatment, dragging is a subtractive distressing technique in which a fine dry brush is gently dragged through a thin wet glaze to produce a series of parallel lines where the ground colour is exposed. On walls it makes a refined backdrop for a sophisticated interior. It's best, too, on smooth surfaces, since the dragged effect will only exaggerate any imperfections. For this reason, while dragging will enhance a sound, well-proportioned room, it is not a good way to disguise irregularities.

Traditionally, dragging is carried out vertically, making an even texture reminiscent of woven fabric. But by using more than one glaze and distressing horizontally or diagonally, as well as vertically, a whole range of different effects can be created, from an open-weave homespun look to something more akin to shot silk.

Apart from walls, any flat surface can be dragged if it is suitably prepared. Dragging is particularly effective on woodwork, doors and furniture, provided the strokes run in the direction of the wood grain. This is a good way of adding colour without sacrificing the impression of graininess.

A well-established professional technique, dragging does

Far left: Glazes for dragging are usually assumed to be of one colour, but this treatment opens up new possibilities. Over a creamy-yellow background massive zigzag stripes were loosely painted all around the walls, using white paint diluted with solvent and coloured brown, rust and orange with artists' oils. The walls were then dragged, and this subtle, almost Italianate effect was the result.

Left and below: Classical dragging at its best. The pink glaze is peculiarly perfect for this elegant paint effect.

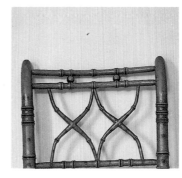

require a degree of expertise. To achieve success you need a steady hand – practising first on small areas like cupboard doors and tables may help. You must also be prepared to spend money on a quality dragging brush – the bristles are flexible enough to avoid a mechanical pinstriped effect. If you can't afford the outlay, wallpaper brushes or jamb brushes make acceptable compromises, although the finish will lack a degree of definition. Dragging, like all subtractive techniques, can be made much easier by enlisting the help of a friend. One person applies the glaze or wash while the other distresses it before it becomes unworkable.

Using oil-based paint

Prepare the surface and apply a base coat in the required colour. Mix the glaze to the right consistency and apply it in vertical strips 60 cm (2 feet) wide, with a 10 cm (4 in.) brush.

Using a dragging brush (or suitable substitute), distress the glaze by dragging through the paint in continuous vertical strokes. As a guide, you can draw vertical lines in blue chalk on the ground coat or suspend a plumb-line from a picture rail. Stop short 15 cm (6 in.) from the leading edge of the glaze, distressing this strip when the next application of glaze has been made.

Using water-based paint

As with all subtractive techniques, washes of emulsion dry too quickly for a consistent finish. The drying time can be slowed by applying the wash over a vinyl silk ground, which will also dry to a slight sheen. The ground could also be flat oil or undercoat, provided it is clean, dry and degreased. A small amount of glycerine added to water-based paint will also retard drying. Do not over-thin the wash or it will run off the surface. The help of a second person makes the distressing of water-based washes considerably easier.

Combing

Combing, a close relative of dragging, is a bold, versatile, subtractive technique that offers considerable scope in its application. The striking patterns you can achieve are particularly suited to decorating floors, where the subtleties of a dragged finish would be lost underfoot.

The characteristics of this finish are a direct function of the distressing tool, the comb. Although you can buy combs in a variety of sizes and materials from paint suppliers or decorators' shops, this is an unnecessary expenditure. Creating a pattern that bears the signature of a comb you have made can be very satisfying.

Tools and techniques

If the room is very high, stop at waist height and then drag upwards from the floor. Stagger the place where you stop and feather the joins. Dragging upwards for 30 cm (12 in.) at the bottom of each strip will prevent a build-up of glaze near the skirting board.

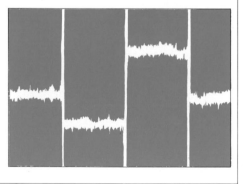

Dragging

Dragging is most easily carried out by two people. Apply a base coat and allow to dry (1). One person paints on a glaze or wash in vertical strips 60 cm (2 ft) wide (2). While this is still wet, the other person distresses the surface by drawing a dry dragging brush down through the paint, stopping short 15 cm (6 in.) from the leading, wet, edge.

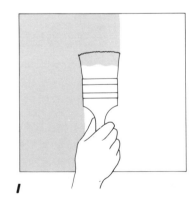

1

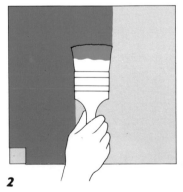

2

3

These kitchen units had a red glaze applied over an off-white base colour, which was then freely distressed with a bought graining comb. The combing technique reveals a lot of the base coat, and in the process a great deal of glaze is displaced: wrapping a rag around the comb will soak up some of this excess, and prevent large deposits of paint at the edges.

The size of the teeth will give the scale of the pattern. The larger the pattern, the bolder the colours can be. In such cases, you will also need to reduce the transparency of the glaze or wash, leaving it more opaque. Combing can never achieve the lightness and refinement of a dragged finish, so it is often better to exploit its directness and forcefulness. Varying the pattern by using different combs can add interest.

Types of paint

With a few exceptions, the combing technique is the same as that of dragging. Most importantly, the undercoat must be substantial enough to withstand abrasion by the comb.

For oil-based paint, the base undercoat should be trade eggshell, which will dry with a slight sheen. For emulsion, use vinyl silk, which also has a sheen finish. These harder surfaces withstand distressing better and allow paint to be more easily moved around on top. When using oil-based paint, there is the added advantage that the top coat will not dry out so quickly, prolonging the distressing time. Apply the glaze in sections that can be easily worked while the glaze is wet.

Protective coats of polyurethane varnish should then be applied. This is very important where the surface will be subject to heavy wear, such as a floor, or walls in kitchens.

Combs

Combs are available commercially from decorators' shops (above) but it is easy and satisfying to make your own (right). Use semi-rigid materials like rubber, hardboard or perspex; experiment by cutting teeth at different intervals and thicknesses.

Combing

Apply a base coat over a suitably prepared surface. When this is dry, apply a glaze or wash, thinned to the required consistency, adjusting the drying time if necessary. While this is still wet, draw the comb down over the surface to create the pattern. If the surface will be exposed to heavy wear, protective coats of polyurethane varnish should then be applied.

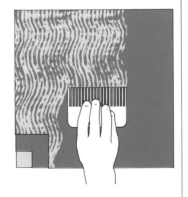

SPATTERING AND CISSING

Spattering

Spattering is a simple additive technique which consists of showering flecks of paint over a uniformly coloured ground. Since there is no one tool to define the method and no formal rules governing the size, colour, density or position of the paint flecks, the scope is vast. The effect can range from a fine misting of colour to a more cavalier treatment where blobs of paint are flung at a surface. It's versatile, too – spattering can be applied to almost any surface, from walls to lamp bases, mirror frames or fireplaces.

The limiting factor is your imagination. Experiment with a range of different techniques and colours on lining paper or a sheet of hardboard. Primary colours over a white ground will give a gay, light-hearted look; subtle differences of tone, such as mauve over grey, are more sophisticated. Where several colours are used, you can set off a couple of close shades like cream and light brown with a sparse application of black. Colour is not the only consideration: contrasting the texture of the paints – for example, spattering matt paint over a mid-sheen or gloss ground – gives you another range of interesting options.

Because this is an additive technique, oil- and water-based paints are equally effective, although the speed at which emulsions dry gives them an advantage when multiple overlaps of colour are required.

Spattering with a brush

Virtually any stiff-bristled brush mounted on a shaft is suitable. A large stencilling brush, with its squared end, is most effective for large surfaces; for detailed work a toothbrush is hard to beat. Release the paint flecks by running your finger over the bristles or by striking the shaft of the brush on a straight edge. Running the brush over fine chicken wire will also give the same effect.

The density and size of the flecks is a function of the paint dilution, the distance from the surface and the force applied to the bristles or shaft of the brush, and prior experimentation is important. This is a messy technique, so take adequate precautions against spilling and splashing.

Safety precautions
To avoid inhaling the spray when spattering with paint atomizers or spray guns, it is essential to wear a mask and goggles. It is also a good idea to keep a window open to allow fumes to escape.

Right: Spattering techniques have been used in this room with great delicacy, so much so that it almost has the stamp of more subtle broken colour effects like sponging. A cheap spray gun was used to spatter pink, cream, grey and a little raspberry paint over a base of blue-grey. The result makes the room quietly inviting and harmonious, and successfully avoids the busy effect that spattering can sometimes produce.

Below: Here blue paint has been spattered very regularly over white, producing a homogeneous effect that is the hallmark of the technique.

Spattering with a spray

For a fine, misted effect, spattering can be carried out using a paint atomizer, a simple instrument available from any model-making shop. A cheap alternative is an ordinary perfume spray. The scale of the tool and delicacy of the spatter means that application is limited to furniture or to picking out fine detail.

For work on a larger scale, you could hire an electric spray gun. Experiment with different nozzles, pressures and paint densities to get the effect you want. It is essential to wear goggles and a mask to avoid inhaling the spray.

Cissing

A variation of spattering is a distressing technique known as cissing. The bristles of a spattering brush are dipped in neat solvent – either water or white spirit, depending on which type of paint is used – and the solvent is then flicked on to a surface glaze or wash. The glaze or wash, which should still be wet and workable, will actually open up, forming pools of diluted colour. The effect can vary from a light, regularly

Using a spray

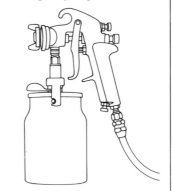

Paint atomizers, available from model-making shops, produce a misted effect. Even cheap ones give a good effect. Perfume sprays are an alternative.

Stencil brush

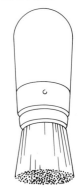

The best tool for spattering and cissing is the square-ended stencil brush, although any stiff-bristled brush with a squared end will do the job efficiently.

Spattering

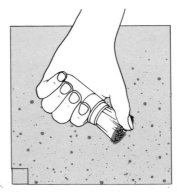

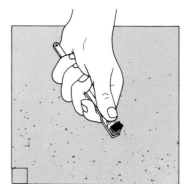

1. Apply a base coat to a suitably prepared surface and allow to dry. Mix up a glaze or wash and experiment with different dilutions to get the effect you want. Dip the squared end of a stencil brush, or similar, into the paint. Release flecks by striking the shaft on a straight edge.

2. An alternative method is to run your thumb over the end of the stencil brush to release the paint. Vary the distance between brush and surface.

3. For really fine results, dip a toothbrush into the paint and draw your thumb over the bristles to release tiny flecks of glaze or wash.

patterned texture reminiscent of porphyry to the random cloudiness often exhibited by marble. With oil-based paint, methylated spirit can be used as an alternative to solvent to create larger 'pools'; an atomizer will provide greater control.

Cissing should always be carried out on horizontal surfaces, otherwise the diluted paint will drip. A clean dry cloth or sponge can be used to control the effect and mop up any excess solvent, and you could also use it to brush out and soften the pools to make an even more blurred finish. Goggles are again recommended protective equipment.

You can achieve a similar effect to cissing without going to the trouble of painting on a base coat and a glaze: there is a proprietary brand of paint called Hammerite which will do the work for you. This is a metallic paint available in a range of colours which, when brushed over a surface, forms itself into a tight, uniform pattern and creates an effect very similar to that of regular cissing (follow the manufacturer's instructions). Used with sensitivity and imagination this can be truly stunning, but as always experiment with it first in case it is too bold for the surface you had in mind.

Spattering just the details in a room can be supremely effective, for the technique often looks its best when carried out with restraint. Mask out surrounding areas with tape and newspaper, and take care not to flick paint outside your chosen area. Here a beam draws the eye towards a mezzanine study, and the heavy black gloss paint on the ladder and balustrade makes an excellent contrast to the fine, understated spattering.

Cissing

Paint on a base coat and allow to dry. Then apply a glaze or wash. While this is still wet, spatter with the appropriate solvent – either water or white spirit. Cissing is easiest on horizontal surfaces: control the effect by mopping up excess dribbles of glaze with a dry cloth.

MARBLING

Marble has always presented a challenge to the craftsman. The cool, serene beauty of this natural stone has long been appreciated, but the high cost and difficulty of transporting and handling the material means that there has always been a demand for decorative simulation.

Marble was originally formed when rivers of molten limestone cooled and solidified under great pressure, a process which gives the stone its stratified crystalline structure. Simulating marble involves suggesting its essential characteristics of translucency, depth, cloudiness and motion, using a combination of broken colour techniques, including ragging, sponging, cissing and spattering.

Inspiration for colour and pattern should be drawn from the tremendous range of shades and textures offered by the natural material. Examining marble fireplaces, tiles and floors will give you some idea of this variety and also suggest ways of applying the technique. Since marble is such a heavy, dense stone, it is particularly suitable for flooring, work surfaces and tiling; avoid applying the technique to such surfaces as ceilings where the real material would never be used.

Using oil-based paint

Achieving translucency and depth: Apply a white or pale base coat of eggshell. Mix up a thin glaze with artist's oils, tinted to a slightly darker shade. A dirty white glaze (with very small amounts of raw umber or black added) over a white base coat will give the effect of the popular white marble.

Apply the glaze with a brush or cloth and rag-roll to expose one-half to two-thirds of the ground (pages 20-3). Soften with a damp or dry sponge or cloth. The glaze can also be rolled on, which gives a slightly sharper pattern. Translucency and depth are achieved by distressing several layers of glaze, each tinted to contrast slightly with the ground colour. Pastels over white are particularly effective.

Achieving cloudiness: While the surface glazes are still workable, a cloudy effect can be achieved by cissing the surface with white spirit (see page 31). This is often known as 'fossilized marbling'. The effect involves spattering flecks of

Opposite, above: A bathroom wall is an obvious candidate for a marbled paint finish. This wall has a strong diagonal accent created by the complicated veining patterns. A white background was ragged over patchily with several glazes, and the veins, in black, red, brown and white, loosely follow this pattern.

Opposite below: Use marbling techniques to create visual witticisms like this dado. Matt black eggshell was used for the background, and white and grey for the veins. The result is both stylized and stylish.

Left: These fake marble slabs are deceptively easy to achieve. The background is a yellow glaze washed over a white ground, and the veins and blocks were painted in a single colour over the top. The result far exceeds the time and effort gone into it: all it requires is a little patience and a straight-edging tool.

solvent randomly over the surface to dissolve the paint glaze into pools of colour. When more than one coloured glaze has been used, the colours merge to form extraordinary patterns and colours. Methylated or white spirit can be used; the former further accentuates the effect. You can control the process to some extent by mopping up excess solvent with a clean dry cloth, but do not attempt cissing on vertical surfaces, for the paint will drip.

To achieve the effect of cloudiness on vertical surfaces, dab with a cloth or sponge, either dry or wetted with water and wrung out thoroughly.

Veining: Perhaps the most striking characteristic of marble is veining, a series of jagged lines which describe a course over the surface and always suggest motion. They usually appear within bands of slightly darker marble. To simulate veining, it might help you to back-light a twig: the shadows projected on the wall can be used for the veining pattern. Choose a colour in artist's oils which contrasts with the glazes used in your background marbling and apply over a wet surface freehand, using a fine sable brush. These lines should then be softened by dabbing with a dry cloth or by running a dry brush or a feather across in all directions. Small flecks of paint can be spattered at intersections – gold or silver metallic paint is useful as highlights. Suggest depth by trapping the veins between different coloured glazes. Finish with one or two coats polyurethane varnish, thinned three parts varnish to one part white spirit.

Make sure that you dispose of all cloths soaked in solvent or glaze very carefully to avoid creating a fire hazard.

Using water-based paint

First apply a matt white base coat in emulsion. Then rag-roll a pastel wash of mid-sheen emulsion over the top. For the veining, use the base colour or a contrasting shade in matt emulsion; metallic paint can also give a dramatic effect. Paint in the veins freehand, using an artist's brush, as above. Smudge or soften these with a cloth and spatter the intersections with a contrasting colour. Repeat the veining process in another colour, following a different path. Protect with polyurethane varnish as for oil-based paint.

Porphyry

Porphyry is a granite-like rock whose surface can be simulated using spattering techniques (pages 28-31) with oil- or water-based paints. Commonly used on fire surrounds and table tops, the predominant colour is red, although green, violet grey and brown types exist. The rock often contains flecks of fool's gold and exhibits a characteristic known as clouding. Simulated porphyry need not slavishly follow nature: unlikely colour combinations can be very pleasing, so don't feel constrained by that suggested here.

The effect of porphyry is very simple to achieve. Sponge a terracotta colour on to a base coat of beige. Then spatter over the entire surface with ivory and black paint, speckling it uniformly but quite sparsely. It can be effective to spatter in metallic paint, although this should be handled carefully as the effect is powerful and can easily detract from the authenticity of the finish. Cissing with water or white spirit (depending on type of paint used) can be undertaken on horizontal surfaces to enhance the effect.

Finish with a varnish when dry, if required.

Marbling is one technique that benefits by a little creative interpretation. This example uses soft browns and neutrals, which find an echo in the pale pink of the walls above the rail. For the marble, three layers of paint were each rag-rolled off and then softened with a dry brush; white 'veins' were then applied. The result is a long way from the chilly feel of real marble, and makes welcoming a dark hallway.

Marbling

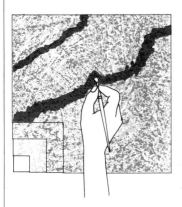

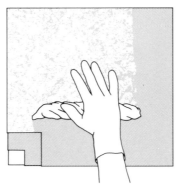

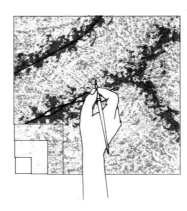

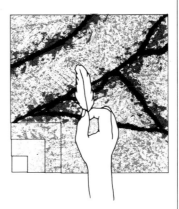

1. Apply a white or pale base coat. Then mix a slightly darker glaze or wash and paint this over the surface using a standard brush.

2. While the glaze or wash is still wet, rag-roll off to expose one-half to two-thirds of the base colour. For a sharper pattern, roll the glaze on.

3. To achieve the characteristic translucency and depth of marble, repeat the process using successive layers of glaze until you are satisfied.

4. Each glaze should be tinted to contrast slightly with the ground colour and with the other glazes, and rag-rolled off – or on – each time.

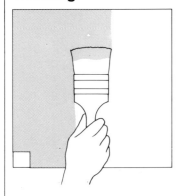

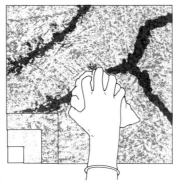

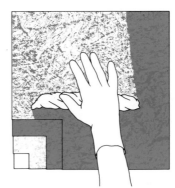

5. Using an artist's brush and a darker glaze or wash, paint on irregular patches about 5 cm (2 in) wide, to suggest areas of compression.

6. While the patches are still wet, rag-roll off to smudge them and preserve the appearance of translucency. Soften with a dry brush.

7. Using a contrasting colour and an artist's brush, paint in the veins freehand, siting them in the darker patches and making them intersect.

8. Soften the veins with a dry brush or feather while still wet. Alternatively, the veins can be painted in with a goose or pheasant's feather.

TORTOISESHELLING

A tortoiseshelled surface is rich and sophisticated. Character-ized by a striking pattern, this treatment is best used in a setting that complements rather than contrasts with its quality of opulence. Tortoiseshelling can make a feature of anony-mous areas such as halls or landings, or highlight details of panelling or furniture. For larger vertical surfaces, it is best to break up the area into regular sections rather than attempt to create an overall pattern.

Novices should think twice before they attempt tortoise-shelling and confine their first attempts to small panels: it requires expertise and practice to make it look stunning.

The traditional colours are warm shades ranging from pale blondes and golden honeys through yellows, reds, browns and blacks. Quite strong colours can be used since the blend-ing process of this technique will soften their impact. Tor-toiseshelling is usually done on a yellow ground coat, but a red or green base colour can also produce fabulous and unusual effects. Build the finish up using the same varnishes and colours as prescribed below for a yellow ground.

The essential characteristic of a tortoiseshelled finish is the blurred diagonal. Diagonal streaks of broken colour are floated on a wet varnish and distressed in a criss-cross fashion. The distressing strokes soften and merge the colours, reinforcing the diagonal accent. Tortoiseshelling is difficult to achieve with water-based paints.

Method

Apply one coat of undercoat (thinned two parts paint to one part white spirit) to a prepared surface. When this has dried, cover with a ground coat of eggshell, traditionally sharp yellow in colour, thinned three parts paint to one part white spirit. Allow to dry and then brush on a liberal coat of glossy polyurethane varnish, tinted dark oak and thinned two parts varnish to one part white spirit.

While the varnish is still wet, use a 25 mm (1 in.) flat artist's brush to create broken diagonal squiggles, fidgeting the brush in a zigzag manner to move the varnish over the surface. Place blobs of the same varnish on and between these marks, to accentuate the diagonal.

Mix a burnt umber colour in artist's oils and apply small diagonal squiggles running in the same direction. Repeat the process using black. All the markings should be random and casual. Soften the surface by stroking with a 10 cm (4 in.) dry flat brush across and with the diagonals, finishing with a final, strong stroke in the direction of the original diagonal.

For an even richer effect, repeat the whole process, be-ginning with the first coat of tinted varnish.

When the finish is dry, seal and protect with two coats clear polyurethane varnish (thinned three parts varnish to one part white spirit).

STENCILLING

Highly versatile, simple and effective, stencilling is a deservedly popular decorative technique. Depending on the colours and design, it can be subtle and evocative, or bold and forthright. Stencilling is a repetitive method of applying a design in paint that involves using a cut-out motif as a mask or stencil. Almost any surface, from walls and floors to furniture, can be decorated in this way.

Planning is essential. Colours must be chosen to complement your existing scheme. Especially in the case of stencilled borders, study the proportions of the room and work out the positioning of the design carefully. If you are going to stencil a pattern on the floor, ensure the design will be seen, not covered up by a large piece of furniture.

Ready-made stencils are available from artists' suppliers and craft shops. Most are traditional motifs that come pre-cut and with suggestions for colour combinations. More satisfying is to make your own stencil – it's not difficult to do and is the best way of achieving a truly personal look.

One of the great advantages of stencilling is that patterns can easily be scaled up or down by constructing a grid or using graph paper. In this way, the same motif in different sizes can be used to co-ordinate walls, floors, furniture and even vases and crockery.

Making your own stencil

The first step is to draw up your design on graph paper and colour it in. Then fix the drawing to a flat surface and overlay it with a piece of tracing paper. Trace around all the areas that are in one particular colour. Repeat this process, using separate overlays for each colour. Templates can now be made in acetate film or oil stencil board, both of which are available from artists' suppliers or craft shops.

To make acetate stencils, pin the tracing on to a drawing board and overlay with a sheet of acetate. Trace the pattern on to the film using a drafting pen and cut it out with a craft knife. Repeat until all templates are cut. To make a stencil from oil stencil board, you must first trace off the pattern from the tracing paper. Cut out the stencils with a craft knife, using a steel rule to guide you. In either case, leave a big

Opposite: A lavatory can provide an opportunity for an extravagant effect inappropriate elsewhere. Tortoiseshell would never be used like this, but with paint anything's possible.

Above: Traditionally stencils are used to create an air of rustic charm. Here a stencil evocative of rural simplicity decorates the panels of the door and bath surround.

enough margin to maintain some rigidity in the template, and make sure that you have lined up your registration marks accurately (see below). If a thick material such as cardboard is used, the edges should be chamfered or bevelled to prevent paint from creeping under the stencil and blurring the outline.

Registration

The crucial element in stencilling is getting each colour in exactly the right position relative to the other colours and to the completed designs. One way to do this when stencilling a frieze round the top or bottom of a room, for example, is to position each separation of the design on the card or acetate in such a way that they have only to be jammed up against the ceiling, picture rail, floor or skirting board to appear at a uniform height. This means you will have to cut each piece of card or acetate to the same size in the first place.

Another way is to draw a line across each piece of tracing paper in exactly the same position relative to the design. Transfer this to the card or acetate. Mark up your wall in blue chalk with an unbroken horizontal line to indicate where the

Two friezes, one pretty and pastel, the other bold and dominating, exemplify a very common and effective application of the stencilling technique. On this page, several stencils from one design were combined, reversed and twisted around to produce a lively, softly coloured border. Opposite, the inspiration for the stencil came from the Egyptian print on the wall. One stencil only was needed, incorporating four of the lily shapes, and this was repeated around the room. Gold paint gives a touch of extravagance – as it is rather runny, it is best to dry it out on a saucer for a while before using it. Notice how in both examples the paint was not applied evenly through the stencil but shaded across each part of the design to soften outlines and give an illusion of depth.

stencil should go (you may need several lines if you are repeating the design vertically), and then match the lines on the card or acetate with the line on the wall.

Applying the stencil

Although any type of paint is suitable, fast-drying types such as acrylics are ideal. If you find acrylic paint is too expensive, emulsion makes a good alternative. You can also use wood dyes on floors. To apply the paint, you will also need to invest in a square-ended stencil brush.

Mark your registration line on the surface with chalk. Ensure that any drops are perfectly vertical by using a plumb-line, and that horizontals are aligned with either the ceiling or the floor, depending on which is nearest.

The paint should be thinned to a creamy consistency. Apply a small amount to the tip of the brush and dab or pounce it on to the surface, rolling the brush slightly. The effect can be one of bold, solid colour, or you can pounce the paint in such a way that a soft, graduated effect emerges. The stencil should be held firm and flat, and cleaned and dried regularly to prevent blurred or smudgy edges. Try to blend two or more colours together on one overlay to produce depth and subtlety, and don't feel constrained by the separations of colour on which you originally decided. Be bold and adventurous, and vary and graduate the colours between and within the stencils. Move the stencils around, flip them over, turn them through 90° – you will be surprised at the range of effects you can create.

Stencilling is usually left as a matt finish, but on floors you will need to protect the pattern with five or six coats of polyurethane varnish.

Using aerosols

Aerosols give a flat and even result but the paint has a tendency to spread under the stencil. They are useful on a small scale, or to achieve graduated shading. Cover the surface first with a recommended primer or sealer and then sand lightly before applying the paint. Use the manufacturer's recommended lacquer to protect and seal the surface.

The stencil motif used all over the walls in this room came from a seventeenth-century French fabric design. It was applied over walls washed with a stone coloured glaze, and the yellow, aged effect was achieved by varnishing the entire surface. Below the dado rail, the walls are dragged. The owner's treasures could not have found a richer backdrop.

Stencilling

1. Draw your design to scale on graph paper and colour it in. Draw registration line.

2. Tape a sheet of tracing paper over the drawing and trace around all the areas that are in one colour. Do this for each colour, and trace off the registration line.

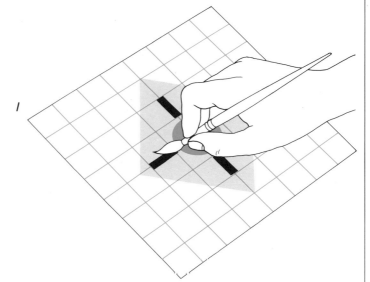

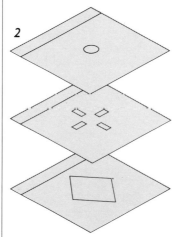

3. Tape each tracing paper overlay over a piece of oil stencil board and trace off the pattern and the line. Alternatively, overlay the tracing paper with a sheet of acetate and trace the pattern on to the film. Score the registration line in the correct place across the acetate.

4. Cut the stencil out of the film or card.

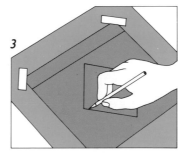

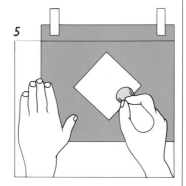

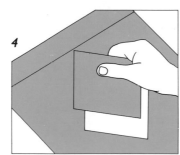

5. Draw a line in blue chalk on the wall where the stencil is to go. Match the line on your stencil card or acetate with this line. Hold the stencil flat, or tape it to the wall, and dab or pounce paint through with a stencil brush.

PAINTING PROCEDURE

Once the surface has been prepared, the first coats of paint can be applied. Bare wood or metal require the application of a primer to seal the raw surface. In all cases, an undercoat is also necessary to provide a suitable base for finishes. This can be either water- or oil-based.

Water-based paints will cover any clean, dry and de-greased surface, except metal (which will rust). On new plaster, the first coat should be emulsion and thinned (one part paint to one part solvent) to act as a primer. The subsequent coat can be full strength. If you are painting over a dark surface, up to three coats may be required.

The order in which you paint is important: generally speaking, you should start nearest the source of natural light, and paint away from it. Paint the ceiling first and the floor last, and the walls before the woodwork (see opposite). Work systematically, laying off strokes on walls and ceilings in the direction of the light. On woodwork, paint should be laid off in the direction of the grain. Laying off consists of a light finishing stroke intended to obliterate brushmarks.

Straight-edging and masking

Professional decorators, with the co-ordination that comes from experience, can paint straight edges and highlight detail freehand. For the amateur, there are certain techniques that ensure paint goes where it is intended. These are particularly important in flat colour schemes where mouldings, plaster-work or panelling are picked out in different colours.

The simplest and most successful way to get a clean, straight edge is to paint against a chamfered piece of thin, stiff material. When painting a moulding, for example, place the chamfered edge right up against the wood and apply paint sparingly to prevent runs. Move the straight edge along as you paint, wiping any excess paint off with a clean cloth.

Masking out the areas not to be painted is essential, particularly when employing broken colour techniques. A few hours spent masking out all wood surrounds with masking tape will be time very well spent, for you should end up with crisp, clean edges. Take care not to damage the paint when you remove the tape, especially if using emulsion.

Basic painting techniques

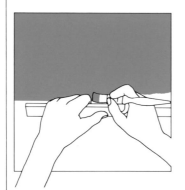

1. Keep a straight edge by running the stock of the brush along a ruler or piece of stiff board held at an angle to the surface being painted.

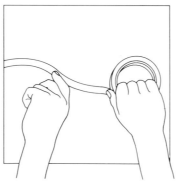

2. When painting a curved shape, mask out surrounding areas with masking tape. Take care not to remove any paint with the tape.

3. Work down the walls in 60 cm (2 ft) sections. 'Lay on' the paint vertically, and use cross strokes to prevent a striped effect.

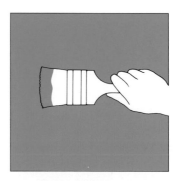

4. The last or 'laying off' stroke should be a light flick with a fairly dry brush across the surface to eliminate any brushmarks.

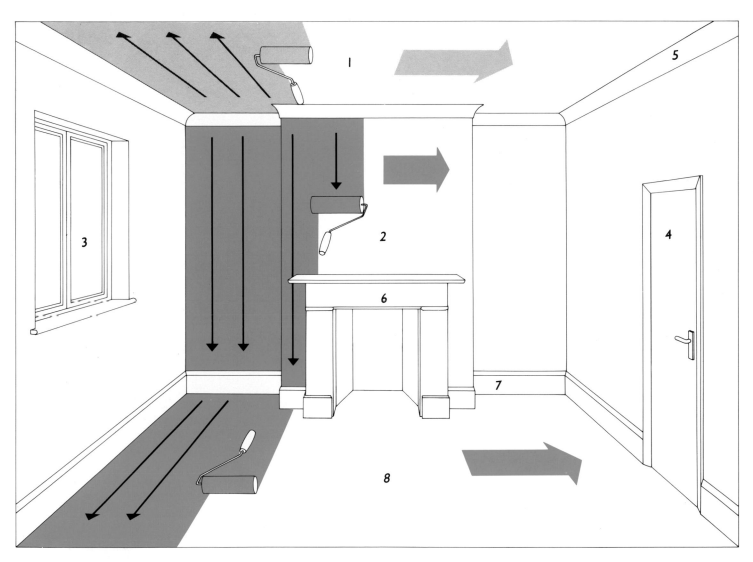

Painting sequence

There is a correct order in which to paint all the elements in a room. First, tackle the ceiling, working in bands away from the main source of natural light (1). Next, paint the walls, again away from the natural light, working in vertical strips 60 cm (2 ft) wide (2). Then paint window frames, starting with the inside of the frame and finishing with the sill (3). For doors, paint panels first, followed by crosspieces and then architraves (4). Next, paint plasterwork details such as cornices and mouldings (5), followed by fireplaces (6). Paint all skirting boards (7). Floors are painted like ceilings, working in bands away from natural light: always work towards an exit (8).

WALLPAPER

As well as the many different paint effects, there are many other wall and ceiling coverings which you can use to create an interesting foundation for a decorative scheme. Wallpapers, paper-backed fabric, hessian, tiles, wood panelling and mirrors can all be applied relatively easily to a surface, adding a textural dimension often lacking in painted finishes.

The range of printed wallpapers is immense – not only in terms of colour and pattern but also in terms of cost, quality and practicability. In general, the cheaper papers tend to be thin and difficult to hang; also, they do not last long. Higher-quality papers are thicker and better-printed. At the extreme end of the market, there are very expensive hand-printed papers, including reproductions of antique designs printed from the original blocks.

Aside from plain white lining paper, which is designed to provide an even surface for decorating, the special attraction of wallpaper lies in the pattern. The range of designs available has enlarged considerably in recent years; it includes traditional varieties, such as Regency stripes and floral motifs, as well as cheerful figurative prints for children's rooms and sophisticated modern geometrics. Many papers are coordinated with fabrics and wall tiles and some are available with contrasting or complementary friezes.

All printed papers are treated to repel moisture and promote maintenance, but the degree of protection varies. 'Spongeable' papers can be wiped down; 'washable' papers, coated with plastic film, can be washed with water. Vinyls – wallpapers coated with thick plastic film – can actually be scrubbed.

Textured papers are useful for covering irregular surfaces. These relief papers are generally embossed with wood and pulp, and are designed to be painted. Other types include the once-fashionable flock paper with a cut-pile surface and relief simulations of panelling or plasterwork.

Other paper-backed coverings available include hessian (burlap), grasses and other natural fibres with paper backing, allowing you to hang them like ordinary wallpaper. Often in neutral shades, these provide a subtle textural interest but tend to be difficult to clean and not very robust.

Wallpapers with definite patterns are either 'straight' (aligned horizontally) or 'drop' (aligned diagonally). Because lengths of paper are laid side by side across the wall (butt-jointed) and not overlapped, the patterns must match along each length of paper.

Cut the first length of paper about 10 cm (4 in.) longer than the depth of the wall; this allows a margin of 5 cm (2 in.) at both top and bottom for trimming. Before cutting the second length, match the pattern with the first, again allowing a 10 cm (4 in.) excess. Number each length consecutively as it is cut and mark which end is the top.

To avoid wastage when cutting 'drop' patterns, it may be necessary to cut alternately from two rolls at once. Even so, wastage is unavoidable.

HANGING WALLPAPER

When you buy your wallpaper ensure that an extra roll with the same batch number will be available. Otherwise, if you need to buy more you may end up with a roll bearing a different batch number and the shades of colour may vary. Wallpaper should be hung on a sound, even, dry surface. Very poor surfaces may need replastering; alternatively, you may just have to line or cross-line with lining paper.

Establishing a vertical
Once you have decided on a starting position, you need to establish a vertical so that the lengths of paper are correctly aligned.

Measure out from the corner of the wall a distance that is 1 cm (½ in.) less than the full width of the paper, and mark it top, middle and bottom.

Hang a plumb line from the top of the wall aligning with the mark nearest the corner and mark along it at intervals. Join up the marks using a straightedge. This pencilled line is the vertical you will use for aligning the first length of paper. The same process must be repeated each time a corner is turned in the room.

Pasting
Some wallpapers are available pre-pasted, but if you are pasting the paper yourself you will need a trestle table or a folding pasting table on which to lay out lengths of paper. To avoid getting paste on the table and the consequent risk of spoiling the next length of paper, some decorators let the paper overhang the table by 2 cm (1 in.), but it can be difficult to paste edges if they have no support. Keep a clean sponge and water on hand, and wipe away any paste which does get onto the table.

Most papers need to be left for a while to allow the paste to soak in. Papers with definite patterns should be pasted and hung one length at a time, so that soaking times do not vary – a length left for too long will stretch irregularly and may not match the previous one. Light- and mediumweight papers will need to be left pasted for two to five minutes, heavyweight types for about ten to twelve.

Large patterns
If the paper has a large pattern, it should be centred on a focal point, such as a chimney breast, or on a wall which is the focus of attention in the room.

From the starting point, work in sequence around the room. Whichever way you go, plan to finish in the least important corner or at a doorway, since it will almost certainly be impossible to match the pattern on the last length. If your wallpaper has a large pattern, ensure that the first length features a complete motif near the top of the wall so that broken motifs are near the floor.

Borders and friezes
Borders and friezes can be applied to any sound surface (not over heavily embossed paper). Use a pencil line as a guide for position and cut a length of border to fit across the entire length of wall. Paste the border and loop it up so that it is easier for you to position correctly. Brush out, letting out the loops as you work along.

Corners – for example, around a door or window frame – should be mitred. Paste the borders in place, overlapping the ends where they meet, and then draw a diagonal line across the corner, using a straightedge. Cut along the line, through both layers, using a sharp knife. Remove the excess pieces and smooth the others back into place.

Special effects
You can create your own wallpaper by using thick writing paper, marbled paper or even photocopies of interesting prints to line a wall. This is best attempted on a small area and the surface should be sealed with a coat of polyurethane (which will yellow with age). An alternative is to stencil your own design on plain wallpaper and seal.

Patterned wallpaper can be used to disguise a multitude of sins, such as uneven plastering.

DESIGNING WITH LIGHT

The real skill of lighting design is to maintain a judicious balance between the practical requirements of illumination and a desire for pleasing or dramatic visual effects. To achieve this, lighting design consultants do considerable groundwork before they even think of specifying luminaires. Careful assessment and analysis of both the home and its occupants is carried out prior to starting the design process.

Invariably, they ask a lot of questions. Which activities take place in which rooms? What plans have already been made for furniture and decor? How old are the occupants? (This is very important, as a sixty-year-old person needs on average fifteen times more light than a child of ten for reading.) How far advanced are the building and decoration of the house? How long do you intend to live in the house? Is energy economy a major factor in how much you are willing to spend? (Lighting is still relatively inexpensive in comparison with other items of home decor expenditure.) What details of your lifestyle will influence the lighting – for example, do you paint or play a musical instrument? How much disruption are you willing to endure during installation? At what times of the day do you use certain rooms? Where are the main entry points of natural light in your home?

Lighting designers have a clear order of priority:

- *Desirability:* for example, do I want to light that surface or object?
- *Practicality:* what equipment do I need? Where shall I position it?
- *Feasibility:* will it work visually in practice? Will it break the budget? Will I be able to change the bulb?

Above all, lighting designers look for opportunities to apply light in a surprising way. If you own, for example, oil paintings, Art Deco pottery or a handsome fireplace, accent them with light to create defined centres of focus. In short, designers look first at what is desirable in terms of effect and then set about trying to achieve it. Functional electrical engineers, in marked contrast, have traditionally looked first at what is feasible and then set about achieving that.

To make the most of your home with lighting, always give desirability a high priority. You can scale down your ambition later, if costs soar or installation proves too tricky. But at the outset, don't be cowed into a cautious provision of light. Look at the full range of equipment available and aim for stimulating, satisfying results.

Lighting is a potent decorative element in the home. This unadorned interior (above) is redesigned with light which creates a sculptural shadow play and vital patterning.

Look for opportunities to apply light in surprising and pleasing ways. A wall light supplemented with candles and an open fire (right) creates an intimate point of focus.

A FRAMEWORK FOR DESIGN

An understanding of the terminology of lighting is an important curtain-raiser to the design process – not least because the terms have become so confused. Not only does the lighting trade call a *lamp* what the public understands to be a *bulb*, but *lighting design* is the expression most commonly used to discuss both the quality of light emanating from the fitting and the product design of the luminaire itself. As a consequence, non-specialists often take more interest in the style of the light fitting than in its performance as a diffuser and distributor of light – and often buy luminaires without having switched them on to see what they look like in action.

To clarify the terms, for the purposes of this book, *lighting design* is, literally, designing in light: the ways light is applied and directed. The design of the instrument which controls the beam is *luminaire design* or *light fittings design*.

Types of lighting

There are four main types of lighting used in the home:
GENERAL LIGHTING Also known as background lighting, this is a direct replacement for natural light and provides a general level of visibility. On its own, it is bland and indiscriminate, but used with other types of lighting, it forms an integral part of an effective lighting scheme.
TASK LIGHTING Well-positioned and well-directed lighting that provides localized light in specific areas for specific tasks. The flexibility of the luminaire and the colour rendering of the light source are particularly important.

ACCENT LIGHTING A key element of creative lighting design, this reveals colour, texture and form by highlighting and painting in the objects around us. Accent lighting can range from a narrow pencil beam to a broad spot.
INFORMATION LIGHTING Also known as orientation or utility lighting, this provides visual information for our safety and comfort. Information lighting is often based in areas of total blackness. The guiding light on the stairwell, a bulkhead by the garage door, and the fluorescent strip above the lift shaft of a block of flats are all examples of information lighting.

Distribution of light

The four different types of lighting – general, task, accent and information – are each achieved by different distributions of light. The distribution depends on the fitting which houses the bulb and which can determine the beam in a wide variety of ways. When choosing a luminaire for your home, consider above all else the way it distributes the light.

There are three major categories of light distribution:
OMNI-DIRECTIONAL A light that disperses in all directions; as from a pendant fitting shaded with a paper globe.
SEMI-DIRECTIONAL The majority of light goes in one direction but a small quantity diffuses in other directions; for example, through the shade of a standard lamp.
DIRECTIONAL All the light travels in one direction, either in a narrow beam (as from a spotlight), or in a broad flood (as in a floodlight), or in a pattern somewhere between the two.

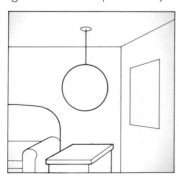

Omni-directional

Semi-directional

Directional

Left: Light distribution can be omni-directional, for general lighting; semi-directional, with light concentrated mainly in one area; or directional, providing a focused beam.

Right: In this open-plan space, mounted fittings supplement light from an uplighter. A downlight links the living area to the kitchen, where spots create efficient task lighting.

Families of light fittings

The categories of light distribution can be applied to the twelve families of light fittings found in the home:

PENDANT LIGHTS The most common type of light fitting offering the greatest variety of designs – from paper lanterns to metal cones. The light distributed can be omni-directional, semi-directional or directional, depending on the shade you choose and the length of flex on which the bulb hangs.

Although the pendant fitting provides abundant general light, it tends to flatten shadows and look obtrusive when used as the sole light source. This fitting should be controlled by a dimmer switch, so the light intensity can be altered.

WALL LIGHTS A wall-mounted light fitting that diffuses light into the room, usually through a translucent housing. Again, the light distributed can be omni-directional, semi-directional or directional. Wall lights vary from opaque metal or ceramic bowls, which push most of the light upwards, to glass or perspex cones, which diffuse light gently. Sturdy bulkhead fittings – information lights by the back door, garage or garden steps – are also wall lights.

WALL WASHERS Used to bathe a wall in an even stream of light. Usually ceiling-mounted, recessed into the ceiling or mounted on a lighting track, these lights are wholly directional, using a reflector or baffle to distribute the light at a certain angle, and are very useful for accent lighting.

Pendant lights offer the widest-style choice, with shades available in materials as diverse as paper, ceramic, fabric and glass.

Wall-mounted fittings range from sturdy weatherproof bulkheads giving omni-directional light, to elegant, semi-directional ceramic shields. A more conventional-looking swing-arm lamp allows some adjustment to the lighting's direction.

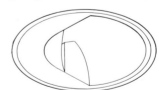

For subtle effects, fully recess wall washers into the ceiling, leaving their silvered reflectors to bathe the wall in a brilliant stream of light.

A pendant light is commonly used as general lighting; the shade over the bulb affects distribution of light.

Wall lights provide discreet accent or background lighting and contribute to the general light level.

A ceiling-recessed wall washer provides directional light angled to flood down the length of the wall.

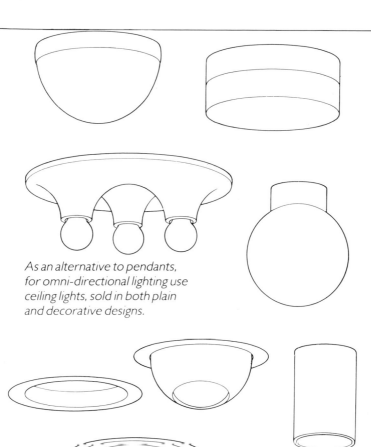

As an alternative to pendants, for omni-directional lighting use ceiling lights, sold in both plain and decorative designs.

Ceiling-mounted downlights can be left prominent or recessed. Swivel 'eyeball' types let you vary the light's direction.

CEILING LIGHTS A ceiling-mounted fitting that is not recessed. Usually a globe, it provides a general omni-directional light like the pendant.

DOWNLIGHTS As the name implies, this family provides directional light in a downward stream. A downlight is normally recessed or semi-recessed in to the ceiling, and when fully recessed is one of the most visually inconspicuous and effective luminaires. Depending on the bulb and housing, it can spread light in a narrow, concentrated beam or a broader flood. Eyeball downlights can be swivelled to avoid the tunnel effect rows of rigid downlights can create.

UPLIGHTERS This type of fitting sends semi-directional and directional light upwards. When the beam is bounced off a wall or ceiling, general lighting is achieved indirectly. Free-standing uplighters are important for accent-lighting schemes: position such fittings with care in a room – in a corner or behind a plant – to create interesting effects. Much in vogue nowadays, uplighters have been the subject of considerable design innovation. They can be fitted with a dimmer and some types are switched on with a foot pedal.

SPOTLIGHTS Ceiling-, wall- or floor-mounted, or attached to a lighting track, the spotlight is a flexible, adjustable luminaire that directs light in a controlled beam. It is a most effective tool for accent lighting and the track – developed

Floor-standing uplighters look like standard lamps, but direct light upwards. Cylindrical versions also provide some light at ground level.

A ceiling-mounted fitting acts as general, omni-directional lighting best supplemented by other sources.

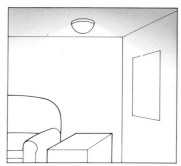

A downlight can be an effective, unobtrusive source of a broad flood or concentrated beam of light.

Uplighters can be arranged at different levels, to accent directly or create softened, reflected light.

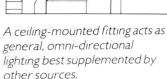

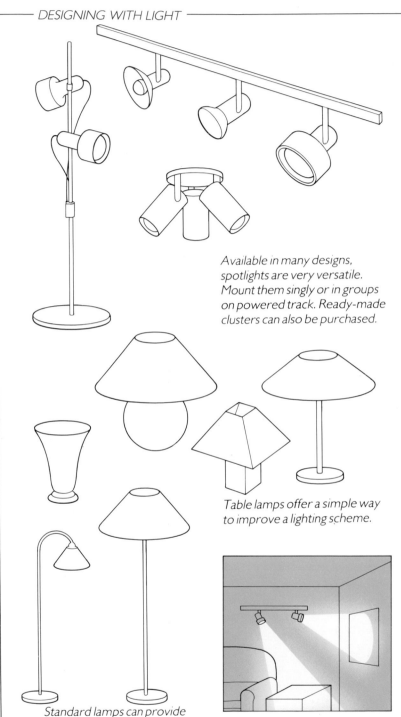

Available in many designs, spotlights are very versatile. Mount them singly or in groups on powered track. Ready-made clusters can also be purchased.

Table lamps offer a simple way to improve a lighting scheme.

Standard lamps can provide both omni-directional and semi-directional light to create a mood.

initially for commercial use – is a useful accessory for creative design. Essentially, the track is an elongated socket which allows you to attach several luminaires to one electrical source and move them about easily and swiftly. The track can be vertically mounted on a wall, as well as horizontally across a ceiling, for added versatility and different effects.

STANDARD LAMPS Decorative light fittings that are free-standing, usually on the floor, standard lamps distribute omni-directional and semi-directional light, depending on the lampshade. They are best used with a dimmer.

TABLE LAMPS A variety of decorative lights which give a soft omni-directional glow. Very popular for both general and accent lighting, table lamps can be used as bedside reading lights as well as for stylistic effect in the living room.

DESK LIGHTS Essential to provide task lighting, the desk light gives a concentrated directional light over a specific area. The best type of desk light has an adjustable arm so you can direct the light exactly where you want it. Again, desk lights have been the focus of much design innovation and their talents are wasted if used only in study or business areas. A desk light is valuable in the kitchen and makes a versatile bedside light.

STRIP LIGHTING Exactly what the name suggests, strip lights distribute omni-directional and semi-directional light and are useful for all kinds of lighting – general, accent, task and information. Most strip lighting is fluorescent (although

Spotlights are versatile, allowing concentrated beams of light to rise or fall from different angles.

A freestanding standard lamp is a useful supplement to other forms of lighting in the room.

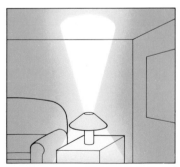

Table lamps provide accent and focus, useful for their decorative effect as well as their function.

tungsten and neon strips can be found in the home). When planning concealed lighting (inside wardrobes, behind bookcases), strip lighting is the most common solution.

VISUAL ODDITIES This heading covers those lights which don't fit into the other eleven categories of luminaire. Usually designed for visual impact rather than the way they distribute light, they provide aesthetic stimulation and amusement. Geese, crescent moons, fabric bag lights, wall-mounted wrapped sweets, giant numbers, and ludicrously large bulbs are just some of the oddities you can buy.

The best lighting design schemes include at least three or four of the twelve families of fittings described here. Deploy them in unusual combinations to banish blandness and develop creative patterns of light.

Frequently, the level of light needed for day-to-day functions is overestimated. Less intense, more subtle and indirect arrangements using three or four light sources in a room will often achieve the same functional level of light while creating a more intimate setting. But, just as knowledge of the existence of paint and brushes won't guarantee a work of art, so the awareness of different luminaires and types of light won't instantly bathe your home in a pleasing glow. As the lighting design professionals will tell you, first you need to examine exactly what you want to achieve.

Ingenious cantilevered and flexible arms give desk lamps an almost sculptural quality.

Fluorescent strip lights are now better designed and provide a softer light than ever before.

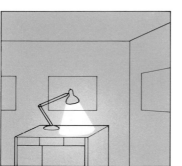

A desk light is a highly efficient form of task lighting, giving a high level of light on a specific area.

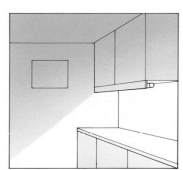

Strip lights perform a variety of functions, with pleasing effect when the source is concealed.

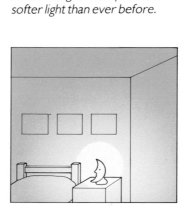

Attractive and eccentric designs for luminaires offer local lighting with a touch of humour.

Providing amusing talking points and unexpected lighting effects, 'novelty' lamps come in all shapes and sizes.

A SENSE OF DRAMA

The application of accent lighting is one of the most important and pleasurable elements of creative lighting design. The possessions that adorn our homes – pottery, plants and paintings, for example – are a direct reflection of our lifestyles and the type of people we are. So why not give them a little limelight and make them points of visual focus in a room?

Accent light on an object can be arranged to provide enough reflected illuminance to do away with characterless general light from a central overhead source. The result is a thrilling sense of theatre in your home. Tungsten halogen, which can provide a narrow, pointing finger of concentrated light, is a very useful source in this context. Take a cue from lighting design professionals: scan your home for opportunities to use accent light, and borrow from the lighting repertoire of the theatre, art gallery and shop window.

Even the most unlikely objects add interest to an interior when lit up. Ask yourself the following:
● What should I light?
● What light source and luminaire should I use?
● From what angle should the object be lit?
Again, improvisation is an important part of the design process, but the following are a few tips in relation to particular objects.

Lighting a ceramic object
Any opaque object will reflect light, not transmit it. A large ceramic vase or sculpture can be dramatically lit as the centrepiece of a well-furnished room.

FROM ABOVE Use the narrow beam of a low-voltage tungsten halogen downlight to pick out the upper contours of a ceramic vase. The contrast of light between top and bottom will make it appear to float theatrically in space.

FROM BELOW Floor-mount a tungsten halogen baby spot behind the object. It will appear in virtual silhouette and there will also be a dramatic shadow on the ceiling.

FROM AN ANGLE Use a wall- or ceiling-mounted spotlight or eyeball downlight to beam on to the object from an angle of thirty-five to forty degrees. This will create a more natural, grazing accent light, less dramatically stark.

Lighting a ceramic object

A direct, concentrated beam of light from a downlight above delineates the upper contours of the object while the lower part remains in shade, giving a dramatic effect of tonal contrast.

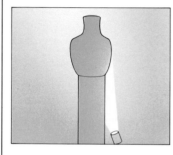

A small spotlight, floor-mounted and casting its beam upwards behind the vase, throws the shape into silhouette, making a mysterious, shadowy form against the background of light.

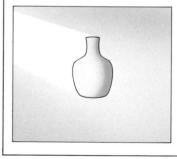

Angled light falling more broadly from one side makes a less theatrical display, but the form is clearly outlined and modelled to show off its natural character. A spotlight or swivelling downlight can be arranged to this effect.

Lighting glassware
The great virtue of glass is its translucence. Exploit its ability to transmit light by lighting glassware from below or behind. Lighting from above ignores its intrinsic qualities.

FROM BELOW If you have glass goblets, place them on a translucent, milky glass shelf. Place a row of low-voltage tungsten halogen spotlights beneath the shelf, or attach a fluorescent strip behind a baffle on the wall. The result is a beautiful 'light box' effect.

FROM BEHIND Use wall-mounted fluorescent strips (tungsten halogen doesn't produce the flat, uniform light needed) to diffuse light gently on to the glassware through a translucent screen of semi-opaque glass, fabric or perspex to achieve an attractive delineation of shape.

Lighting glassware

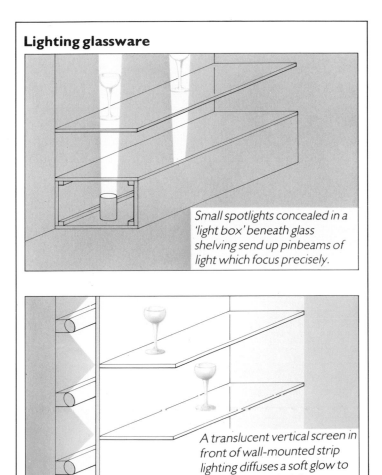

Small spotlights concealed in a 'light box' beneath glass shelving send up pinbeams of light which focus precisely.

A translucent vertical screen in front of wall-mounted strip lighting diffuses a soft glow to illuminate the shelving.

Lighting books

The texture and typographic interest of rows of books are worth accenting, so use wall washers recessed or semi-recessed into the ceiling, to graze your bookshelves with light from an angle, emphasizing effects of shadow and texture. Alternatively, clip spots to the underside of shelves and skim light along their length. Remember to think about the lighting for your books at the same time as you plan your shelving.

Lighting pictures

We have all seen the inadequate illumination, reflections and glare that result when pictures are lit incorrectly. It is a subtle art which demands care and attention; with oil paintings in particular, it is important to avoid accenting the heavier

Ceiling-recessed eyeball downlights throw soft pools of light on books and a decorative wall-hanging – a means of highlighting your favourite possessions with a flourish.

Lighting pictures

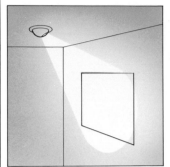

A ceiling-recessed, swivelling eyeball downlight sheds a broad beam over the picture and the area it occupies.

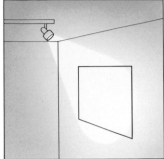

An adjustable spotlight gives a directional spread of light over the appropriate area, tending to centralize the focus.

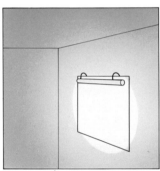

A strip light the width of the painting, mounted on the frame, should cast even light, from top to bottom.

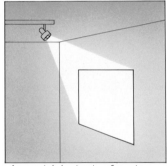

A special device is a framing spot with shutters that lights the picture area exactly, concentrating the attention.

Lighting plants

A broad, angled beam from a spotlight above and behind the plant illuminates its pattern and texture.

An uplighter on the floor bounces soft light off the wall, to create a subtle pattern of light and shade.

texture on the ridges of the brushstrokes – this happens if the angle of the light is too steep. There are four basic options for lighting pictures:

A SWIVELLING EYEBALL DOWNLIGHT, recessed into the ceiling, spreads a broad beam over the painting.

AN ADJUSTABLE SPOTLIGHT on a ceiling track projects a controlled beam on to the painting. Take care to respect the artist's intention in the use of light and shade. (A glance at the Dutch Masters will reveal that they used light in a supremely skilled fashion.) Point the beam at the likeliest focal point of light in the painting.

A SPECIAL PICTURE LIGHT extends over the frame of the painting. You can choose from a range of designs, but try to avoid the imbalance often seen in the picture lighting of stately homes open to the public, whereby the picture is brighter at the top than at the bottom.

A FRAMING SPOT on a ceiling track is a specialist piece of equipment with framing shutters designed to produce a perfect square of light that you can adjust to the size of your picture. This luminaire is accurate but expensive, and therefore best used only if you have a particularly fine or valuable painting and want to make it a special focal point.

Lighting plants

Plants look attractive when revealed by accent lighting, but they also need plenty of light for survival and growth. Place them directly in the line of natural light entering a room, and if there is very limited natural light, shine special plant-

Left: Just as white walls create a more spacious feeling, so a tight or low space is opened out by a wash of light over surfaces. Natural and artificial light give a visual lift to this sloping ceiling.

Below: Dramatic patterns can be created by uplighting a plant from behind. A baby spot on the floor bounces light off the wall, transforming this tall, narrow-stemmed plant.

irradiating light sources on to them after dark to ensure they receive enough ultraviolet light.

There are a number of ways to light plants. If the plant pot is in the corner of a room, place an uplighter or floor-mounted baby spot behind it and allow light to bounce off wall and ceiling, diffusing back through the foliage to create imaginative patterns of shadow. Light a plant from above with a downlight to create a pleasant glow, or place a low-voltage tungsten halogen fitting on a spike in the soil for a fairy-light effect. This is especially useful for tumbling plants in baskets.

Avoid placing the light source too close to foliage or the leaves will burn. With spotlights, use a wide angle of directional beam to fall on the whole shape of a large plant; a narrow beam will light no more than a couple of leaves.

Highlighting architectural features

Use the three-dimensional geometry of your room to advantage, exploiting architectural detail with light to create a new visual aspect. Architectural features fall into two main categories: large planar expanses of wall and ceiling, or smaller elements such as column heads, decorative plaster-work, niches and cornices.

Light the large areas with uplighters and wall washers, using light to soften the surfaces of your room. If you have a sloping cottage roof and oak beams, fix spots to the beams pointing upwards, to create a sense of warmth in the cavernous hollow beneath the roof. Treat architectural detail in the same way you would a solid ceramic object: use tungsten halogen spotlights or eyeball downlights to pick out features.

LIGHTING AREA BY AREA

Your home is essentially made up of a number of discrete but interlinked spaces. Although each room should be treated individually in terms of lighting style, with a design solution to suit the tasks performed in the room and the atmosphere you want to achieve, always observe how the different spaces relate to each other in terms of progression and eye adaptation.

When you step into sunlight after an afternoon spent in the darkness of the cinema, it takes a while for your eyes to adapt to the intensity of light and you are momentarily disoriented. If there are extreme contrasts of this kind between different spaces in your home, the effect is unpleasant and can even be dangerous. Don't allow visitors to plunge headlong from a brightly lit living room into a pitch-black hallway, for instance. Think about how your lighting scheme will work as a totality, linking different moods and fuctions.

This doesn't mean, of course, that you should use exactly the same light levels and types of luminaires throughout your home – even if it's a small apartment. That kind of lighting is a recipe for boredom. Different styles of luminaires with equally different ways of distributing light give a small home visual variety and impact. Simply, when you plan your lighting break down your home into a series of smaller interdependent spaces.

Rooms can be split into two categories: those with a single, fixed functional use and multi-functional spaces that require more flexible lighting design with the accent on decorative style and mood. When planning each room, draw a pencil sketch showing the architectural contours, windows and doors, furniture, shelving, decorative objects and plants. Mark also the angles of entry of natural light and the electrical sockets and switches. All such details are important to your planning – poorly positioned or insensitively styled switches can spoil the effect of a room just as easily as an inappropriate choice of luminaires.

Left: A glass façade gives a clear view of the interdependence of interior spaces. A good lighting scheme takes account of visual links between one room and the next.

Below: A hallway should provide an easy transition between the light levels in adjoining rooms. An internal space can need artificial light during the day.

For each individual space, ask yourself the questions examined earlier in the context of looking at your home as a whole, and weigh up the pros and cons of using different types of light sources and fittings.

There is no single, correct way to light a given space; each room can be lit in half-a-dozen different ways and the solution you find the most comfortable and stylish will be very much up to you. However, there are some cardinal rules you should follow in designing with light:

- *General lighting:* avoid glare and tiring, disorienting extremes of contrast;
- *Task lighting:* always put the light exactly where it is needed – on desk or workbench, for example;
- *Accent lighting:* be clear in your intent and direct attention unambiguously towards those objects and surfaces you want to highlight;
- *Information lighting:* make sure you give the right visual information, and in good time – for example, in lighting a concealed back door step.

In all areas, lighting design comes back to the trio of basic choices: the light source, light fitting, and position of the equipment.

HALLS, STAIRS AND LANDINGS

This staircase is lit by an unconventional method. Lights in the wall above each step send shafts of light along the treads, forming an ascending pattern of haloes opposite.

Hallways, staircases and landings are transitional areas, between rooms and between the interior and exterior. They have a pivotal role to play in any lighting design, to ensure that eye adaptation to different light levels in different parts of the house is progressive and pleasant. Furthermore, these corridor areas are often difficult to furnish imaginatively, so lighting takes on an added significance as the only really potent decorative element that can be utilized. Too often, though, these spaces are neglected in terms of light.

Hallways

In a narrow hall, low pendant lights will get in the way. Try ceiling-recessed downlights and strategically placed mirrors to give an impression of space, or position tungsten wall lights to give a soft, semi-directional glow. Never direct light into the faces of visitors as they come through the front door. Put all hall fittings on a dimmer so you can vary the intensity of light in response to the quality of light outside.

An imaginative way to light up the hall is to conceal fluorescent lighting behind cornices, or behind a wall-mounted decorative object. A narrow-stemmed uplighter which doubles as a coat stand is another polished combination of function and flair.

Staircases

Safety is an important element in plans for staircase lighting. It is unsatisfactory and potentially dangerous either to leave the staircase in darkness or to wash it with light indiscriminately. In both cases you lose definition of the edges of the steps. The most important aim is to create a shadow which reveals the rise and tread of each step. The simplest way to achieve this is to position a luminaire at the top of the flight of stairs – a ceiling light, pendant or downlight. The angle of the staircase will do the rest. If you choose a pendant, make sure the filament of the bulb is not shining nakedly into the eyes of a person coming up the stairs.

More complicated arrangements include tiny, cinema-style recessed lights or concealed fluorescent strips on each step. People with ultra-modern homes sometimes go to the expense of installing coloured neon or fluorescent tubes running the length of the bannisters – but this solution is more style-conscious than safety-conscious.

Two-way delay switches between top and bottom of the staircase are a good idea. So, too, is a mini-fluorescent bulb in the fitting at the top of the staircase: its energy efficiency means that you won't need to change it so often in what is usually an inaccessible spot.

Landings

As with hallways, put all landing luminaires on a dimmer. Soft, omni-directional light is best. Children and guests may appreciate a night light to guide them from bedroom to bathroom, so tiny, low-voltage and low-glow fittings at ankle height will be useful here.

Lighting the stairs

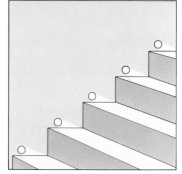

Recessed lights at the side of each step show the treads clearly and make an unusual, stylish feature.

A light source at the top of the stairs sculptures every step in a precise pattern of light and shade.

Ceiling-mounted downlights create attractive pools of light on this landing while lighting from an upper level delineates clearly the rise and tread of each step on the staircase. The effect is warm, comfortable and, above all, safe.

LIVING ROOMS

The living room is the focal point of your entire home: the place where you enjoy a communal life with the other members of your family, watch television, work and play. You will probably spend more time in it than in any other room in the house. You may therefore be willing to spend more money on furnishing it and naturally this room has the greatest demands placed on it in terms of lighting.

The sheer diversity of activity that goes on in the living room means that your lighting scheme should combine general, task and accent lighting and be an intelligent synthesis of all the points discussed earlier in this chapter. Review it not only in terms of general and task lighting suited to your needs, but also with emphasis on atmosphere, style and any special effects you wish to create.

Two views of the same room, from opposite ends, show how the lighting creates different focal points, moods and spatial relationships within the space. Ceiling-mounted spotlights accent-light pictures and books (below) with lamps and candles making soft pools of local light. At the other end of the room (right) the spotlights are used as general lighting, with a single table lamp creating a defined focal point.

Look first at the architectural contours of the room. Is it too small or too big? Can lighting improve this aspect? How do your decor plans relate to the colour qualities of the light sources and style of luminaires? What decorative objects are worth accenting with light? What jobs do you intend to do in your living room that will require special task lighting?

The options open to you are many. But bear in mind one cardinal rule: keep your design flexible.

Keep it flexible

In a living room which must adapt to a series of different emotional moods and physical requirements, it is important to avoid fixed relationships between the lighting and the furniture. You may want to change your mind about how to hang a painting and where to position the sofa. Furthermore, as decor products become more and more like couture clothing, changing with the seasons, you may wish to acquire new furnishing accessories, replace or give a new look to even the major items of furniture.

Portable fittings – table lamps, desklights, standard lamps and freestanding uplighters – are very useful and flexible design tools, creating intimate rings of light. So too are spotlights that you can reposition at will along a track.

Generally speaking, don't decide on ceiling-recessed downlights unless you are absolutely sure about the long-term uses and style of the room. Make design decisions that are easily reversed – an uplighter standing on a carpet and plugged into a wall socket leaves your options open; a hole cut in the ceiling does not.

Tungsten and tungsten halogen are the best light sources for the living room. Concealed accent lighting behind cornices, bookshelves, and glassware displays make an effective complement to the general level of lighting. Put all lights on dimmers – the variety of moods you will require, and the subtle balances of artificial light with incoming natural light, make this imperative.

As well as creating accent lighting for plants, books and paintings, don't forget to position a useful task light close to the stereo, video rack, computer and record collection. This could be a spot mounted on a short piece of track or clipped to the edge of a book or record shelf, or a wall-mounted adjustable-arm fitting.

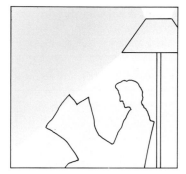

No shadow falls across reading matter if it is lit from above and behind.

A tall uplighter placed behind the television (far left) won't interfere with the screen image. For reading, a broad spread of light from a lamp at one side (left) is efficient and relaxing.

Lighting and decor dovetail in this arrangement of mirror and wall lights.

Watching television

Never watch television without additional lighting. The extreme brightness of the screen in contrast to the darkness of the room will damage your eyes. Equally, avoid positioning luminaires where they cause reflections on the screen, as happens if they are close by the viewer, for example. The best solutions are to place a light behind the television set or deploy light sources elsewhere in the room to bounce indirect general light off walls and other surfaces.

Reading

Focusing on a printed text in a bright pool of light surrounded by complete blackness is very tiring for the eyes. A light source positioned too close to the reader is tiring in itself. Directional fittings such as spotlights are not suited to comfortable, relaxed reading: the best solutions are traditional standard and table lamps positioned beside or some way behind the reader. These luminaires give off a soft, omni-directional glow but will throw enough direct light on to the page for reading. Supplement the general light level with other light sources glowing in the background.

Fitting a dimmer

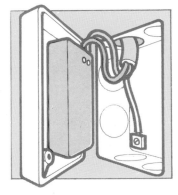

To replace an existing light switch with a dimmer, turn off the power at the mains, undo the screws in the switch's face plate and ease it away from the wall. Disconnect the red and black wires from the *switch terminals, and connect them to the dimmer's terminals according to the manufacturer's instructions. Finally, screw the dimmer to the original switch mounting box and restore the power.*

DINING ROOMS

A deep shade on the pendant directs a pool of light on the dining table without glare from the bulb. Other sources of light spread a warm ring that reinforces the central focus.

You can be the greatest cook in the world, but if poor lighting in your dining room makes your vegetables look tired and the chicken look synthetic, then your meal is off to a bad start. If you're lucky enough to have a self-contained room reserved solely for the purpose of dining, you have a golden opportunity to create a cosy, dramatic, singular setting which enhances the quality of the food and stimulates relaxed conversation.

You don't need a general level of background lighting in your dining room, unless the table regularly doubles as a work surface. Concentrate all light on to the dining table. The most common fitting performing this function is a rise-and-fall pendant. When you are giving a candlelit dinner, the pendant can be lifted up out of sight. When you bring it in low, remember to position it at a level that does not obstruct the eye contact of your guests but is not so high that it exposes the glare of the bulb. Avoid a harsh quality of strong light from a central source that will cast unflattering shadows. For everyday dining, fix a level that is effective and comfortable for all members of the family.

Experiment to find the right balance. Put the pendant on a dimmer and choose a luminaire which houses the light source high up inside the fitting. The level of light is important: too bright, and the reflections from cutlery and glassware will be painful: too dim, and the diners' faces will recede into the gloom. A good lighting design can be subtle without seeming anonymous; it can add brilliance without being intrusive.

An alternative lighting scheme is eyeball tungsten halogen downlights in the ceiling augmented with candles around the perimeter of the room. Concealed fluorescent strips above the serving hatch and behind a corner cabinet will not detract from the visual focus.

It is important to use tungsten and tungsten halogen sources in the dining room because of the excellence of the colour rendering. If a tomato and avocado salad takes on a uniform muddy tone, it looks unreal and unappetizing. The appearance of food is just as important as the taste, whether the occasion is a quiet family supper or a formal dinner with business associates.

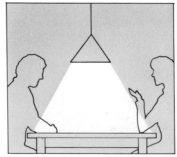

A pendant light should be hung at a level that lights the table clearly without obstructing the line of vision.

A downlight creates an attractive central focus on the table and can be supplemented by other sources.

The cool, uncluttered feel of this dining room is carried through in the fine, white, vase-shaped lamps and the delicate ceramic shade for a pendant hung at just the right height.

KITCHENS

Safety

DO
- supplement general light with task lighting on work surfaces, cooker and other fixed equipment

DON'T
- use portable fittings which overload sockets already occupied by other electrical appliances
- allow flexes to trail across worktops or close to the sink
- position light sources where they may dazzle you as you carry hot pans or sharp knives

The kitchen is a functional work centre composed of fixed elements. You can plan permanent lighting in relation to the position of the work surfaces, cupboards and appliances without the need to cater for changing moods as in, say, the living room.

Kitchen lighting has been almost defined by the single fluorescent strip, but in fact this room needs much more than just one source of general light. A high level of shadow-free general lighting, important in an area where you are handling sharp knives and scalding hot pans, should always be supplemented with task lighting focused precisely where it is needed – on the sink, cooker, refrigerator and food preparation surfaces.

Colour rendering is extremely important so you can see that your ingredients are fresh. Fluorescent light has deservedly acquired a bad reputation in the past, due to poor colour rendering and a harsh appearance, but there is a pleasant alternative to positioning a fluorescent strip across the centre of the ceiling. Concealed strips on top of your wall-mounted kitchen units, fixed at the back and against the wall, transmit light upwards so it reflects back from a white-painted ceiling, creating an effective glow.

Downlights recessed into the ceiling provide pleasing pools of general light and the light sources have excellent colour-rendering properties. This solution has a significant advantage in that the luminaire is hidden and less likely to attract dirt and grease, in a room which already has a lot of equipment which needs cleaning.

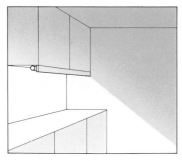

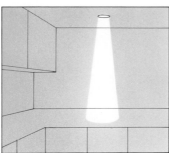

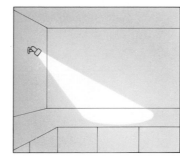

Unusual concealment for a pendant (far left) in a suspended rack surrounding the light source. Task lighting is fitted to the underside of wall units. In a streamlined white kitchen (above) ceiling downlights provide general lighting; a low pendant illuminates the adjoining dining area.

A strip light mounted underneath a cupboard and behind a baffle spreads even light on the work surface below.

A downlight placed to shed light exactly where it is needed is in itself a neat and unobtrusive source.

An adjustable spotlight mounted on the wall is a covenient and flexible source of task lighting.

The fixed elements in the kitchen allow a minimum of flexibility. Ceiling downlights throw a warm pool of light on the dining bar of this compact kitchen/diner (below).

Task lighting can add warmth to an otherwise coolly efficient kitchen, as in the sunny glow of these strip lights (right) baffle-mounted under the shelving.

Fitting a downlight

Fully recessing a downlight into a ceiling is not a very difficult job, but it does need care. Always follow any instructions supplied with the light to the letter, and if you are at all unsure on any point, particularly when it comes to providing the power supply and making the electrical connections, call in a qualified electrician – it's safer!

1. Mark out the hole for the downlight as accurately as possible on the ceiling – a template is often supplied with the light to make this easier.

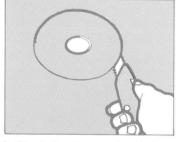

2. Check that the required hole will not be interrupted by any ceiling joists, then cut it out using a padsaw. Make good the edges of the hole with filler.

3. Turn off the power at the mains, and connect the downlight up to the cable supplying it with power according to the instructions.

Supplementary lighting

There are various possibilities for task lighting, adaptable according to the amount of space in the room as a whole and the particular arrangement of appliances and storage units. You can utilize the underside of a wall-mounted kitchen unit, illuminating the gap between unit and work surface, by recessing downlights into the bottom of the cupboard. Alternatively, place fluorescent strips around the rim of the underside, concealed by a baffle. Flexible spotlights on wall- or ceiling-mounted track can be directed towards the areas where particular chores are carried out. Adjustable-arm desk lights – wall-mounted, clipped to the edge of the kitchen table, or freestanding on their own base – provide clear directional light, but make sure the fitting will not prove an obstacle as you move around between work areas.

The kitchen may also double as a dining area, in which case you may want to create a less functional, more relaxed environment. Do this by judicious use of accent light, using track-mounted spotlights; gleaming kitchen utensils on metal grids are a good target. If you have concealed strips mounted above the units, position attractive glass jars and bottles along the top of the units, so they are lit from behind to create a decorative sparkle.

A combination including more than one type of light source gives the kitchen environment a varied, less monochromatic quality. You may also do much more than just prepare food in the kitchen – read, sew, or work on domestic administration, for example – so arrange suitable lighting for all these tasks. But remember that the kitchen is already cluttered with appliances: plan to create the best effect without the need for a lot of prominent hardware.

Some of the most stylish solutions have been achieved with industrial luminaires – fittings normally found in shops and offices. These often go well in the kitchen because of the predominance of laminates and metalware in the setting. So look beyond the normal home decor retail outlets for your kitchen lighting – the wider range of products for commercial interiors may well provide you with the fittings you want without spoiling the aesthetics of the room.

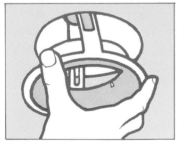

4. Ease the downlight into its hole, making sure it fits snugly against the ceiling surface, and fix in place – the method used depends on the light's design.

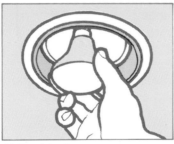

5. Double check that all is secure before fitting the lamp and restoring the power. Check that the light and its switching work correctly.

BEDROOMS

Ease and comfort are all-important in the bedroom and well-placed task lighting meets a variety of needs. Concealed lighting inside a cupboard (below left) reveals its contents clearly. Adjustable fittings wall-mounted above the bed (below) provide versatility. The more conventional bedside lamp (right) gives a pleasant, intimate glow.

Like the living room, the bedroom is an intimate setting for much varied activity: reading, relaxing, rummaging in cupboards, sleeping, dressing and working. A high level of general light should be supplemented by task lighting relevant to your bedroom-based pastimes – typing or playing a musical instrument, for instance – plus mood lighting capable of being dimmed and varied in keeping with pursuits of a more romantic nature.

A pendant luminaire is not ideal for distribution of general bedroom lighting. Stand between this light source and a drawn curtain or blind and your silhouetted naked form will unwittingly provide a shadow play for the neighbours. Much better solutions are recessed downlights or dimmer-controlled wall lights. These should provide a good level of visibility: when you're dressing, for example, you need light that will show up the torn hem of a dress or soup stains on your jacket.

Bedside lighting

Much innovation has gone into lighting controls at the bedhead, so make sure that you can switch off all bedroom lights without getting out of bed. Plan bedside lights so that either you or your partner can read on while the other sleeps. For that reason, a single tungsten strip behind a bedhead baffle is not such a good idea, even if it casts a pleasing glow on both partners. Provide individual control with two wall-mounted spotlights, one on each side of the bed, each with its own on-off switch. But spotlighting also has a drawback: it creates a rather severe contrast between the beam of light and the dark surroundings and, coming from one side, it dictates your position if you want clear, even light on your reading matter.

A good solution is a freestanding adjustable-arm luminaire with sturdy base and stem, placed on the bedside table with the bulb pointing at the wall. Less severe indirect light will

bounce down on to your bedtime book without disturbing your partner. An equally good solution is to use two translucent globe table lights, which give off a gentle omni-directional glow.

If you can wall-mount your bedside reading light, you create more space on your bedside table for books, the radio alarm clock and so on. An adjustable-arm fitting or globe light can be clamped to the wall. Another space-saving device is lighting strips built directly into the bedhead. This is a good idea in principle, but many of the marketed designs have been rather vulgar in taste. If you can't find one you like, consider customizing a more appealing design.

Storage lighting

A proportion of your bedroom space will be given over to storing your clothes and other possessions, and you'll spend a fair amount of time nosing into wardrobes and drawers. Fix a tungsten or fluorescent strip inside the wardrobe, protect it behind a baffle board and connect it up so that, operated by a pressure switch, it comes on automatically when you open the door.

If your storage cupboard is too small or awkwardly made to house internal lighting, position a couple of spotlights on a small piece of track mounted on an adjacent wall. Arrange them to shine directly into the cupboard from an angle when the door is open. If you also use spots to create task lights for dressing in front of a full-length mirror, always direct the light towards yourself and never on to the mirror.

Your dressing table may be part of an entire wall of storage units. If so, take the opportunity to fix tungsten downlights into the underside of the unit hanging above the table, or install a tungsten strip along the lower rim. In this area you can light a mirror in the same way as in the bathroom, to give good light for dry shaving or applying make-up.

BATHROOMS

Safety

DO

- follow required safety standards to keep water and electricity well apart
- recess fittings into wall or ceiling wherever possible
- put the main switch outside the door
- fit a dimmer to give low light intensity for late-night trips to the bathroom
- install a small light in the bathroom cabinet where razor blades, medicines, etc are housed

DON'T

- install hanging or adjustable fittings which you may touch or splash with water accidentally
- arrange lighting in a way that causes glaring reflections off shiny surfaces
- install conventional switches, sockets or loose flexes

Once bathrooms were regarded as stark, white and utilitarian. Today their decor is being given unprecedented attention, to make them much more comfortable and appealing. With this more luxurious concept, bathroom lighting is a design element which it is difficult to get right. Not only does the abundance of shiny reflective surfaces increase the potential for glare, but electrical safety regulations impose necessary restrictions. Electricity and water must be kept well away from each other.

Therefore a hanging central pendant, which you might brush with a wet arm as you get out of the bath, is inappropriate. So too are spotlights – it is far too tempting to adjust them by hand. The most suitable fittings are double insulated with not only all metal parts covered, but the bulb completely covered, too. A splash of cold water on a hot tungsten bulb, for example, may shatter it. Ceiling lights in the form of fixed bowls or recessed downlights are an ideal solution, achieving a high level of light that dispels early-morning miseries.

In the bathroom, it is important not to delude yourself with soft, flattering mood lighting. On the other hand, too stark and bright a light will create an unbearably pallid and ghastly effect. Light distribution, colour rendering and colour temperature are all very important, to achieve a balance that shows you to yourself in a true light that isn't too harsh – of itself and on you.

Arrange dimmer switches outside your bathroom so that you can pop in for a glass of water in the night without exposing your eyes to the full intensity of light. String-pull cords, a standard item in many bathrooms, are not attractive and can be made obsolete simply by positioning all main switches outside the bathroom.

Shower lighting

When you draw the shower curtain, make sure that it doesn't block the main source of light, leaving you to shower in gloom. Try to avoid fixing a special shower light by clever placing of the ceiling lights; but if you must light the shower itself, then a waterproof outdoor bulkhead fitting is the safest solution. Ask your supplier for advice.

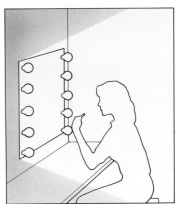

Bare bulbs mounted around three sides of a mirror are not intended merely to evoke the atmosphere of a theatre dressing room – they actually provide a very efficient spread of clear but not harsh light (above) for tasks such as shaving or applying make-up. In a confined space (top) the effect is also warming and decorative.

Well-planned distribution of light and good colour rendering create an impression of even, natural light in this spacious bathroom (left). The lights are recessed for safety's sake. A shower light concealed behind a baffle (below) accents the decorative pattern of the tiles.

Mirror lighting

Adopt the actor's style: all theatre dressing rooms have a row of bare bulbs around the edge of the mirror. Despite the glamorous image, the effect is purely functional – light shining on your face from above, below and either side of the mirror makes shaving or applying make-up much easier. A simple strip light above the mirror is a standard fitting, but it creates ridges of shadow below the nose and mouth.

As in bedroom storage, put concealed strip lighting inside bathroom cupboards – you won't want to grope in the dark for a medicine bottle or open razor. If you fit adjustable eyeball downlights in the ceiling, you can introduce an element of accent lighting – highlighting ornate taps, sparkling bottles of bath oil, wall-hanging baskets of plants or any other decorative feature. There's plenty of opportunity to create an attractive, relaxing atmosphere. You can even obtain coloured ceramic luminaires, to coordinate with sanitary-ware and bathroom furnishings.

WORKROOMS

Task lighting is an important feature in any type of workroom. Both the light sources and styles of luminaires should be chosen to suit the specific function of the room.

The home office

Whether you are writing a novel, running a mail order business, or simply totting up domestic bills, your home office should have a distinct identity, created by lighting which separates that space from the rest of the house. The enclosure of your desk within a tight ring of light, for instance, will aid concentration and creative thought. So underplay the general surroundings in your office or study. Use ceiling-mounted wall washers to brush bookcases and filing cabinets with gentle light, or deploy discreet uplighters to give an indirect glow.

Desk lighting
Concentrate your task light on the desk and invest in a quality luminaire. The designers' favourite is the adjustable-arm desk lamp, whether strictly functional or a complex piece of industrial sculpture, as exemplified in recent Italian designs. It is the more useful if the head swivels independently.

When seated at the desk, place the luminaire not directly in front of you but on a far corner of the desk so that light shines diagonally across your papers. Position the fitting where you can't see the glare of the bulb. Be careful in the initial choice of your light source: tungsten and linear mini-fluorescent bulbs provide soft but effective task lighting.

Visual display screens
If you work at home with a computer terminal and visual display screen, you can avoid constant headaches caused by glare, screen reflections and extremes of contrast. Block out sunlight effectively with thick curtains or blinds and use uplighters to provide soft, general and indirect artificial light. It is possible to buy task lights specially designed for computer screens. Good colour rendering and lack of flicker are the important factors here.

Whether you work with a traditional sewing machine or advanced computer terminal, task lighting should aim a tight ring of light on the work area to assist concentration.

A desk light on a flexible arm mounted above the study area (right) distributes light exactly as it is needed, lowered to direct a focused beam or raised to provide a generous pool of light.

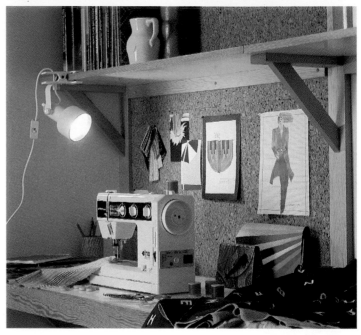

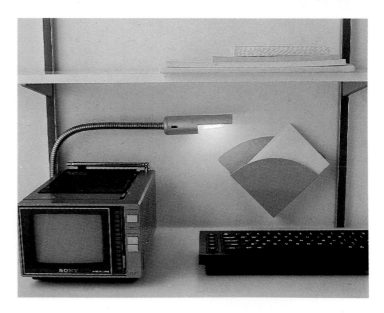

Utility rooms

Utility rooms – attic, storage room, basement, garage and workshop – require lighting that is functional, long-lasting and energy efficient rather than decorative, versatile and mood-inducing. The time you spend in such areas is put to a specific purpose and you certainly won't be entertaining guests in a utility room, so dimming, flexibility and colour appearance are not paramount considerations.

However, you must provide a good general level of visibility and, in the case of a storage basement or attic, delineate corners and steps clearly with information lighting.

Fluorescent strip on the ceiling and mini-fluorescent fittings on walls are a good option. Sturdy industrial fixtures commonly used in factories and shops are equally useful for large domestic utility areas. Once again, explore lighting outlets beyond the general run of home decor retailers. Deep bowl pendant fittings, known as hi-bays and lo-bays in the trade, are heavy and visually obtrusive but provide powerful lighting for a giant garage or storage area. Wall bulkheads are ideal for garages; they give enough light to get under the car bonnet.

Lighting a workbench

When your work involves use of industrial tools, poor lighting can result in accidents. Take care to avoid shadows, or a general light level which is gloomy or glaring. Ceiling mount a fluorescent strip directly above or just behind where you stand so that a bright, even, patternless light spills down on to the bench from both sides of you.

For industrial handywork in which colour rendering is very important – making jewellery, for example – supplement general lighting from the fluorescent strip with tungsten light from an adjustable-arm luminaire. Clip it to the corner of the workbench or let it stand on the surface on a firm base, in a position where it will not be affected by vibration or knocked over as you move and handle the necessary equipment.

ENTERTAINING WITH LIGHT

The ability of light to convey a sense of occasion and festivity is an important asset for all kinds of entertaining in the home. Parties provide a golden opportunity to supplement your conventional lighting arrangements with temporary solutions – adventurous, colourful ideas that you may not want to live with all the year round, but which are great fun for an afternoon, evening or a couple of days.

Eating outdoors
The focal point of a barbecue will be the live flame, heat, smoke and food. Take this as your cue and use smoke flares on the lawn and camping-gas lamps behind the bushes to create an atmospheric effect – a warm glow in the distant vista or a close ring of light.

Whatever the occasion small amounts of well-placed light in the blackness of your garden will have an extraordinarily dramatic effect, given the sheer extent of contrast, but take care where you position the sources. If you have an old wall covered with ivy, wash it with light from a spotlight to reveal the interesting texture. If you have a swimming pool or jacuzzi, switch on the underwater lights.

Above all, aim to create silhouettes, shapes and small pockets of visual focus. Uplighting behind bushes adjacent to the eating area is useful to produce moving shadows. But allow enough light to avoid the problem of guests stumbling around in the dark with plates of food. By improvising with light, you will amaze not only your guests, but also your neighbours, who know your garden well by daylight but will see it in a brand new light at night.

Christmas
Christmas lighting should be ethereal rather than overt, to create a sense of wonder in young children and a feeling of intimacy for the whole family. Low-voltage tungsten halogen 'sparkler' fittings are useful to supplement the cosy, warm appeal of strings of fairy and silver lights. Avoid brashly coloured bulbs as they destroy a delicate atmosphere.

One way to make more use of your Christmas decorative lights is to buy a string of fairy-light fittings which are

Special lighting effects can be appropriate and still surprising. Strands of sparkling fairy lights coiled into perspex boxes (above) are a clever new trick with a traditional form. Colourful flares on the lawn (left) are an alluring background to a barbecue outdoors.

The pleasures of eating outdoors are enhanced by magical,
temporary lighting effects. An
array of candles can be relied
upon to add an air of enchant-
ment. Glass containers shield
the flames and contribute their
own sparkle to the occasion.

weatherproof and suitable for outdoor use. You can string them up outside for summer evening parties and bring them indoors to adorn the Christmas tree in winter. To add dramatic impact to your Christmas tree, uplight it from behind with a floor-mounted baby spot or uplighter Reflected light will create pleasing foliage patterns on the ceiling.

Candles are an essential feature of Christmas lighting. Arrange them in elegant groupings on coloured trays, decorate them with foliage and dried flowers, and they will bring a warm, magical feeling to the festivities.

Children's parties

It is important to keep the lighting bright: a sophisticated, smoochy atmosphere is inappropriate and, anyway, you need to keep an eye on the kids. Candles and flares are dangerous when young children are around and delicate, temporary lighting structures invariably get knocked over.

The safest, jolliest solution is to replace the tungsten bulbs in your ordinary fittings – desk lights, wall lights, pendants – with brightly coloured light sources. Also, to hold the attention of the generation of tiny TV addicts, project cartoons, videos and slides on to walls or screens.

Dinner parties

Candlelight creates a glowing, sympathetic ambience for dinner parties. It brings a warm sparkle to silverware and glassware, it creates a private pool of light and provides a focus for intimate conversation. It also has a cosmetic effect, in that it leaves large areas of the room in discreet shadow, to conceal dirty dishes, serving bowls and so on: this contributes to your image as a natural host or hostess.

If you are worried that candlelight will provide insufficient illumination – for example, when entertaining more than twelve guests – supplement it with dimmable tungsten halogen downlights which create appealing and dramatic shards of light. Switch off all your usual accent lights on plants and books so that the dinner table becomes the uncontested focal point.

A rise-and-fall pendant fitting on a flex is useful for entertaining. If you bring it in low, position candles around the perimeter of the room rather than on the table.

The important point to remember with a pendant is that you must position it exactly, placing the pendant high enough to give unobstructed view to each dinner guest but low enough to conceal the gleaming bulb. With that in mind, it is best to choose a pendant which houses the bulb high up inside the fitting, and put the pendant on a dimmer switch.

Candlelight is a welcome feature of entertaining in the evening; elegant groupings strike the right note (below).

A soft, discreetly positioned lamp (left) is a good supplement to candlelight at dinner.

Disco

Unless you're a technical genius it is best to hire a light show from a specialist firm, but avoid being palmed off with the standard package – a bank of static flashing lights or a couple of stock, clichéd effects.

Disco equipment provides the opportunity to bring all your party rooms alive with light, not just the dancing area. Help out the disco lighting equipment by putting a light under the sofa so that the furniture looks as though it is about to lift off. Strongly accent light your possessions to create all kinds of interesting shadows.

Sound-to-light units will produce flashing lights in time with pulsating music. Strobe lighting causes excitement, but don't overplay it all night long as it can get monotonous and is disturbing to some people. Image projection is another good idea – project videos or slides on to giant screens or white walls to build the party mood. Above all, aim for colour, movement and excitement.

FLOORS AND FLOORING

The floor sets the tone in any living space. One-sixth of the surface area of a room, it is literally the base for the interior as a whole, for furniture, ornaments and decoration. No matter how carefully everything else is put together, if the floor is wrong the overall effect will be uneasy and disjointed.

Since the floor plays such a fundamental role in creating the style and atmosphere in a home, there's a good argument for making it your first choice and designing the rest of your scheme around it. Even if you don't have the opportunity to plan a whole room or home from scratch, you can stand back and take a long, critical look at what you already have to see if it can be improved.

Don't just worry about the overall picture – 'God is in the details' as one famous architect observed. Inexpert laying, a poor finish or lack of maintenance will undermine the wisest choice. It's foolish to lay cork and then not bother to seal it properly; to fit a carpet without adequate underlay; to leave the junction between two types of flooring unresolved.

A floor must work harder than any other surface in your home. It must be safe, provide a degree of comfort and withstand a reasonable amount of wear. It may have to act as a sound or heat insulator. When you choose a floor, select a type that is practical and fulfils your particular requirements.

Luckily there is an enormous variety of floors from which to choose – a wide enough range to satisfy both stylistic and practical needs, and, importantly, to accommodate most budgets. Traditional floorings such as carpet are more versatile and hard-wearing than ever before, while utilitarian materials such as vinyl and linoleum are now available in specially designed ranges; so research all the alternatives.

Although the floor surfaces differ in material – quarry tiles, wood and rug – toning colours create a harmonious yet varied whole.

CARPETS

Warm and comfortable underfoot, available in a wide range of colours, patterns and textures, carpet is deservedly popular. A fitted carpet can do more to enhance and unify a decorative scheme than almost any other type of floor; and modern fibres will stand a high degree of wear.

In terms of durability and appearance, there is almost nothing to choose between *good quality* (well-constructed) carpets of a similar pile weight. The price and performance of a carpet is more likely to relate to the type and amount of fibre used and to the *quality* of construction, rather than the method of manufacture, though tufted carpets, for example, are generally cheaper than woven.

Woven carpets

Fibres available include all-wool, all-synthetic and mixes. The backing and pile are constructed at the same time. Three types of warp yarns are intertwined into the side-to-side frame of weft yarns. *Chain* warps go over and under the weft yarns to bind them; *stuffers* run through the centre of the carpet to fill it out and stengthen it; and *pile* warps form the carpet surface.

WILTON can be plain or patterned. As well as the smooth-cut pile usually associated with Wilton, there is Brussels weave (uncut loop pile), cord carpet (low loop pile) or a mixture of cut and looped pile. The pile warp yarn is continuous and carried underneath the weft, then over a wire which pushes it to a variable height above the backing in a loop and fixes it. These loops can be left uncut, or sliced to produce a thick, smooth pile surface. By mixing cut and uncut loops, sculptured effects can be achieved; by using long wires, 'shag' style Wilton carpets are produced.

To obtain pattern, up to five colours of pile yarns are run through the weave, controlled by a punched card-operated jacquard, which lifts the correct colour from its frame, carrying the others through the backing as in fair isle knitting. All this extra fibre means patterned Wiltons are usually heavy top grade, but very classy plain ones are made with the jacquard process.

Lower quality plain Wiltons are made by the face-to-face

Carpet fibre chart
Dots indicate quality and performance

	Price	Feel and appearance	Ease of cleaning	Dirt performance	Dur…
Acrylic (Acrilan, Courtelle, Orlon etc.)	Fairly costly	● ● ● ● ●	● ● ● ●	● ● ● ●	●
Cotton	Cheap	● ● ● ● ●	● ● ● ● ●	● ● ● ●	●
Nylon (Timbrelle, Enkalon, Antron etc.)	Good quality will be costly	● ● ●	● ● ● ●	● ● ● ●	● ●
Polyester (Terylene, Dacron, Trevira etc.)	Cheap	● ● ● ●	● ● ● ● ●	● ● ●	● ●
Polypropylene (Propathene, Fibrite, Olefin etc.)	Cheap	● ● ●	● ● ● ● ● ●	● ● ● ● ● ●	●
Sisal	Cheap	● ●	● ●	● ● ●	● ● ●
Viscose rayon	Cheap	● ● ● ●	● ● ● ● ●	● ●	●
Wool	Costly to very costly	● ● ● ● ● ●	● ● ● ● ● ●	● ● ●	● ●

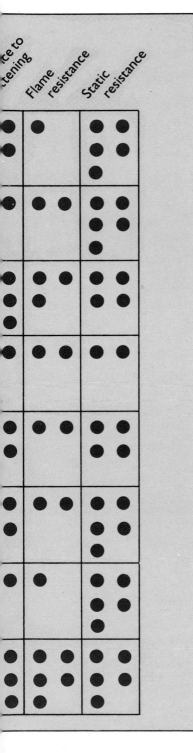

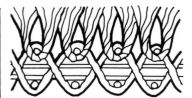

Wilton cut pile. *This is woven on a loom in loop form, the loops being cut to make the pile.*

Wilton loop. *Known also as Brussels weave, it is woven as cut pile, but the loops are uncut.*

Axminster cut pile. *Each tuft is separately inserted into the backing before being cut.*

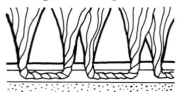

Tufted cut pile. *A fairly new type of carpet, cheaper than Axminster or Wilton.*

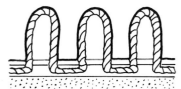

Tufted loop. *Basically, the same as the cut pile with the loops uncut.*

method in which one set of pile warp yarns is shared between sets of backing yarns. As the sandwich is made, it is sliced through the centre to separate it into two carpets.

AXMINSTER For gripper Axminsters, each tuft is separately inserted into the backing by grippers and then cut, which means that no unused yarn runs through the carpet and that a large number of colours can be used – usually about eight, sometimes as many as sixteen – all controlled by jacquards.

Less tightly woven, but more highly coloured, are spool Axminsters: the yarn is wound on spools arranged over the loom in as many rows as needed for pattern repeat, and these clank round continuously. Up to thirty to forty colours can be used this way – sometimes with regrettable results! The back of gripper Axminster is ridged and the pattern does not show. The back of spool Axminster is smooth, usually with the pattern showing through.

Tufted carpets

Introduced about thirty years ago, tufted carpets are made by inserting pile yarn (synthetic or wool), threaded through a row of needles poised above the machine, into the prepared backing. Once in, the hooks hold back enough yarn to make a loop while the needles are pulled out and the process repeated. For cut pile, the loops are sliced as they are made. The carpet backing is then coated with adhesive to secure the tufts in position, and usually another backing is applied, too. In recent years it has become possible to achieve flecked effects, and even simple patterns. Most patterned carpets in the United States are printed tufteds.

Non-woven carpets

These carpets can be *needlepunched* and fixed with a coating of adhesive. Or they can be *bonded* – by adhesive which fixes pile fibres on the pre-manufactured backing, in ridges for a cord effect. This can be done simultaneously on to two sets of backing which are then sliced through the centre to make two smooth-faced carpets at once. Or they can be electrostatically *flocked* in which (usually nylon) short fibres are electrostatically attracted to the backing.

Laying carpet

Measuring for carpets

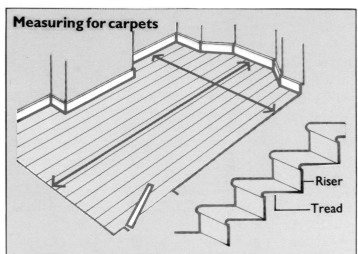

Riser

Tread

For a square or rectangular room, multiply the length by the width. Few rooms are absolutely square, so take the longest wall in each direction if there is a difference. This calculation gives you the number of square feet, yards or metres according to your measuring system. To convert square feet into square yards, divide the number of square feet by nine. For strip carpet priced by the linear yard, decide which way the carpet is to run. Ideally, it should be laid at right angles to the main source of natural light, to minimize the joins visually. It is also a good idea to lay it in the same direction as the room's traffic movement. In practical terms, lay it whichever way requires the fewest strips to be cut. Measure the width (or length) of the room in inches, then divide by 26 or 36 (according to the width of the carpet) to arrive at the number of strips needed. Multiply this number by the yard length (or width) of the room, for the number of linear yards needed. For patterned carpet, allow one matching repeat per strip.

For stairs, measure each stair separately. Calculate the length of carpet by running string from top to bottom of the staircase, down the risers and over the treads. Add an extra 60cm (24in) so the carpet can be moved up and down to even out the wear and tear.

On the whole, carpet laying is a job for the professional. If you want to attempt it yourself remember you'll be dealing with unwieldy, heavy rolls of material which may be hard to cut and must be stretched to fit – a tricky process. The correct equipment is important too, and not cheap. However, some manufacturers produce kits designed for the do-it-yourself fitter and other manufacturers supply instruction manuals.

Ordering a carpet

It's a good idea to measure the space to be carpeted before shopping around, so you can compare carpet prices and estimates accurately. This will just be a rough guide – the supplier or carpet fitter will take exact measurements to prevent any subsequent disputes.

Work out the rough price by multiplying your square metre (yard) figure by the price per square metre (yard) and adding on the amount for underlay, fitting and any purchase (value added) tax. Another approach is to work backwards from a budget limit to find out how much you can afford per square metre (yard) laid.

With fitted carpet you probably won't be able to avoid either wastage or seams and minimizing both at the same time can be tricky: the art of laying carpet involves resolving these sometimes contradictory demands. Making a plan of the spaces to be carpeted will help.

Before the floor is ordered and laid, assuming you aren't laying the carpet yourself, the carpet suppliers should give you an estimate. This should state: the type and amount of carpet (by manufacturer's name, code, with width and colour specified) and a similarly exact description of any underlay; the rooms/area to be covered; the cost of the carpet, underlay, fitting and tax, separately detailed.

The fitters should give you a date and time for delivery and fitting and specify whether their charge includes moving furniture, removing doors and so on. Some fitters will supply you with a diagram of where the seams will go, but you should at least discuss it beforehand. This important point relates to the width of carpet you have chosen: it would be foolish to take a narrow width for a large space. Further, with velour or

Carpet tiles

These are small squares of sealed-edged carpet available in several sizes, materials and colours, both plain and patterned. Most common are 40cm (15½in) and 50cm (19½in) squares, but 30cm (12in) and 45cm (18in) squares are also available. Carpet tiles are made in a wide range of fibres, including wool, other animal hair, synthetic fibres and mixes. Backings can be of PVC, polypropylene, natural and synthetic rubber and bitumen impregnated felt. Whichever sort you choose, it should possess guaranted dimensional stability. Carpet tiles laid in a single colour will resemble broadloom carpet; chequerboard effects can be created by using two colours, and other, more complicated patterns are possible. They can be stuck down, or loose laid for easy replacement, and are ideal for dining rooms and children's rooms, where dirt, damage and general wear and tear are likely. In very worn-out areas, though, a single, new carpet tile can be as conspicuous as a damaged one; moving the tiles around regularly is often a better solution. Carpet tiles allow access to under-floor services.

patterned pile, you can't just add in extra pieces – the pattern repeat and pile direction must match up. The method of fitting dictates cost, too – sewn seams cost more than stuck seams, for example.

Types of underlay

It really is worth spending money on a good quality underlay – even if the carpet is cheap, underlay may extend its life as well as improving the way it feels underfoot. Foam-backed carpet does not need underlay, but should be laid on felt paper (very cheap) to prevent the foam sticking to the floor.

Underlay absorbs pressure on the carpet, lessens wear, cushions the carpet from unevenness in the floor, prevents dirt from working up from the floorboards and protects the carpet from rot. It insulates for heat and from noise and is pleasant to walk on. Beware, however, of buying a too-thick underlay: heavy furniture may sink in and pull the carpet out of shape; also doors will have to be trimmed.

FELT underlay is usually made of jute or animal hair, or a mixture of the two. Jute felt, while cheaper, can flatten, harden or break down. Hair felt is generally stronger, more resilient and durable. A mixture is reasonably strong and cheap. The weight and thickness of this underlay should be at least 1628g per square metre (48oz per square yard) in a heavily used room, and underlay should have been moth-proofed by the manufacturer.

FOAM OR RUBBER underlay is made from natural or synthetic materials. Both types are fairly springy and don't shed fibres, but they can rot in damp, may perish on an overheated sub-floor, and are unsuitable for heavily seamed areas or stairs. They are best with a hessian or mesh nylon/polypropylene backing fabric or a textured surface. To test quality, rub a foam underlay firmly with your thumb – it should not crumble at all. Reject it if it does.

RUBBERIZED FELT theoretically combines the advantages of both rubber and felt.

BONDED UNDERLAY is similarly made from wool, synthetic fibres and latex rubber.

Preparation

As always, lay only on a sound, dry surface. Remove all old tacks and nails or hammer nails in flat. Fix loose floorboards and correct severe unevenness in the floor. Cover floors in bad condition with hardboard. Do not lay carpet direct on thermoplastic tiles; moisture cannot escape and will eventually damage the carpet.

Laying woven carpet

Woven carpet is best laid by fitting it to gripper rods. These are quite expensive but can be re-used, and the laid carpet looks smooth to the edges. The gripper is a strip of light wood 2.5cm (1in) or so wide, with pins protruding at an angle; is nailed or stuck around the edges of the floor with the pins facing the wall. The carpet is stretched, hooked on the pins, and tacked neatly down into the gap. Where the carpet does not run up to a wall a binder bar is used: the carpet is pulled on to the pins and then covered by a curved metal strip. Double binder bars are used where two carpets meet.

To fit pre-nailed gripper rods, use a hammer similar to a carpet fitter's hammer, with a small striking face on a heavy head so you avoid striking and blunting the gripping points. To follow curved recesses in the room, cut the strip into very short lengths.

TACKING is a traditional, cheaper method of laying which involves stretching the carpet, turning its edges in and tacking them down every 7.5 to 10cm (3 to 4in) with 2cm (¾in) tacks, 2.5cm (1in) where the carpet is very thick. But the indentations can look untidy and will collect dirt.

RING AND PIN is a type of laying that enables the carpet to

Laying woven carpet

  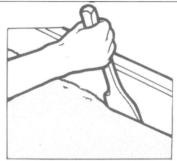 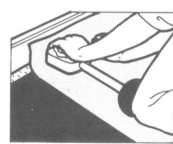

1. Nail gripper strips around room. Leave gap between strips and skirting boards.

2. Fix underlay up to gripper strips. Secure with tacks or strong staples.

3. Fix carpet over gripper strips. Push down to fill gap so it butts up to the skirting.

4. With knee kicker, gradually stretch carpet to opposing walls until it hooks gripper.

Laying foam-backed carpet

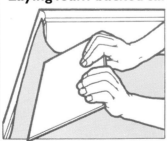 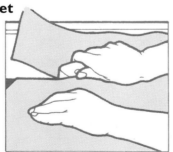  

1. Line floor with felt paper. Push carpet firmly into position using a board.

2. Cut carpet with a small overlap. Allow it to settle for a week, then trim it to fit.

3. Butt edges of two strips as close together as possible, using double-sided tape.

4. In awkward corners, fold carpet back over board. With ruler, extend wall line and cut.

A good-quality fitted carpet is a sensible investment for stairs; it looks attractive and muffles sound. For safety and long-lasting wear, fit the carpet securely. To use gripper strips, fit one on each riser and one on each tread, with the pins facing the angle between. Make the gap between the two strips twice the thickness of the carpet. Once the strips are in position, fit the tread underlay mats between the grippers. Tack, stick or staple each mat securely, then fit the carpet starting from the bottom of the stairs and working upwards. Stretch the carpet and hook it on to each gripper as you move up the steps. Stair rods, fitted across the carpet where each riser and tread meet, are another alternative.

A runner can be a less expensive alternative to a fitted carpet, but depends for its beauty on the exposed staircase being well finished. It, too, needs secure fixing.

be taken up for cleaning but is expensive and must be done professionally. Rings are sewn into the carpet's backing and then fixed over pins or a gripper strip in the floor.

FIXING UNDERLAY The underlay should stop just short of the gripper rods and (unless it's foam) be fixed with tacks, although staples, if you can obtain a stapling hammer, are better. Cut the underlay slightly oversize, fix it, then trim to fit along the guiding inner edge of the gripper strip. On concrete or similar floors stick it around the edges of the room.

FIXING CARPET Begin in a corner. Let the carpet ride up the wall a little and smooth it on to gripping pins by hand. Using a fitting hammer or similar tool, push it down on to the points and draw it along the wall, forcing it into the gulley. Do this for the two walls that meet in the starting corner.

Then stretch and hook carpet on to the gripper strip on opposite walls. If you can borrow, hire or even make a carpet stretcher do so, but practise first – you could hurt yourself and chew up the carpet. The 'teeth' of this device dig into the carpet and a push with the knee stretches the carpet a little, a process which is repeated until the carpet stretches enough to fit over the gripper strip, after which it contracts and stays in place. If you don't have a stretcher, push the carpet along with your feet, making little jumps. Knock in tacks lightly to help hold the surplus you've pushed along.

For alcoves, cut carpet long enough to reach to the end, then make a cut on both sides at right angles so a tongue of carpet falls into the alcove. The same principles apply to tufted and non-woven carpets.

Laying foam-backed carpet

Foam-backed carpet does not need to be stretched. Cut the carpet just slightly larger than the room – 2.5cm (1in) or so extra at each wall. Trim to fit. To join at seams, use wide carpet seaming tape.

Foam-backed carpet, needlefelt and carpet tiles can be stuck down all over with adhesive, or loose-laid and secured with double-sided tape. Foam-backed carpets should never be laid directly on to polished, varnished or vinyl floors or they will stick permanently – lay paper felt first.

MATTING

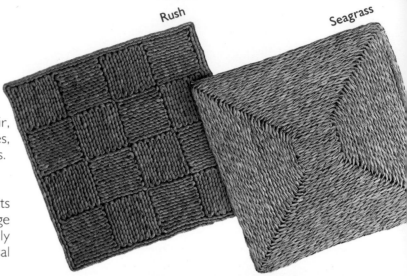

Rush

Seagrass

As wall-to-wall flooring or cheerful scatter mats, sisal, coir, rush, seagrass and maize, as well as synthetic plastic types, make cheap, easy alternatives to more traditional surfaces.

Sisal and coir

Both cheap, hard-wearing fibres, coir comes from coconuts and sisal from the leaves of the agave plant. Colours range from pale brown to dark brown, though coir most usually comes in a honey gold. Now it is also possible to dye sisal many beautiful shades, although not all are fast.

Both fibres can be uncomfortable, and may crumble and shed fibres and dust. Better varieties are latex- or vinyl-backed to prevent dust and dirt falling through to the floor beneath and make for greater durability. Good for stairs (but ensure the surface doesn't become hard and slippery), corridors and as a base throughout the house, but avoid using in the kitchen or under dining tables because of food spills.

LAYING After cutting slightly oversize, allow to acclimatize to room for twenty-four hours. For wall-to-wall laying, pick one of the broadloom types, stitch narrower lengths together, or butt edges firmly together, using double-sided tape underneath. You can loose-lay but it is better to stick down using double-sided tape or carpet adhesive. Tacking down edges may cause slight bumping and troughing.

Rush, seagrass, maize

Natural materials of varying fineness of texture, these vegetable fibres have plenty of cool charm. Maize is the finest and palest in colour. Woven squares can be sewn together into mats using fine twine, and there are many attractive weaves. Don't expect them to take heavy wear; they may be quickly shredded if there are cats in the family.

LAYING Do not need underlay. Also look good scattered over other flooring.

Plastic

Woven plastic matting comes in bright colours and has a jolly, cheerful appeal. It is very cheap and fairly durable. Avoid direct heat, strong chemicals and abrasive cleaners.

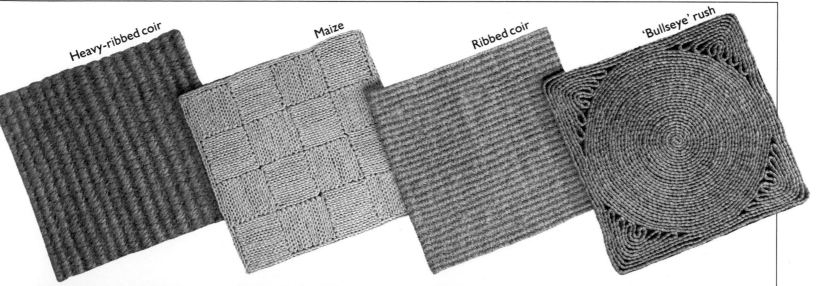

Heavy-ribbed coir   Maize   Ribbed coir   'Bullseye' rush

Care of matting

SISAL AND COIR
Vacuum clean. Loose matting can be taken up and beaten, and scrubbed with soapless detergent. Clean underneath now and then if you can.

RUSH, SEA-GRASS, MAIZE
Deteriorate if too dry, so moisten occasionally with a plant sprayer. Lift and sweep beneath and snip off flaking ends. Bind edges if they start to fray.

Far left: The sea-grass matting squares add definition to the sleeping area and provide the visual and physical warmth lacking in the ceramic tiles.

Left: Practical and hardwearing, coir matting can be used in a bathroom. Here, its natural colour sets off the vivid blue of the traditional-style bath, and complements the cream of the walls and cupboards.

OLD WOOD

A wooden floor, treated in one of the many ways that costs little but effort, should be durable and economical as well as attractive. Rugs can be added as you wish, which makes for flexibility. While you shouldn't underestimate the amount of time and work that may be needed to execute a finish properly, the sense of creativity can be immensely satisfying. When choosing a finish, consider the room as a whole: the cleverest treatment may only look fussy if everything else is jostling for attention too.

Types of floor

SUSPENDED WOODEN PLANK FLOORS consist of planks supported on joists, support beams which run at right-angles to the planks. Assuming that the joists, and the timber wall plates that support them, are free of rot and damp (which should be checked by a surveyor), the state of the planks will dictate your next move.

Planks come in many widths and generally in cheap, strong wood such as pine or deal. There is a great difference between wide, old solid oak planks and worn, splintery, pine boards; most floors are somewhere in between.

SOLID WOOD FLOORS consist of hardwood parquet, wood strips, tiles or blocks laid on solid floors, usually concrete over hardcore. In upper storey rooms, however, the floor will probably be a suspended one. Solid floors are very durable, but much depends on whether the wood is solid or veneered, and, if veneered, on how thick the skin is, and on the type of base material. Veneered plywood, for example, is not suitable for machine stripping.

Preparation

MAKING GOOD Take up existing floor covering, if any, and inspect the boards carefully. Look out for springy or saggy areas, squeaking boards, wide gaps between boards, flaking and badly pitted surfaces.

If boards are springy or saggy the joists may be at fault; lift the boards to inspect. If they are in a bad condition, seriously damaged or rotten, call in a builder to replace or repair. If they squeak, the boards may not be hammered down

Making good

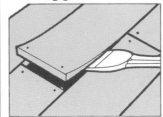

If you need to replace a floorboard, use a special chisel to lever it up.

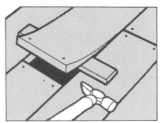

Use a block of wood to prevent the board springing back while you lever it up.

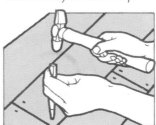

Always sink the head of the nail below the surface of the board, using a nail punch.

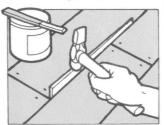

Use wood fillets to fill gaps between boards. Or for tiny gaps try papier mâché or wood filler.

properly: fix them firmly on the joists with nails, punching them down so that a small space is left above the nail head.

If there are many wide gaps between boards, you would be better off covering the floor with hardboard, but if the gaps are not too serious, fill with wood fillets. Cut matching wood in wedge shapes to fit tightly, glue the edges and tap down smartly into the gaps. Plane until all is level. Smaller gaps can be filled with a homemade papier maché (wet, drained newspaper pulp mixed with glue size); or with a proprietary woodwork filler; or, if you plan to polyurethane the floor, with a polyurethane filler. These filling materials may 'take' stains, varnishes and so on in a slightly different way to the surrounding boards, though you can buy stopping in a range of tints or try to match it yourself using a drop or two of stain.

CLEANING There are easier ways to clean than sanding. Even if it turns out that you have to sand anyway, cleaning will reveal the real condition of the surface and it may emerge that hand sanding will be enough.

First, punch down any protruding nails at least 3mm (⅛in) below surface, using a nail punch. For a professional finish, fill holes with stopping, and if there is a heavy deposit of wax on the floor, remove it with wire wool and white spirit. Wear gloves and scrub thoroughly, but not too wetly, with very hot water and strong detergent. Wetting the wood like this will raise the grain, and, even if you find there's no real need to sand, the raised grain will need rubbing down once the floor dries. Rub down with medium, then fine, glasspaper in the direction of the grain using long smooth strokes. Particularly if the boards have been protected by a carpet or lino you may find they come up very well or with just a few stains and paint splashes which you can deal with individually.

Part of the charm of these old wood floorboards lies in their imperfections – the variations in colour, odd splits and knotting. As with furniture the finish of an old wooden floor is a kind of patina that develops over many years.

Stripping, sanding and sealing

Power sanding

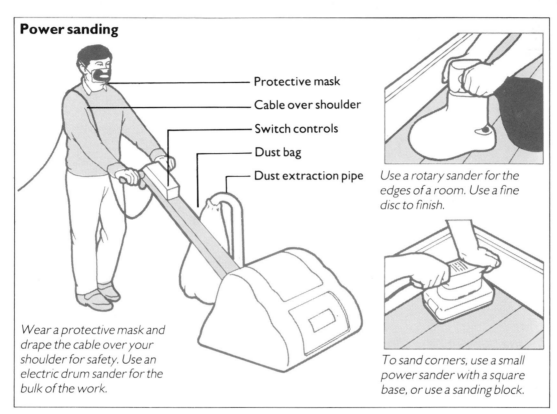

- Protective mask
- Cable over shoulder
- Switch controls
- Dust bag
- Dust extraction pipe

Wear a protective mask and drape the cable over your shoulder for safety. Use an electric drum sander for the bulk of the work.

Use a rotary sander for the edges of a room. Use a fine disc to finish.

To sand corners, use a small power sander with a square base, or use a sanding block.

Stripping

For small areas of floor or stair treads that have been painted, try a proprietary chemical stripper or hot air stripper, and follow the directions exactly. Work quickly, scraping off the softened paint before giving an all-over scrub with white spirit. You could use a blow lamp if you are very skilled, but there's a great danger of burning or scorching the wood badly. If the boards have been treated with a tenacious varnish (or a stain) don't try to clean it off: it may sink in and make matters worse. Sanding is the solution here.

Hand sanding

If the floor displays only a few patches of stubborn stain after cleaning, use coarse, medium and fine glasspaper, in that order, wrapped round a sanding block, rubbing in the direction of the grain. When sanding parquet, sand twice, the second time at right angles to the first. This is because parquet is laid in opposite directions. Give a final, thorough sanding with fine sandpaper.

Power sanding

Boards that are in a truly poor condition, badly stained and uneven, will need power sanding. If there are several floors or a very large area to do at once, power sanding is also a sensible option. If you're dealing with a wood strip or parquet floor, pull up a section to check whether, if it's veneer, the veneer is thick enough to cope with sanding. Glue down any loose pieces with appropriate adhesive.

grooves in the boards: tilt it up at the beginning and end of rows. Remember that softwood floors will be sanded away quicker than hardwood, but don't be tempted to 'deep sand' stubborn spots: you may end up with potholes. Go over frequently and lightly, finishing with a fine sanding sheet in the direction of the grain. But before the last run with the big sander, deal with the margins of the room with the edging sander, again going in line with the grain. Give a final clean with white spirit: dust must be removed before further treatment.

Sealing

Soft, clean boards must be protected. If you want to decorate or colour them, keep them covered until you have finished and are ready to seal the decoration in. Otherwise, seal immediately. Some traditional wood treatments – oiling, waxing and coating with so-called button polish (shellac) – are not recommended by timber experts for use on floors.

There is no such thing as an ideal seal, but several are equally useful. Oleo-resinous seals, sometimes called clear varnishes, are the result of a reaction between a resin (often a phenolic) and an oil (often tung oil). They are very hard wearing and easy to apply. The almost identical, widely available 'polyurethanes' in a single can are basically oleo-resinous with a small amount of urethane resin added. These two, and most resin solution types, are no more noxious than gloss paints, but some other seals may produce nasty fumes or react badly on skin. Wear protective clothing, a face mask, have proper ventilation, obey the manufacturer's instructions and avoid contact with flame – all seals are flammable.

Urea formaldehydes are lacquers that either have to be catalyzed into effectiveness by separately stored 'acid' or come as one-can 'self-curing' mixtures. They are hard wearing and good for pale woods such as maple since they dry to a colourless film. Other two-can seals are epoxy resin and a heavier duty polyurethane, both durable but slow drying.

Apply seals with brush or pad of non-fluffy cloth, working well into the grain. Do not allow drips or ridges to occur. Seals take a while to cure, so don't subject the floor to heavy wear too soon.

You'll need two sanders: a large upright one with a dust collector, and an edging sander. Wear a face mask and goggles. Using a medium grit belt (or coarse grade if the deposits are thick) on the larger machine, sand at forty-five degrees to the board, then again in the opposite direction (still at forty-five degrees). After this, sand in the direction of the grain, moving progressively to fine sandpaper. If the deposits are light, you need go in the direction of the grain only, but this can create furrows if you do it for too long. Start each sanding run a few centimetres (inches) away from the last to avoid making start marks. Sweep up the dust that settles with a slightly damp cloth. (Do not burn this, or the sawdust that you collect, or you may create a flash fire.)

Do not allow the machine to run on the spot as it will chew

NEW WOOD

New wooden floors are classic, contemporary, attractive, warm underfoot and durable. They can be laid structurally in soft or hardwood strips or boards of varying thickness, or in factory-made 'tile' systems. Only stiletto heels and cigarette burns are likely to cause lasting damage.

Selecting flooring timber

If you plan to go to the trouble of laying a new floor, you must also go to the trouble of selecting good quality, properly dried and seasoned timber. The harder softwoods and a wide range of hardwoods are all suitable for floors. Avoid softwood not impregnated against rot and woodworm; softwood with too high a resin content that will 'weep'; sapwood and the heart of hardwood logs (too soft and likely to split, shrink or twist); badly dried or badly stacked timber; over-warped or cracked timber; timber with dead knots; damp timber. Kiln-dried timber should be ready to use. Old timber, occasionally available when buildings are demolished (and sometimes at bargain prices), may be well seasoned and solid – or it may re-saw badly.

Flooring wood must contain roughly the same amount of moisture as exists in the atmosphere of the room in which it will be laid. Wood that is too dry may regain moisture from the atmosphere during the summer and swell; wood that is too wet may dry out *in situ* and shrink. Where there is underfloor heating, the moisture content must be in the range of 6 to 8 per cent; if there is ordinary central heating, the moisture content should be between 10 and 14 per cent. Wood for flooring also must have a density (at 15 per cent moisture content) of around 700 or more – this is measured on an internationally agreed scale.

Once you have selected your timber, check in which widths it is available. Wide boards look rugged, reminiscent of ships' timbers. Narrower boards will give a more refined look. Most wood comes in standard widths, so specifying odd sizes may mean a high degree of wastage.

Natural wood floors are very attractive and available in a wide range of grains and colours. Finding your favourite needs patience and a big budget.

Beech

Mahogany

Light oak

Walnut   Maple   Elm   Dark oak   Pine

Ready-made wood floors

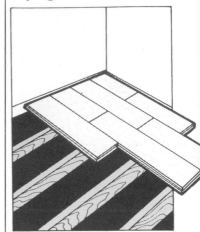

1. Lay the wood from the corner at right angles to the joists.

Tongue & groove fixing

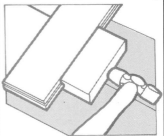

Strips can be gently knocked into place using a spare piece of tongue-and-groove flooring as a buffer.

To attach strips to a timber sub-floor, 'secret nail' at a 45° angle through tongue.

Manufactured wood floors include hardwood strip, wood mosaic (usually in a basket-weave pattern) and wood block. Price varies according to quality and finish – but compares favourably with quarry or ceramic tiles. Many systems interlock and come in different stains or natural colours so that patterns can be made. They are often ready sealed by the manufacturer.

Some types are best professionally laid and finished; others are easy to fit yourself. All of these floors must be laid on completely smooth, level, damp-free sub-floors – either concrete, or timber, ply, chipboard or hardboard. For ground-level floors with a concrete base you will need a damp-proof membrane, overlaid with a self-smoothing screed. The screed material is poured on to a clean, grease-free floor, levelled by trowel then left to level itself by settling. Do not lay this type of floor if you haven't protected against damp. Once laid and sealed it is easy to maintain by sweeping, wiping and occasionally polishing.

Hardwood strip

These floors are composed of strips of solid hardwood or veneered softwood. Provided the veneer is thick enough this flooring should be perfectly durable. If there is underfloor heating, a stable wood is best – merbau, iroko, or teak. Other good woods are oak, hard maple, keruing and mahogany. All should be treated with preservative.

Fixing will vary from system to system: on a sub-floor adhesive is often used. Do not push strip against strip if laying with adhesive: the adhesive will seep up through the joints. Instead set the strip down carefully to butt the next one, and wipe off any excess adhesive immediately.

Other systems interlock and can be dry-laid except for the last few panels. Some can be fixed with panel pins if there is a wooden sub-floor: drive pins diagonally through the tongue of each strip or through the flaps which protrude from the sides. Beware, however, of knocking a long pin through a pipe or wire beneath the boards. Strips can also be secret-nailed to softwood joists or battens running at right-angles to the strip flooring.

Laying wood blocks

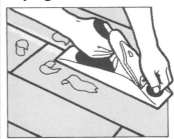

1. Ensure that the surface is flat. Any raised edges should be levelled with a plane.

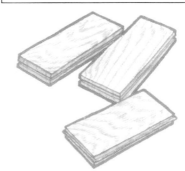

Solid wood blocks. Very hard-wearing. Particularly suitable for industrial use.

 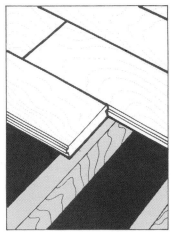

2. When ends are tongued and grooved, they can meet in the spaces between the joists.

3. Flat ended strips must join on a joist. Strips are usually fixed by secret nailing.

Laying mosaic tile panels

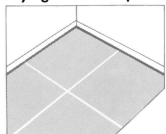 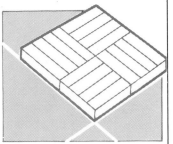

1. Stretch chalked string from the centres of opposite walls, crossing at right angles. Snap to transfer chalk line to floor.

2. Working from the centre, dry lay tiles to check fit, then attach with adhesive. Leave fractional expansion gap.

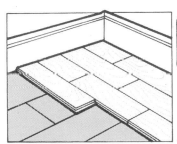 

2. Blocks should be laid at right angles across existing boards. Joints should be staggered.

3. A bitumen adhesive can be used instead of nails. It may cut down squeaks.

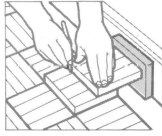 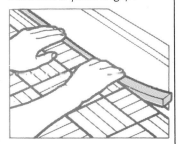

3. Cut tiles to fit edge. (See page 109.) Keep correct expansion gap using batten.

4. Measure expansion gap. Cut a cork strip to fit it and stick firmly down.

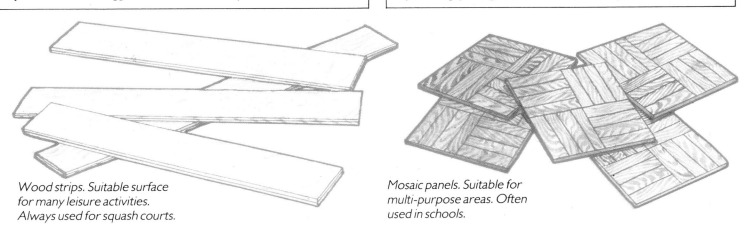

Wood strips. Suitable surface for many leisure activities. Always used for squash courts.

Mosaic panels. Suitable for multi-purpose areas. Often used in schools.

TILES

Tiles represent a convenient way of manufacturing and handling the type of heavy or brittle material that would be difficult to make and manage in sheet form. Well-laid tiles – whether they are ceramic, cork, quarry or vinyl – have a regularity and a rhythm that is classic, soothing and stylish. Available in a huge range of materials, textures, colours, sizes, shapes – and prices – tiles not only make good utility floors for kitchens, bathrooms and laundries but can be used imaginatively in many other areas of the home, too.

Depending on their size and whether they are laid across a room or lengthwise, they can alter the impression of a room's dimensions and emphasize its overall style. Very large tiles give a grand look to living rooms and halls – a crisp white-tiled floor teamed with colourful rugs has a cool elegant, Mediterranean style. Small square tiles, on the other hand, would look fussy in a big room because of the number of intersecting lines but their neat gridded appearance is perfect for a small kitchen or bathroom. Small rectangular tiles have a busy pace that suits high-tech interiors,

There are many ways to vary the look of a tiled floor. Borders in a contrasting colour, size or material lend definition. Patterns, from the simple and formal to more complex arrangements, are particularly effective and can be used to emphasize a particular area of a room or highlight a special feature.

Practically speaking, tiles also come in enough variety to meet most needs. Some are warm underfoot, such as cork and rubber; others hard and cold, notably ceramic and quarry. Some are lightweight, others so heavy that the sub-floor must be surveyed to check that it can bear the load. Some are easy to lay; for others you should call in professional help.

Right: Warm underfoot, non-slip cork tiles are a superb natural flooring for a bathroom.

Far right: White ceramic floor tiles with contrasting trim make a pretty and easily cleaned floor for a kitchen that opens to greenery.

Calculating tiles

To calculate the amount of tiles neded, work in metric if the tiles are made in metric dimensions, or imperial if the tiles are imperial. Measure the square area of the room (see Measuring for Carpets page 88). Work out how many tiles fit into a square metre or yard, and multiply this by the total number of square metres or yards necessary. Allow extra for breakage and wastage. If the room is irregularly shaped, draw a plan of the room on graph paper. Map out the central area, calculate the number of tiles needed, then work out the number of tiles needed for alcoves, bays and odd corners, and add the calculations together for the total number of tiles. If you are using coving tiles around the edge of the floor, calculate these separately.

Types of tile

Big, pale quarry tiles make a warm-toned, hard-wearing kitchen floor. Tile variation and uneven grouting result in a hand-crafted look.

Ceramic tiles

To make ceramic tiles, clay dust is pressed into moulds under very high pressure, and then baked at high temperatures. This produces tiles of extreme hardness and strength. The range of styles, finishes, colours and textures is vast: shapes include rectangular, square and Provençal; finishes can be shiny, dull, transparent, opaque and unglazed; decoration can be handpainted (irregular and charming) or machine-made (cheaper but precise). Textures range from smooth, embossed and relief patterns to 'anti-slip' surfaces such as raised squares, pinheads or ridges. Interesting colours include the very pale shades and greens, black and blue, as well as the more common warm rustic tones of brown, buff, red and yellow. Browse through the stock of the major manufacturers. Most good ranges have matching coving tiles for a smooth wall-to-floor transition.

As well as being extremely hard, ceramic tiles are also cold and noisy. You will break what you drop, and may well chip the tiles too, particularly if you drop something hard and heavy. Some people find these tiles tiring to stand on. Tiles for outside use must be fully vitrified to be frost-proof.

Since these tiles are heavy and can place a strain on suspended timber sub-floors, it is essential to call in a surveyor to check that there is sufficient load-bearing capacity. Obviously, a small room such as a bathroom will have less of a problem than a larger area. The floor must be level and even. Timber floors should be covered with hardboard first; concrete with a cement or sand screed is also recommended as a sub-floor, but any smooth floor with a latex screed will do.

Ceramic tiles are embedded in mortar (normally a professional job) or fixed with a special adhesive. Use waterproof adhesive in bathrooms, kitchens or utility rooms. Check that tiles chosen for the kitchen are also fat- and oil-resistant.

For after-care, a mild detergent solution will usually do – rinse well afterwards. If the surface of glazed tiles becomes dulled, try a water-softener. Commercial tile bleach will probably solve stubborn stains and refresh dirty grout.

Quarry tiles

Quarry tiles, terracotta and similar rustic-looking varieties from countries such as Mexico and Portugal, are made from unrefined high silica alumina clay, extruded into a tile mould. They usually come in earth colours such as brickish reds, browns and gold. Though extremely durable, quarries have a very slightly softer surface than ceramic tiles; after years of use they can become a little worn and pitted – but this is not unattractive. There is a wide price range; much depends on thickness. Like ceramic tiles, quarries are cold underfoot and noisy. You will break what you drop.

If the manufacturer allows sealing, use a mixture of one part linseed oil to four parts turpentine. Paint on the seal, let it soak in, cover with brown paper and leave for forty-eight hours. Don't seal with simple polyurethane: it will probably peel away or chip away. Sweep and wash, polish if desired, but take care not to make the floor slippery. If white patches appear, wash with a dash of vinegar in water; do not rinse. Clean stains with dilute liquid abrasive cleaner.

Symmetrical informality is the theme of this entrance hall, achieved by the use of bright blue and yellow ceramic tiles. This bold combination gives impact to the hallway.

Cork

Cork is very versatile and provides a warm neutral base, ideal for displaying bright rugs. If well laid and properly sealed, it is a practical floor for kitchens, bathrooms, children's rooms and cloakrooms, and can also be smart in entrance halls or sitting areas. The colour range is narrow – light honey to dark brown – and tiles tend to be plain, but some are patterned with stripes or squares in a contrasting colour.

Made from natural cork, compressed with binders and baked, these tiles come in a variety of thicknesses and densities. It is essential to use flooring grade. Good quality cork looks dense and even, and is springy underfoot but, if you're laying on hardboard and feeling cost-conscious, thinner grades will be adequate. The toughest type of all has a clear vinyl surface. Cork is fairly warm and resilient but not impervious to cuts, cigarette burns or strong chemicals. It may fade after prolonged exposure to strong sunlight.

Simple, quick and light to cut and work with, cork should be laid on a smooth floor, such as hardboard, rather than uneven floorboards. Store tiles flat and dry in the room in which they are to be laid, for a day or two if possible.

Proper sealing with several coats of polyurethane is essential. Wear a mask if the sealer is a strong one. A light sanding before the last coat is a good idea. Allow the seal to 'cure' thoroughly for a day or so after the seal is dry. Even pre-sealed tiles will benefit from a coat or two of seal to prevent liquid seeping between the joints, however tightly you have butted them together. Sweep and wash lightly; occasionally emulsion polish. Avoid spirit-based chemical cleaners.

Linoleum

Once a thin, brittle material prone to cracking and often luridly patterned, good flooring lino today is thick, glossy and durable. Made from linseed oil, ground cork, wood flour and resins, baked slowly at high temperatures and pressed on to a jute, hessian or fibreglass backing, it can be plain, mottled, marbled, patterned or glittery. Many architects and designers value its toughness and use it to make 'inlaid' patterns with different plain colours – sheet lino is better for curved shapes but tiles could be used to make interesting geometric ones. Fairly warm underfoot and resilient, lino also has a good resistance to dilute acids, alkalis and household chemicals but will eventually rot if water gets underneath. Since it is slightly thicker than vinyl, sub-floor deficiencies will be less damaging, and it can be used over underfloor heating.

Lay on a smooth, dry, level sub-floor – on hardboard or chipboard rather than on floorboards, which may vary in position and cause the lino to crack along ridges. Butt tiles close up against each other – lino seams get tighter with age, which prevents liquids from penetrating.

No sealing is necessary but lino can be polished. You can use the manufacturer's own dressing or a special lino dressing. Sweep and polish lightly. Dilute washing soda can be used occasionally to bring up surface colour. Rub away crayon marks with silver metal polish; try emulsion floor polish on scuff marks.

Plastic

Plastic flooring, borrowed for high-tech homes from sports halls and swimming pools, is hardly classic but can be a lot of fun. It tends to come in plain, strong colours – black, white and grey, and bright primaries – and is available in sheet form and matting as well as open-work grid or duckboard-type tiles, some of which snap together. While not necessarily cheap, it is a surprisingly comfortable surface. Unless ultraviolet light stabilizers are incorporated, it might fade if continually exposed to strong sunlight. Lay on an impervious sub-floor as water will seep through and take a while to evaporate.

No sealing is necessary. Wash with plain hot water and soap-based cleaner if stained. Don't use heavy abrasive cleaners, chemicals, acids, petroleum, undiluted bleach or acetone. Dirt will fall through holed varieties, and is difficult to remove without a powerful vacuum cleaner.

Rubber/synthetic rubber

First used in industrial and contract work where its tough, non-slip, burn-resistant and soundproofing surface made attractive railway station and airport floors, rubber tiles are

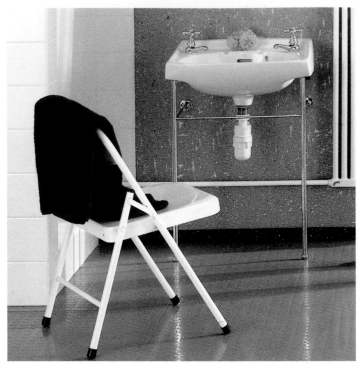

Studded rubber floor tiles make a smart, water-resistant non-slip floor. They are ideal in bathrooms but less suitable in kitchens as sticky spills and crumbs are hard to remove.

increasingly popular in the home, especially for utility areas. Made of different blends of natural and synthetic materials, rubber varies in grade, thickness and hence price, but is rarely cheap, although some thinner, easy to lay, but slightly stretchy varieties cost no more than a medium-quality vinyl. These tiles are normally plain coloured but there are two-toned and marble-effect types. Pattern is generally lent by the texture – round raised studs are common. But beware: when installed in kitchens, there is a tendency for scraps of food to build up tenacious deposits around studs and other relief textures. Narrow tiles are available for stairs.

Thermoplastic

Sometimes referred to as asphalt tiles, these thin, hard tiles are made from asphaltic binders, asbestos fibres, mineral fillers and pigments. A workhorse surface, durable and cheap, these tiles tend to come only in dark browns and blacks, sometimes with a little white vinyl resin thrown in.

Vinylized thermoplastic, with PVC added, is more flexible

Lino tiles give a tough and elegant floor for a classically furnished study. A dull view is counteracted by the brilliant hue and illusion of depth in the pattern of the tiles.

Vinyl tiles come in a huge range of patterns and colours. These classic chequered tiles, set in a diagonal pattern, echo the colour scheme of this Victorian-style kitchen.

and highly durable, is available in many more colours and sizes, and slightly more expensive.

Vinyl asbestos
Made from plasticized vinyl resins, asbestos fibres, mineral fillers and pigments, these tiles are tough, flexible, and impervious. They come in a wide range of plain colours, marbled or embossed effects.

Vinyl
Vinyl is an excellent all-purpose material for kitchens, kitchen-diners, bathrooms and corridors but it is not always cheap – the best quality is as expensive as very good quality carpet. 'Vinyl' is a shortened form of polyvinyl chloride (PVC) but the amount of PVC in the material can vary from 25 to 85 per cent – you can usually tell by the price (PVC is expensive). Very versatile, vinyl is produced in varying degrees of flexibility from soft and rubbery to hard, and in tile or sheet form. It can be absolutely smooth but more usually is textured.

There is a vast range of patterns and colours, many of which simulate 'real' floors such as ceramic and quarry tiles, sometimes very effectively, sometimes not. Newer vinyls have borrowed the idea from industrial flooring of suspending glitter or tiny crystals in the clear surface layer.

Some vinyls have inbuilt underlays or a 'cushioned' sandwich filling layer for greater sound and heat insulation and greater resilience. Waterproof, resistant to oil and fat and most domestic chemicals, vinyl is not immune to burns or to abrasion by grit.

In winter, vinyl must be warmed before laying – cold makes it brittle. To clean, check manufacturers' recommendations – washing with warm, soapy water and rinsing to avoid a dulling film is usual. Try a pencil rubber or emulsion floor polish to remove scuff marks. Do not use petrol, paraffin, white spirit or wax polish. Manufacturers of vinyl always say they wish their customers would not use harsh, abrasive detergents: one of the main causes of surface damage.

Laying hard tiles

When laying a hard tile floor, it is particularly important to remember that the floor covering will only be successful if the floor beneath is properly prepared. Ceramic and quarry tiles, which have no flexibility, will be uneven unless laid over a completely level surface. Timber floors should be covered with hardboard first. Concrete sub-floors need a cement or sand screed. Tiles can then be bedded in mortar – the correct mix of which is essential – or with adhesive. Hard tiles are not as easy to lay as soft tiles and are more expensive on the whole, but they are very hard-wearing and should last for a long time. Ceramic tiles are not easy to cut and instructions should be followed closely. It is worth investing in the correct tools. The wrong cutters can very easily cause broken and damaged tiles.

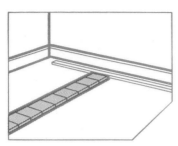

1. Mark line at right angles from door centre to far wall. Dry lay using spacers. Adjust so border tiles not too narrow. Fix batten at 90° where last full tile ends.

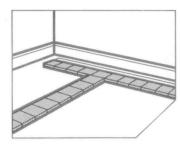

2. Dry lay tiles along batten to either end, again adjusting so border tiles not much less than half-size. Fix second batten at right angles to the first.

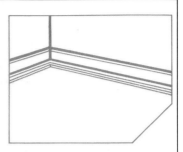

3. Remove all dry tiles. Start tiling in corner formed by the two battens. If using mortar, ensure mix is correct. Otherwise adhesive can be used.

4. With a notched spreader, spread a thin layer of adhesive across a small area. Press down tiles using spacers to separate them.

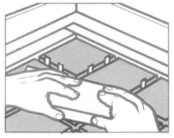

5. Work back towards the door along both battens. Ensure that the surface is quite even by laying a batten across it. Or use a spirit level.

6. Using a set square, periodically check the angle of the tiles. Leave them for 24 hours. Then remove the spacers and finish the borders.

Cutting ceramic tiles

1. Score a firm line through glazed surface and edges of tile, running tile cutter against a rule. Hold unwanted section over table edge. Snap off.

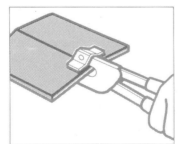

2. Or, when the tile has been scored, use plier cutters. Centre and press evenly on both sides so that the tile snaps in the required place.

Grouting

1. Grouting can be bought ready-made or in powder form. Spread it over tiles with a malleable spreader or sponge until all the joints are well filled.

2. Wipe off the excess with a damp cloth before it sets. Finally, remove any hardened grout left on the surface and buff up with a soft, clean cloth.

Laying soft tiles

As a general rule, soft tiles are rather easier to lay than hard tiles. They are lighter to work with and much easier to cut to shape. Like hard tiles they need to be laid on an even surface and a chipboard or hardboard covering provides an ideal base – certainly better than uneven floorboards. Because they are light they are suitable for use in rooms with suspended floors, such as children's bedrooms and bathrooms on first or second floors, where support may be insufficient for harder, heavier tiles. Many cork and vinyl tiles are self-adhesive which makes them easier to lay, although care has to be taken to position them correctly before pressing them down. Soft tiles are now surprisingly durable, and stand up well to everyday wear and tear. Cleaning instructions must be followed as the wrong cleaner can damage the tile.

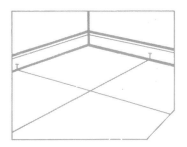

1. Fix chalked line between centres of both pairs of opposite walls. Snap line down so chalk marks cross at right angles. (Check with set square.)

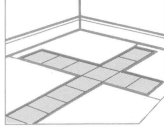

2. Dry lay tiles tightly adjacent along the lines, starting at the centre. Border tiles should be as near full-size as possible: adjust from centre for this.

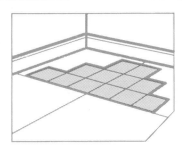

3. Glue the tiles in place, working outwards from the centre in a pyramidal pattern until the field is completed and only the border remains.

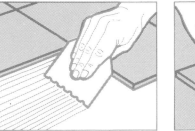

4. Spread glue over slightly larger area than five or six tiles at a time, with notched spreader. Press tiles downwards and tightly together.

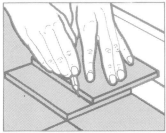

5. For borders, place tile to be cut on the last complete tile, then a third flush with the wall. Using this as an edge, mark the second tile then cut and fit it.

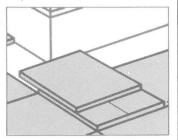

6. Cut corner tiles in the same way. Move the tile first against one wall, then, without turning it, against the other. Mark and cut second tile as before.

Making a template

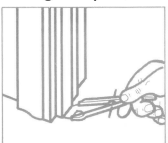

1. Templates are used when cutting around architraves or other awkward shapes in a room. Using a compass, measure shape exactly.

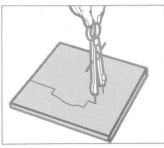

2. Transfer each measurement exactly to a piece of thin card or paper. Cut out the resulting shape carefully. Ensure it fits snugly in position.

3. Place the template on the tile, and mark around it exactly, using sharp pencil or tile cutter wheel. Then, cut the tile with great care.

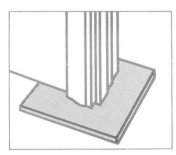

4. Place the tile in position, smoothing any rough edges, and make sure that it fits perfectly. Then stick as with other tiles.

SHEET FLOORING

Below: A cool, marbled sheet lino loses its period conno-tations by being set in a modern high-tech style. It becomes a perfect partner for a chrome-edged chair and picture.

Right: Sheet vinyl in plain geometric patterns makes a smart, easily cleaned kitchen floor. Vinyl is also relatively warm and soft, added assets if there are children in the family.

The virtue of sheet flooring is that a larger area can be covered quickly and with a minimum of seams – but since the material can be heavy and unwieldy, it is more difficult for the amateur to lay. Vinyl, lino and rubber are all available in rolls as wide as 4m (13ft), which helps to minimize the chances of water seeping between joints and promotes a smooth overall look. Paradoxically, quite a few sheet vinyls are printed with a simulated tile pattern but the aim is just to achieve the tiled look more easily.

Sheet lino is also the best choice if you want to create a floor pattern involving curves since different shapes can be cut out of it. However, dealing with hefty rolls is not easy. Unless you're confident, it is probably a good idea to call in professional help. Nothing is worse than a length of vinyl that has been cut too small or with an embarrassingly wobbly edge.

Before laying, decide which way the sheet will run. Avoid ending up with a seam in the middle of a doorway. If the flooring is laid at right-angles to a window the seams will not be as noticeable. If the sheet is going directly on to floor-boards, it should run at right-angles to them, but it is best to lay it on hardboard, to avoid uneven wear. Measure the room to establish how much sheet you need and how wide it should be in order to minimize cost and wastage and match up patterns.

Laying sheet flooring

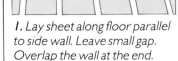

1. Lay sheet along floor parallel to side wall. Leave small gap. Overlap the wall at the end.

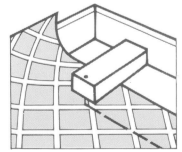

2. Using scriber – wood block with nail protruding – pull along wall scratching sheet. Cut.

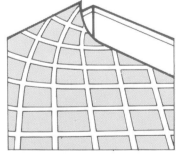

3. Slide cut side to wall. The fit should be exact. Keep the overlap on the end wall.

4. To trim ends, measure back a distance of about 200mm from the wall and mark the flooring.

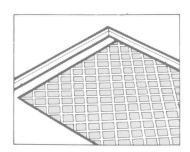

5. Pull the end back keeping it straight against the other wall and lay flat.

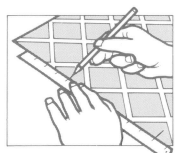

6. Make a second mark, again 200mm, from the first, towards the end of the sheet.

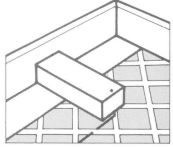

7. Adjust sheet so scriber point falls on second mark. Scratch sheet pushing scriber along wall.

To complete the process, cut along the scratched line and fit the flooring against the wall. Repeat at the other end.

Where it is necessary to lay more than one sheet of flooring, overlap the two sheets slightly, matching the pattern. Leave to settle for a few days, then trim the second sheet. Butt edges. Attach to floor at seams and perimeters with double-sided tape.

BRICK

Flooring bricks must be the type suitable for paving, otherwise the surface will quickly degrade. Either clay or calcium silicate bricks will do. While bricks are normally rectangular in shape, sizes vary and thicknesses range from the standard 6.5cm (2½in) to thin paviors of 2.5 to 5cm (1 to 2in). Colours include warm buffs, goldens, greys, reds, browns, and cool blues, greens and grey shades, as well as speckled mixtures. Surface texture can vary as can porosity – some bricks can absorb as much as 20 per cent of their own mass. Brick is a reasonably priced material and is available secondhand, but check that quality is appropriate and clean before use.

Indoors, brick makes a durable, but hard and noisy floor. It looks equally good right through the house, in hall, kitchen and sitting room, from the front door to the patio.

Lay it on concrete cured for a minimum of 28 days, on a damp-proof course on a ground floor, into a stiff mortar bed 2.5 to 3cm (1 to 1¼in) deep, with mortar jointing carried out simultaneously. Absorbent bricks should be briefly ducked in water before laying so that they don't suck too much water out of the mortar. Don't seal, oil or polish. Sweep, wash with mild detergent and rinse carefully.

Outdoors, brick is one of the most sympathetic materials for town and country garden alike. It can look crisp and regular or softer and more rustic, depending on how it is used. As well as paths, patios and terraces it is also suitable for slopes, steps, walls or mixed with other materials. Thin paviors can be used on roof terraces. Make sure outdoor bricks are frost-resistant.

Outdoors it does not need to be laid as precisely as indoors. Lay on a bed of firm even sand 2 to 4cm (¾ to 1½in) deep, on top of a layer of consolidated hardcore or ash. Margin bricks can be bedded in mortar to keep stretches of brick fixed firmly in place. Sand-laid bricks need to be pointed, a fiddly procedure which can stain the brick surface. Try a dry sand and cement mix, brush between joints, clean off surplus, water and allow to set. Don't be tempted to over-fill the joints: they really look best scooped lightly below the brick surface, so that the different shades of the individual bricks stand out cleanly.

Laying Bricks Outdoors

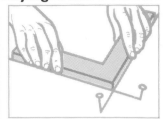
1. Set out dimensions with pegs and string, checking that the corners are right angles.

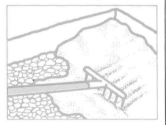
2. Dig to required depth. Backfill with consolidated hardcore. Sand. Rake level.

3. Lay bricks with narrow joints. Carefully brush in a dry mix of cement and sand.

4. Using a watering can with a fine rose, or a fine spray from a hose, water the brickwork to set the mortar.

With their warm colour and inherent variations, old bricks bring charm to any environment. This stretcher bond pattern unifies this whole area, and has a pleasant, soothing look.

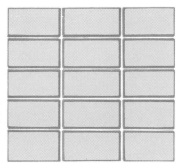

Stack bond Bricks in straight rows. Easiest of all to lay. Ideal for small, unfussy areas.

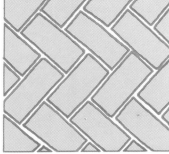

Herringbone A very popular pattern. Pleasing to look at, it is also easy to lay.

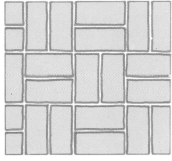

Basket weave Visually pleasing. Somehow manages to look inwards. Good as a path.

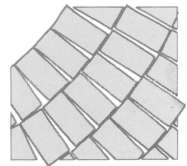

Radial Ideal as a surround to curved or circular features. Comparatively easy to lay.

Patterns

Part of the charm of brick derives from its human scale, which also enables a variety of patterns to be created easily. These include bond patterns, herringbone and basket-weave. Patterns are partly dependent on whether brick is laid on its bed (largest) face or on an edge. Fewer bricks will be needed for face laying, which gives a proportion of length to width of two to one as opposed to three to one of edge laying, and therefore demands forty standard bricks as opposed to sixty for each square metre (yard).

NATURAL STONE

Crazy paving

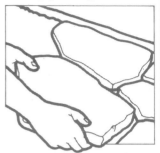

1. Dig down to depth of stones. Flatten. Dry lay. Use regular stones for edges.

2. Remove a few stones and put by. Lay down 25mm (1 in) of mortar. Replace stones.

3. When the slabs have been laid, with small gap between each, fill joints with mortar using trowel, and smooth.

Natural stone is a sympathetic material, full of character and available in as many shades and textures as there are types of quarried stone. New, it literally costs the earth.

Stone flags are the traditional flooring for country houses and cottages, especially in kitchen, hall and utility areas, but are rarer in new homes. Despite being impervious, tremendously hard-wearing and attractive, such floors are also heavy, cold, hard underfoot and need very strong sub-floors. Types include warm coloured sandstones, grey York stone, granite setts, creamy Portland stone, porous limestone and reconstituted stone slabs, as well as stone chippings mixed with cement and cast in slabs. These should be laid in mortar indoors, over a damp-proof membrane. If you inherit a flagstone floor, you may need to lift, damp-proof underneath, clean the slabs and replace. Sweeping and scrubbing are all the maintenance the floor should need, but porous types may stain and can sometimes be sealed – get expert advice.

Patios, porches, greenhouses, conservatories and paths are all suitable locations for stone floors. Thin sliced stone could be interesting for a roof garden (but check the load-bearing capacity of the roof first). Lay garden stone in sand: its own weight will keep it in place. Ensure foundations are firm and well-drained and that slabs are settled evenly on foundations. Fill joints with mortar, sand, gravel or earth and plants. Secondhand stone, broken or cracked, is a cheap alternative, suitable for crazy paving. This should not look too crazy – jigsaw it together neatly and with evenly sized joints.

Granite

Granite is a very hard rock – often dark blue-grey or mottled white – available in many colours, with a rich texture and a faintly crystalline appearance. Surfaces are often slightly irregular but can be honed, polished, flame-textured or sawn.

Granite is also available in paving stones known as setts. These can be laid in similar patterns to bricks although they are larger and rather more uneven, and also look good laid randomly or in irregular shapes. Granite is maintenance free but, if polished, can be washed and buffed.

Slate

Slate is a beautiful, evocative material which, bizarrely, can manage to look bogus if badly handled – especially if used in too small an area. It has a slightly rippled surface and comes in deep greys, grey-blues and grey-greens, though slightly reddish shades also exist. Quarried in mountain regions, it is very durable if properly cut: it can be sliced into thin layers, varying from about 1 to 10cm (½ to 4in). Although expensive, cold, brittle, heavy, hard underfoot and noisy, it makes a uniquely dramatic floor, a stunning foil for rugs.

Lay it in a concrete bed on a concrete sub-floor. Slate can be polished but it's best to leave it alone. Because of its slow water absorption slate is particularly good for outdoor use.

Left: A 'carpet' made of stone – large flagstones, smaller pebbles – works well in this country-house kitchen. The central ring of pebbles marks out and gives emphasis to the dining area.

Above: Two different shades of natural stone, laid in a pattern, focus the attention on the central working/eating area. The pleasant, overall effect is one of controlled informality.

UNUSUAL SOLUTIONS

Left: Shaped plywood, stained in soft, watery colours, makes a startlingly original floor with a three-dimensional quality. Although time-consuming to achieve, the effect is well worth the effort.

Above: This eye-catching trompe l'oeil hearth-rug is made of concrete set in the wood flooring. It focuses attention on the fireplace, and unlike a real rug is immune to flying sparks.

Right: This chequered floor is easily achieved by juxtaposing dark and light cork tiles. They are easy to cut and can make striking borders echoing the main floor pattern.

Below: This highly original floor is made up of rectangles of sheet vinyl in bold colours: a practical, budget-conscious, but stylish solution for a living room needing little other decoration.

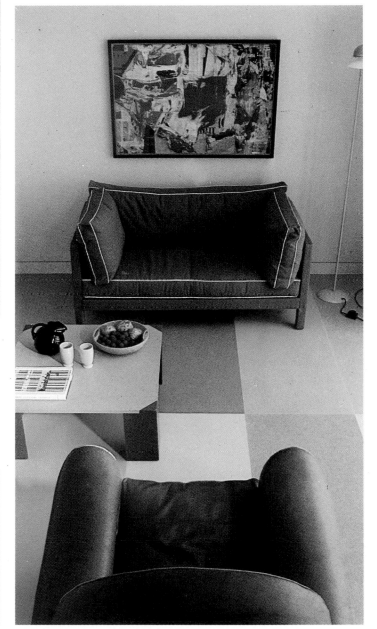

STORAGE WITH STYLE

Careful planning is needed if storage provision is to match to both the style of your home and your budget. It takes time to evolve an individual and distinctive style and your home should complement and reflect your own interests and way of life. Its appearance makes a statement about how you choose the things you live with and assemble the different elements – colour, lighting, furnishings.

Finding the happy balance between personal taste and practical function also means juggling with available funds. Financial restraints often lead to better solutions. Limited resources force you to stop and assess each purchase or decorating decision.

Don't be deceived by those interiors that look thrown together but work as if by magic: it is likely that more thought has gone into them than you would ever imagine. Before deciding on a furnishing and decorative scheme, work out as clearly as possible how each room relates to the next and how they are individually used. Storage must be part of these initial plans as it may affect the colours, shapes and patterns you choose or the types of lighting you select. Be practical and alert to the combination of function and attractive design. Display shelves that include stereo housing need electrical outlets close by or built into the wall itself: the effect of a subtle wallpaper may be spoiled by the presence of a large imposing wardrobe, but a built-in cupboard with doors decorated in the same paper can look perfectly sympathetic.

Build into your plans a degree of flexibility too; a small pile of books quickly grows into a sizeable library and several pieces of delicate china could easily develop into a collecting habit. Know yourself; if you're naturally untidy, don't think that stringent storage will change the habits of a lifetime. Chaotically packed shelves that can be instantly concealed with blinds and a vast wardrobe where clothes are simply hooked or hung rather than carefully folded are good storage solutions that don't make extra work.

Providing well-designed storage has to be an integral part of the initial planning of all interior spaces and, in today's smaller homes, it's essential to make the most of every inch of available space. Clever use of colour and light has helped to make the most of this tiny sleeping area, but it is the carefully designed and well-organized storage that actually makes the whole scheme work. This room has been divided into two areas, one providing a generous, open space for dining and entertaining visitors. The other end has been meticulously planned to integrate a sleeping platform with desk space, a library in the alcove above the bed, with a wardrobe space concealed by drapes on the right of the platform. Further clothes' storage is provided by generous-sized drawers under the platform at the foot of the bed. Two mini chests of drawers make perfectly proportioned jewellery boxes and side tables for the desk lamp which doubles up as a bedside reading light. Cane blinds adjusted by a simple pulley can be lowered to conceal the whole or just part of this arrangement.

BUILT-IN AND FREE-STANDING FURNITURE

When making a choice between built-in and freestanding storage, you need to consider the appearance you would like it to have and balance this with the style and structural characteristics of the interior architecture. There is also the important choice between permanence and mobility. Whichever you choose, the storage system should add visual interest to a room as well as performing a function for you. It need not be obtrusive or seem to crowd in on the living space. One wall of a living room filled with custom-built shelves may provide all the storage you need, make an interesting focal point and free the rest of the room from clutter, thus creating an illusion of more space than is actually there.

In older homes, with alcoves either side of the chimney breast, irregular walls, protruding skirting and picture rails, building-in is a possible solution but the quirks and individuality of each room deserve consideration too. Built-in means the furniture is there to stay and should look as though it has always been there. This means continuing cornices, picture rails and skirtings around floor-to-ceiling storage. Hardwood mouldings glued to plywood doors and shelf edges before painting often supply new furniture with a style in keeping with other structural details.

Radiators are not an original feature of most homes and, though essential, may be far from attractive. They can be disguised by storage units built above and around them. Once painted to match the walls, both storage and radiator blend into the background.

A modern house or flat with basic box dimensions may cry out for some architectural definition. Simple alcoves filled with shelves fitted between plasterboard partitions can improve the room's original proportions. A permanent partition can divide one room into two more interesting spaces, with storage combining a variety of functions on either side – a bar above a wine cupboard, a desk in a bookshelf unit. Tailor your storage to the possessions you have and those you are likely to accumulate. Customized storage designed for a music library must have flexibility; you are hardly likely to stop collecting records just because all the

Left: Built-in furniture needs to take into account the architectural style of a room. The numerous partitions of this library follow similar lines in the room's casement windows.

Below: This awkward gap has wisely been chosen to conceal a radiator behind a rattan panel. Two simple shelves above it make no attempt to fill the remaining space.

shelves originally built have been filled.

It is difficult to visualize permanent storage and you could try experimenting with a freestanding item of similar dimensions borrowed from another room. Study neighbouring homes to see how others have solved storage problems, but bring a critical eye to bear and learn by their mistakes.

Traditional, reproduction and antique furniture, usually acquired for appearance rather than function, should still work to enhance and complement a room. It may take a long time to find a piece that is exactly right. Keep the measurements of a particular recess or specific wall with you wherever you go. An expensive antique may not be such a wise investment if it does not fit where you intended it should – it may not even be persuaded to go through your front door.

Self-assembly units

Most of today's freestanding storage is designed and made for quick assembly. Self-assembly, knock-down or flat-pack are all terms used by manufacturers to describe the type of furniture you put together yourself at home. On the whole such units tend to be cheaper, but only because, packed flat, they take up less space in shops and warehouses and need fewer staff to handle them. Less expensive does not necessarily mean less good. Also, it is far easier to take home a large shelving system in kit form than to negotiate tight corners and narrow staircases with a pre-assembled unit. As an added bonus, of course, even sturdy and quite complex items can be dismantled and re-erected if you move house.

Self-assembly open shelving units, particularly those with adjustable shelves, are practical for displaying a whole range of different items and make simple but very functional room dividers, with easy access from both sides. More flexible storage is achieved with those systems which consist of different individual units – open shelves, cupboards with glass or wood doors and drawers. They can be combined as you like, added to or rearranged if your lifestyle alters, you move or you simply feel like a change. These systems have so many permutations they can easily be adapted to meet any new situation.

Self-assembly furniture

DON'T

- order furniture by mail order if there is no opportunity to see before you buy. Glossy advertisements and catalogues often disguise inferior quality; photographs can give a distorted view of size and proportions.

- take away a self-assembly pack from a showroom or warehouse without checking that all the components, including a full set of instructions, are there.

- deal with a large item of furniture single-handed. You might damage yourself or the unit, and two heads are better than one for deciphering cryptic instructions.

- tighten screws fully until the whole assembly is complete unless instructions state otherwise.

- be tempted to modify the construction until you have put it together as instructed to see how the design works.

DO

- examine a fully assembled sample before you buy. Check that the dimensions will fit the intended space and look at the small print for details such as adjustable shelving.

- unpack the components carefully and keep them together near the place where the assembled unit will stand. Put them on a soft rug or blanket if the floor is not carpeted.

- read all instructions carefully before you get to work. Run them through in your mind and if they are unclear contact the manufacturer or supplier for further advice.

- make sure you have the right tools to hand; usually a screwdriver is all that is necessary and specific items such as keys or spanners may be supplied with the kit.

- lift the assembled furniture into place without pulling or dragging to avoid stresses that may loosen fixings or damage parts.

- go back to the store and complain if you are dissatisfied with the result or some of the components are damaged.

Below: This storage system and room divider is assembled exactly where it is to be used.

Bottom: Entire self-assembly kitchens are also available but need special care when fitting.

Below: Mobile storage relieves the congestion of overcrowded kitchen work surfaces.

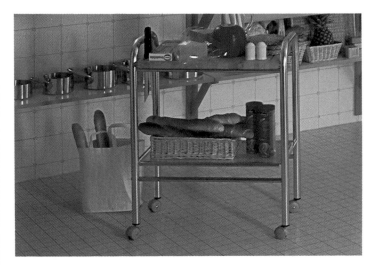

Movable storage

Furniture that is even more flexible than freestanding units is the type of storage actually designed to be moved. The simple trolley is the solution for a vast range of items suitably kept on wheels. For example, hi-fi, television and video are bulky, heavy items, often needing a change of position for better sound and vision. They are more safely moved on wheeled bases.

Drinks and food trolleys move from the dining room to kitchen, kitchen to living room. They make useful serving tops and mobile side-tables, as well as providing a convenient method of clearing away. You can keep bottles and glasses or heavy serving dishes permanently stored on a trolley when they are out of use. In the kitchen, you can use a mobile work table with built-in chopping boards and knife racks, but check that wheels can be locked when necessary or the constant mobility will be an extreme disadvantage.

Vegetables are kept well ventilated in wire grid racks on castors, can be neatly stored under worktops, moved out for re-stocking and brought close to the sink for cleaning. These handy mobile baskets provide ingenious solutions for storage anywhere in the home. The best systems are those found at catering equipment and shopfitting suppliers.

MODULAR AND SPECIFIC STORAGE

Modular and specific furniture are in many ways at opposite ends of the storage spectrum. Your choice to some extent depends on whether you prefer the appearance of purpose-built furniture which proclaims its specific function, or more anonymous, streamlined units used to conceal or display the items stored in them. Other important factors are the amount of space available and the immediacy of particular storage requirements.

Modular storage

Modular storage offers you the convenience of adding units as and when finances or space permit; many systems can also be easily rearranged and moved from room to room. One of the best and most flexible is the cube system. Based on a simple wooden or plastic box, open or shelved, contents may be freely displayed or concealed by the addition of extra details such as deep or shallow drawers or cupboard fronts. This system offers many possible configurations: two units side by side as a bedside chest; one on top of another as a plant stand; four in a square as a low living room table; eight stacked together as a tall bookcase. Other designs offer a wider selection of basic units, including cabinets with transparent or opaque doors, often with adjustable shelves, and flap-down tops on open cases and drawer units. With complete systems like these you can create library storage or display cabinets.

In the better quality furniture of this kind, the units are well finished at the backs, so storage pieces can be placed at right-angles to the wall or as freestanding room dividers. A system arranged in this way may improve the dimensions of a large room, giving greater flexibility and saving wall space for other purposes. Cheaper modular furniture may be dramatically improved by a couple of coats of paint or by changing door and drawer handles for ones of superior quality.

Furniture for a specific purpose

Modular storage systems have evolved over the past few decades to meet the changing and growing needs of modern living. Old storage furniture tends to fall into specific cate-

Modular storage is flexible, can be built up over a period·of time, and is useful where space is at a premium or for filling awkward corners. This unit has been used to display glasses, books, and a vase of flowers, but closed units can be added to hide away unsightly jumble. The wood of the unit blends with that of the table, window shutters and floor.

Modular shelving

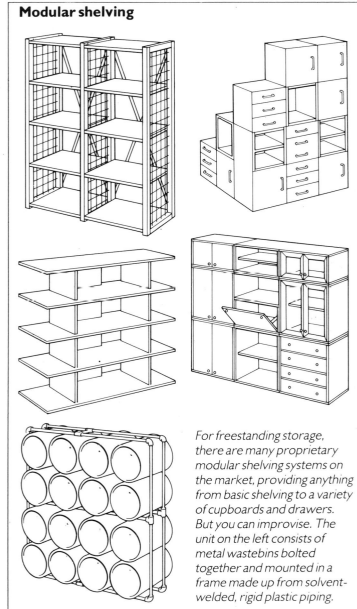

For freestanding storage, there are many proprietary modular shelving systems on the market, providing anything from basic shelving to a variety of cupboards and drawers. But you can improvise. The unit on the left consists of metal wastebins bolted together and mounted in a frame made up from solvent-welded, rigid plastic piping.

Left: The fine craftsmanship and strong character of old furniture can often be adapted to suit modern needs without drastically changing the original design or function. In this Victorian-style bathroom, an old-fashioned washstand has been brought up to date by plumbing in taps and setting a basin into the marble top. Though drawer space is lost, the washstand still provides storage in the generous cupboard beneath the sink.

Above: This chest was probably part of the fittings of an old grocer's or chemist's shop and its numerous drawers of all shapes and sizes make an ideal place to store dress-making equipment.

Clothes, otherwise draped across a bedroom, are simply hung from this wigwam of sticks: a practical addition to guest rooms or for taking the bulge from a crammed wardrobe.

gories, from a time when natural materials like wood were more plentiful and therefore cheaper, and when homes were filled with much more furniture than is the preference today. Late nineteenth-century fashion, for example, adored dark mahogany pieces cluttering up the rooms – which was all well and good in generously proportioned homes with live-in housekeepers to keep them well polished. Much of this old furniture is massive, but solid and beautifully made, and individual pieces can work just as well in contemporary settings. The popularity of the appearance and fine craftsmanship of old furniture has increasingly led to new designs built on old models and contemporary pieces are available that have the same sense of solidity combined with elegance.

Besides providing an interesting focal point to a room, much of this furniture may be used for purposes other than those for which it was specifically designed. It's worth remembering that outdated furniture can often be turned to a new use if you put your mind to it. For instance, in a dining or living room a mahogany linen press can make an elegant drinks cupboard with drawers used to store table linen and silver. A small pine dresser may be just the thing for a child's room, displaying treasured objects and toys on the shelves, with clothes stored in the cupboards or drawers beneath. A pedestal desk with a mass of tiny drawers turns into a perfect dressing table with storage of just the right size for cosmetics, perfumes and jewellery.

Contemporary designs for specific types of furniture tend to feature largely in the kitchen, where practicality usually dictates a function for every inch of space. Wire grocery drawers, carousel shelves for corner cupboards and tiered vegetable trolleys are adaptable as ideal modular systems for clothes, cosmetics and toys, and for storage in the home office. Furniture designed specifically for one type of storage is in fact often multi-functional, bearing in mind what best suits your needs, taste and budget. An all-purpose tubular steel trolley may not be so desirable, or so mobile, in a home with thick rugs on bare floors or in a room furnished throughout with antiques.

AREA BY AREA

One of the most important aspects of home interior design is the use of space. Unfortunately, not all rooms are the size and shape we'd like them to be. Clever use of colour and light can help to create the illusion of space, but in reality it is well-planned and organized storage that actually makes space for space – and this has to be the ultimate luxury in most of today's smaller homes. How we utilize different areas of our homes largely dictates how much we enjoy living in them. Smaller homes demand less furniture, which in turn has to be more versatile and practical.

Modern storage furniture has to fulfil more than one function and be flexible enough to be used in several rooms. Beds with integral drawers, low chests that form coffee tables, seating that disguises cupboards or shelving: all these are practical ways of overcoming space restrictions. Apart from the furniture, the living spaces need to be made multi-functional, too. A dining room can double up as an extra bedroom or playroom, a boxroom can be halved and made to serve as a tiny home office and a walk-in wardrobe. The important criterion is to make your space adaptable to the needs of its regular occupants.

The same principle can be applied to well-designed storage. A working wall of shelves, for example, can be tailored to store and display all sorts of items, whereas separate storage for different possessions means floorspace is crowded with bookcases, magazine racks, cupboards and supports for the stereo units. Well-planned shelving means those items regularly used are within easy reach – and the plan should also include spotlights for highlighting treasured possessions or making it easy to select records or videotapes.

Look for ingenious solutions to make more of the storage space you already have – wire pull-out drawers can dramatically reorganize a wardrobe or larder; dividing up existing drawers with special inserts or plywood divisions allows small items to be found more easily. The secret of successful storage lies in taking plenty of time both to determine your lifestyle and to select very carefully the type of furniture that not only suits your personal taste and needs but allows you to make the most of your home and possessions.

When you're looking to buy a house or apartment, one of the most important points to check is a property's storage potential. You really need carefully to assess the space in each room and consider the relationship of one room to another, because storage should relate to how the spaces are used and combined. Top marks go to the architect who designed this split-level home in Germany. Its layout perfectly illustrates the principles of good interior planning. Rooms are divided not by walls but an open-plan pine wood storage system which echoes the timber construction of the house and blends with the quarry-tiled floors on each level. The kitchen/breakfast room is situated on a level just above this dining room, a family living area is on the floor below and, under that, a children's playroom. All the floors are linked together by short runs of open-plan stairs.

LIVING ROOMS

A living room should be the easiest room to plan and organize – the only real constraints are your budget and available space. But it is that freedom, in terms of style and type of furnishings, that makes decisions the more perplexing.

A further complication is a certain ambiguity of function. In the past, houses were built with a front parlour reserved for 'best' and a back room for everyday living. Now the two have been combined: the living room is the showpiece of a home, the area most frequently seen by outsiders, but also the room that you come home to for total relaxation in privacy and comfort. Other rooms make more stringent demands with regard to function and practicality. Large appliances in the kitchen often dictate how space may be most economically used; so, too, do bathroom fittings and bedroom furniture. But the living room gives you a free hand to create exactly what you and your family want, according to your lifestyle. The danger here is that it is tempting to gloss over the importance of planning the layout, and rush straight into colour schemes and soft furnishings. Storage is often an afterthought, but together with lighting and heating, it forms an important and integral part of a relaxing, easy and comfortable room. These three basic aspects should be considered together.

Central heating is now a modern essential rather than a luxury; if a system is well planned, with good, flexible controls, it can have more effect than any other home improvement. Standard radiators do have limitations – most are visually unappealing and take up valuable wall space. There are designs which run the length of walls at skirting level, which are less obtrusive and free the walls above for built-in storage or simple shelving. A conventional radiator can be disguised by painting it the same colour as the walls. A shelf, the same width and depth as the radiator, fixed about 10cm (4in) above it, can be used to display attractive objects, drawing attention away from the less attractive radiator beneath. If it is close to a window this shelf makes an ideal home for tropical plants, given sufficient humidity. Radiators can be moved or changed for more efficient types or sizes

The best and most creative use of available storage space is achieved by positioning a stylish, floor-to-ceiling set of open display shelves between closed cupboards. The marble-look shelves are an elegant display case for objets d'art and ornaments. Even small paintings, spotlit from within, are on show. To create even more space, some of the shelves have been subdivided into three to display objects too small to be featured on their own. Those items too unsightly to be displayed are hidden behind the closed doors of the complementary grey cupboards. This combination of functional and decorative storage is a very attractive way of using space. Additional storage is provided by the wooden chest, which also serves as a coffee table.

Economy is no bar to style: by using one colour for all components of this living room, and by reducing decoration to a handful of well-displayed objects, a simple elegance is achieved. An illusion of space is enhanced by inserting the alcove shelves into the wall before finish-plastering, for a cantilevered look, by rejecting a traditional fireplace in favour of a simple recessed type.

and this is a worthwhile consideration if the installation you have inhibits a room's heat efficiency or makes a sensible storage layout impossible.

Using the space

Really spacious living rooms are a joy in summer but can be freezing expanses in winter. Sometimes it is wiser to accommodate these seasonal weather changes rather than fight them. Furniture chosen for flexibility offers the opportunity to move seating further into the room when it is colder so that storage such as bookcases and modular units can be put against outside walls for added insulation. A large room may also be partitioned in winter with freestanding storage. Make use of the window side during the day, when it's warmer, and retreat to the other side of the divider at night, where the space can be heated more easily.

Smaller living rooms are naturally cosy; the problem here is how to, visually at least, gain space. Avoid large pieces of dark heavy furniture that tower overhead. If you install shelving, only fit it to the depth you actually need and if possible restrict

storage to one wall or limited area. Shelves always look better grouped together, giving the impression of being planned rather than merely thrown up at random. Store only what you really need or want to display, to leave more space free for comfortable and generous seating.

Older homes have fireplaces which once made natural focal points to the rooms; and although the fireplace may not house the heat source any more, it is still likely to be an attractive feature. The mantelpiece is tailormade for display. An uplighter concealed in the fireplace itself accentuates a beautiful surround and highlights plants standing in the grate. On either side of the chimney breast, alcoves give scope for considerable storage. Display shelves are easily built within each space and doors fixed to lower shelves combine concealed with open storage. In traditional or period style rooms, visually incompatible equipment such as sound systems, the television and video may look better behind closed doors. Deeply spaced shelves that pull out on runners allow more flexibility in the positioning of the television, with the video recorder above or below it.

Without visible means of support, these glass shelves seem to float against the walls of the alcoves. Careful choice of the material for the shelf itself enhances a display.

Permanent storage

When building shelves or units to house electrical equipment, remember to consider the positions and capacity of electrical outlets. Overloaded adaptors are dangerous and, if sockets are at skirting height and the stereo at waist-level, there will be trailing wires that must be kept unentangled and concealed.

Good modern storage for home entertainment is gradually emerging but many designs have severe limitations. Units built to house a television and video have little, or unsuitable, space for tapes; audio storage often allows room for thirty albums and no more, completely ignoring a section for cassettes. Collections always expand and many expensive units have almost built-in redundancy.

Speakers, a vital part of any sound system, need careful positioning if they're to be effective; one day, perhaps, architects will start planning homes with built-in facilities for concealing them. Until then, we have to improvise and find places at the right height with sufficient space between for reasonable sound balance. Speakers should never be placed directly on the floor where part of the sound is absorbed and can annoy neighbours beneath.

Living-room storage can contribute to making space for casual meals. The ubiquitous coffee table, though handy, is much more useful when it features low-level shelves or compartments. Magazines and books are quickly stored below, clearing the top for plates and cups. Cube storage is ideal for this purpose and can be moved easily; combine several cubes to make one large, low table or use single or paired units as perfect one-place settings.

Whatever you are storing or displaying needs careful positioning in the room. Central heating can be damaging; protection can be provided by a correct-output humidifier, which puts sufficient moisture back into the air to counter the heating's drying effect. Avoid putting anything made of wood too close to a radiator or in strong, direct sunlight; audio and video cassettes can also be badly affected by excess heat or light. Ornaments on display near a window should be regularly moved or they will leave marks on the surface.

DINING ROOMS

Delicious food, an imaginatively decorated table, intimate lighting and gentle music are the ingredients for successful entertaining. How and what you eat is much more important than where you eat – a relaxed, comfortable atmosphere puts both you and your guests at ease, whether you dine in the kitchen, living or dining room, or even in the hall.

Preparing food should be a joy not a chore, but the less confident or inhibited chef may feel more relaxed if formal dining is kept apart from the cooking operation. A room reserved solely for dining is an expensive waste of space and in most homes the room in which meals are taken almost certainly has a dual role.

Living and dining

A combined living and dining room is a very popular option and the dining area can be partitioned off by folding doors, a screen or a room divider mainly consisting of shelving. The room may be too small to take a permanent, full-sized dining table comfortably, but there's a wide choice of designs with extension leaves or flaps that fold out, or you can opt for the simple trestle version that's put up only when you need it and is otherwise stored neatly away. Folding chairs that also store flat will stop the room looking overcrowded or cluttered.

Kitchen/diners

The added bonus of an attractive, well-planned kitchen is that you'll almost certainly want to eat there, too. Even if you have a separate dining room, some meals are just more coveniently eaten in the room where the food is prepared. Gone are the days when the cook was banished to the kitchen to churn out endless meals single-handed, joining the dining table in between tending to the different courses. Meal times are far more relaxed and sociable occasions when the opportunity to meet and talk is as important as the meal itself.

Unless your kitchen is fitted into a cupboard there's always a way to find space for somewhere to sit and eat. Some kitchen designs incorporate retractable dining tables within base units; a cheaper alternative is to mount a large hinged shelf on a wall where it can be folded down when not in use.

Nothing matches exactly but everything blends beautifully in this elegant dining/kitchen room. By stopping the run of the fitted kitchen units, and using a different, freestanding, style of furniture to store china and glass, the two areas of the room are emphatically separated. The shelves of an otherwise formal cabinet have been softened by the sensitive addition of fabric.

Left: To appreciate the delicate patterns on china plates, they are best displayed upright. As a safety measure, fix a batten along the back edge of shelves to prevent them slipping or toppling over. This display is deliberately arranged so that regularly used china is to the front and on lower, more accessible levels.

Right: The dining table is the focus of attention in this rustic but practical kitchen. Ample storage space is provided by the wall units, and baskets of all shapes and sizes, filled with herbs, plants and dried flowers, look delightful hanging from the ceiling beams.

An instant breakfast bar is made by combining a simple worktop with narrow stools or folding chairs.

In busy family kitchens, it's wise to keep young children out of the cooking and preparation zones, but still confined within the room where you can keep an eye on them. A run of low-level units forming a peninsula divides the kitchen practically and safely. The counter provides a serving area and additional table top. Sensible designs include cupboards with doors that open on both sides, so items such as china and glass can be taken to the table from one side and returned, via the sink, from the other.

Storage of china, cutlery and glass should be planned according to how and when they are used. Everyday items are most practically kept near the sink, so they can be put away effortlessly; precious glasses, silver and dinner services reserved only for special occasions need not be stored here at all. China and glass that are rarely used make a beautiful and almost permanent decorative display on the open shelves of a dresser or behind the dust-proof protection of glass doors.

Table-top appliances, such as the toaster and coffee-maker, are appropriately placed near the dining table, to save you getting up to refill cups or hovering around the grill. Jams, sauces, spreads and condiments need to be kept together somewhere near the serving and preparation zones. A narrow cupboard or shelves at the end of a peninsula puts them equidistant between the two.

Dining rooms

If a separate room is used regularly for dining, make sure it's well heated, close to and on the same level as the kitchen. This room, permanently equipped with a sizeable, sturdy table, is also ideal for homework, hobbies and sewing. The amount of storage you need depends on your interests and equipment, of course, but allow sufficient space to conceal the typewriter, computer or sewing machine as well as the china, cutlery and glass needed for dinner parties. A con-

ventional sideboard takes up a lot of space and offers limited storage. A dresser combining concealing cupboards and display glass cabinets gives good vertical storage; it may come in two parts, one sitting on top of the other. If the glass cabinet at the top can be wall-mounted, the flat-topped cupboard below makes a useful sideboard.

A practical way of combining extra seating with permanent storage is to build in a fitted cupboard the length of the table, the height and depth of a chair seat. Add seat and back cushions and you have a comfortable bench with lots of hidden space to store things below.

If the room is only occasionally used it will probably be cooler than the rest of the house and can provide space at the right temperature for storing your wine. Keep the bottles in simple wood or metal wine racks, sufficiently portable to be moved out if you are heating the room for any length of time.

Preparing food in advance leaves you free to entertain guests and a mobile heated trolley may be worth considera-tion. You will have to adapt your cooking techniques slightly and choose your menu with care, as most food suffers from being kept hot. Vegetables should be undercooked as they'll continue cooking in a hot cabinet, whereas roast meats appreciate a 'set' time of about fifteen minutes before carving.

A wide, fixed shelf at table height with electric sockets above forms a serving counter where you can plug in hot trays, plate warmers or an electric wok for stir-frying on the spot. The shelf doubles as a desk or worktop when needed for other pursuits. A mobile drinks cabinet with an integrated refrigerator provides a separate place to serve drinks and to keep cold desserts chilled until serving.

If the room overlooks a garden or balcony, more adven-turous cooks can make space for a barbecue and enjoy al fresco food nearly all year round. Whatever its aspect, put on some relaxing music, light the candles or lower the light above the table, and you're dining in style.

KITCHENS

The kitchen is usually the greediest area for storage, demanding not only sufficient space for a vast and diverse range of equipment and edibles, but also in specific places if the room is going to have any sense of order about it. It is easier to find room for everything if your kitchen is well designed and thoroughly planned from the outset. Good looks are, of course, an important aspect but efficient function, safety and economy of movement must be worked into the scheme too.

Planning or simply reorganizing a kitchen involves a network of decisions and you need to give a great deal of thought to how and what you like to cook in order to achieve the sort of kitchen in which you'll feel at home. The best way to tackle the situation is to consider the position of the basic elements: sink, cooker and refrigerator. The tried and tested formula for an efficient and safe work pattern between major items is: prepare; cook; serve/prepare; clean; prepare. This pattern can take the form of one unbroken line or a closely related 'working triangle'.

Planning a kitchen layout
As a rule of thumb, this work sequence should be confined to a space of between 5m (12ft) and 7m (22ft), incorporating enough storage space for all the materials and utensils needed there. These are the essentials of a good, safe working kitchen even if the only cooking you do is to make tea. If space is tight you would do better to consider making room elsewhere for laundry and cleaning equipment, deep freeze and occasional or bulk storage.

The following sequences show how the working triangle can be arranged – the one best suited to you is likely to depend on the size and shape of your kitchen.

In-line layout The simplest arrangement is a single line with everything set against a suitable wall. This sequence is ideal for long narrow rooms or one wall of a studio apartment where the kitchen could be screened off by sliding or folding doors. The most practical sequence is worktop, sink, worktop, hob, worktop, kept within a maximum span of about 6m (20ft).

Safety

DO
- keep chemicals out of children's reach.
- keep a fire blanket and extinguisher by the hob.
- provide adequate lighting over work areas.
- use steps to reach high shelves or cupboards.

DON'T
- interpose a traffic route between cooker and sink.
- place cooker hobs near curtains and blinds.
- fix cupboards over hobs.
- let cupboard doors clash with opening room doors.
- position electrical sockets too near sinks and cooker hobs.
- interrupt worktop runs with full-height units.

Don't be deceived by this romantic, nostalgic kitchen; it has been planned to incorporate all the essential modern coveniences. The rustic beam above the Aga conceals lighting and extractor fan, the deep recess provides ample hanging space for utensils. Recessed downlights illuminate the pretty display of china on the dresser.

Galley layout The galley kitchen has two parallel runs with sink and hob on one side, food storage, including refrigerator, and preparation areas on the other. It is an easy layout to work with but the corridor needs to be around 1.2m (4ft) wide if there's more than one cook; for a single person this gap can be reduced to 76cm (2½ft). This layout is not advisable if the central aisle is a main thoroughfare with doors at both ends.

U-shaped and L-shaped layouts In these layouts the 'working triangle' falls into its natural sequence between either two or three walls and is compatible for both small and large kitchens. In larger rooms the essential triangle should still be kept within the optimum span.

In a kitchen/dining room, one side of the 'U' or 'L' can form a peninsula and visually make the dividing line between the two areas. To emphasize this, the dividing worktop can be split into two levels; a lower counter on the kitchen side with a wide shelf above. This usefully doubles as a serving counter and casual snack bar, also helping to conceal the kitchen when dining is more formal.

Island layout This is a layout favoured by serious cooks and best suited to large rooms. A central work station houses the hob and, if space and finances permit, an extra sink for food preparation. This work station may also become a dining table, or at least a place where family or friends can sit around and watch the cook at work, and it provides an attractive focal point to the room.

Kitchen storage

Having worked out a suitable layout, plan how materials and utensils can be stored in relation to the work zones where they are first needed, and where they can be logically returned. Putting things back in place is a chore that even modern technology hasn't yet resolved, but with common sense you can make it relatively quick and easy. Sometimes good planning obviates the need to put everything away, and attractive items can be displayed.

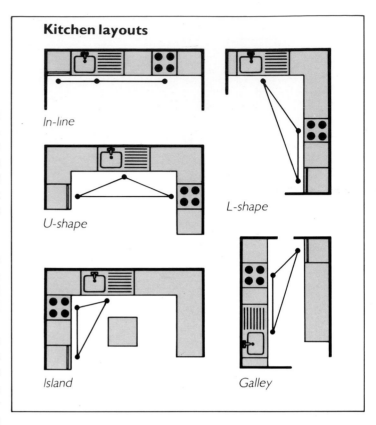

Kitchen layouts

In-line

U-shape

L-shape

Island

Galley

Washing zone – the sink

If space permits a double sink is best, particularly for the busy cook. One bowl can be covered with a chopping board and when food preparation is finished, the washing up is done in one bowl, rinsed and drained in the other. In a tight space a single sink can be freed to work if the washing up is left to drain on a rack above it. It's not only hygienic and saves drying up, the rack provides practical storage for everyday china, especially if hooks are fitted to hold cups and mugs.

If you prefer to keep everything behind closed doors, china can drain on a rack hidden away inside a bottomless wall cupboard. Ensure that the cupboard is hung in a position that allows the drips to go into the sink, not down the wall or on to the floor.

A rubbish bin of appropriate size needs to be close to the sink; housed in a long, deep drawer beneath the worktop, it leaves both your hands free to scrape plates or scoop vegetable peelings from sink to bin.

Any plumbed-in appliances are economically housed near

Left: A simple wooden drainer is designed so that dishes can drip dry and be stored in one place, conveniently above the sink. Baking tins used only occasionally are kept higher up on the rack. Glass shelves are held safely in place by special brackets with upturned lips and the mirrored wall visually enlarges this narrow galley kitchen. Cutlery is kept well organized in old ceramic mustard jars.

Above: A wooden grid is suspended from the ceiling and makes a practical solution for storing mis-matched utensils, drying herbs and the cook's string of garlic.

Far left: An industrial wire grid used for the reinforcement of cement structures has been adapted to make a display of kitchen utensils, simply attached by butchers' hooks.

Left: End of unit shelves make china easily accessible.

Below: A hob is given a canopied extractor hood, neatly disguised.

the sink. You may not consider a dishwasher top priority, but it's a very hygienic method of washing up and saves time on a boring job.

Washing machines were traditionally housed in kitchens before technology developed automatic programming. From the point of view of hygiene, they are really incompatible with the kitchen and are far more logically installed in a utility area. Modern designs have the advantage of space-saving features such as washing machine and tumble-drier combined.

Washing-up detergent and pan scourers should be within easy reach of the sink and these can neatly fit into a rack hung inside a cupboard door. Cleaning items used less frequently need not be stored here. Space beneath the sink, particularly if it's on an outside wall, can easily be ventilated to provide a cool, dark larder for vegetables conveniently close to hand.

Drying cloths on telescopic towel rails fit neatly into a narrow cupboard or gap beneath the worktop, often a space where trays of awkward shape and large chopping boards can also be stacked.

Cooking zone – oven, hob or combination

In a large family kitchen the 'split-level' separate oven and hob is a practical choice. Oven, grill and microwave can be moved out of the 'working triangle' and built into a tall housing unit where they're out of reach of children but on eye level for the cook. Heavy pots and casseroles are safely stored beneath the ovens and a heat-resistant glove should be within easy reach. Near the hob you need to store all the items actually used during cooking – that includes herbs, seasonings and stirring utensils as well as saucepans and frying pans.

In smaller kitchens a combined hob with built-in oven is more space-saving. Remember to allow 30cm (1ft) of heat-resistant worktop, preferably on both sides of the hob.

Whatever the size of your kitchen a modern essential is an extractor hood fitted over the cooker or hob. There are two types – one recycles air through a charcoal filter, the other, more efficient type, removes smoke and steam through a vent pipe to the outside, leaving the kitchen free from lingering food smells and damaging condensation.

Preparation zone – refrigerator

The size and type of refrigerator you need largely depends on how and what you eat. Fresh foods, other than dairy and meat products, appreciate a less cool temperature and many new designs for fridges now incorporate three zones – larder, refrigerator and deep freeze, to keep the various contents in peak condition. A well-designed refrigerator should use every scrap of space for maximum efficiency and energy-saving, and that includes adjustable shelving both inside the cabinet and on the back of the door. If you are having the refrigerator built in, be sure that it can be adequately ventilated from behind or has a top-mounted venting, and site it well away from other appliances that generate heat.

Food stuffs not kept in the fridge or freezer should be stored in close proximity to the preparation zone for easy access. Pull-out larder cupboards filled with adjustable shelves make everyday basics clearly visible and easily accessible from both sides. Conventional base units can be fitted with wire baskets on runners to save you from groping in the back of dark cupboards. In a narrow galley kitchen, wide, open shelves and a couple of low, deep drawers make more accessible storage than conventional cabinets.

Different types of surfaces are needed for preparing food – wooden boards for chopping, marble slabs for pastry-making. They can be built into the worktops themselves; if separate, they take up less space standing vertically or slid into a shallow shelf under wall units. Some sophisticated kitchens have pull-out worktops to increase counter space.

Food preparation counters must be kept squeaky clean, and this is made easier if they are kept free of clutter. Use the wall space immediately above worktops for hanging utensils either on fixed battens or on individual hooks. A wire grid system is a versatile method for storing kitchen paper holders, spice racks and other small accessories.

A good set of super-sharp kitchen knives is a basic essential and for easy food preparation they should be kept in peak condition. Mounted on a magnetic rack, or slid into a wooden block or slots cut into the back of a worktop, they are instantly

Far left: A galley kitchen is an easy layout to work with but safest when access is restricted to one end. A well-lit alcove recess between cupboards is just the right width for storing table-top appliances and books.

Above left: A narrow hinged box pulls out and conveniently stores long French loaves and sharp knives. Lined with a plastic sack, this same unit would also make a practical rubbish bin.

Below left: Kitchen units do not have to be of a uniform width. Thin pull-out drawers make contents easily visible and accessible. The lower section keeps oddly shaped bottles safely upright.

accessible. If you prefer to keep them out of sight, a separate section should be reserved in a drawer, away from other cutlery and utensils but close to the sharpener.

Above the worktop lightweight items can stand on open shelves or in cupboards. Shelving is cheaper and shows off attractive packaging, jars and everyday china but shelves should be limited to about 20cm (8in) deep for easy reach. Cupboards suit the less tidy-minded but still need to be organized with items used regularly at the front and those used less often at the back. The inside face of a wall-cupboard door is often wasted and can be fitted with hooks, racks, narrow shelves, foil and clingfilm dispensers – but don't overload it.

Small electrical appliances are energy-saving and make the

*Far left: A butchers' block
provides an extra work surface
in this well-planned kitchen.*

*Left: Even a tiny kitchen can
house a breakfast bar.*

cook's life easier, but gadgets become gimmicks unless regularly used. An electric coffee-grinder tucked away in a cupboard means you'll soon resort to the instant or ready-ground varieties. Make sure you have enough electrical sockets at worktop height.

How to plan a kitchen

Draw a diagram of the room on graph paper using a sensible scale – 1:20 is practical – and don't forget to mark positions of doors, windows, electrical sockets, radiators, etc. Make scaled cutouts of the appliances you have and are keeping, and of those you intend to buy.

Many kitchen manufacturers and retailers offer a free planning service, but they too will need all the above information. Their advice may prove invaluable, giving you ideas and suggestions you would never have thought of, but the kitchen must be studied carefully. Remember, too, they are in the business of selling kitchen furniture, so don't be fooled into thinking you need all that they'd like to sell you.

Vertical layout

Kitchen units and appliances are standardized at a height of 90cm (2ft 11in) which discriminates unfairly against very tall or short people. Well-designed units have adjustable plinths; those that don't can be removed entirely or raised to a more suitable height. Built-in toe space of at least 75mm (3in) makes it easier to reach the back of worktops and wall cupboards.

Food preparation worktops should be at least 19mm (¾in) proud of base units to make it easier to sweep off crumbs, vegetable peelings and so on. The standard depth of worktop, 60cm (2ft), is not really broad enough and a little extra depth provides useful storage in the preparation zone. Worktops do not have to be all on the same level; washing up is easier at a slightly higher level than jobs such as rolling pastry and chopping vegetables. The right height is what feels right for you.

Wall cupboards should be mounted at least 40cm (1ft 4in) above worktops and 180 degree hinges or up-and-over doors prevent the risk of banging your head.

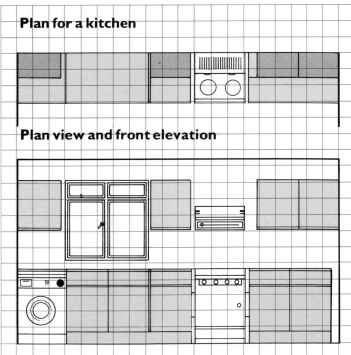

Plan for a kitchen

Plan view and front elevation

BEDROOMS

In the bedroom comfort is top priority, and the atmosphere should be relaxing and secure. Your bed is the only essential piece of furniture here and many people would find their sleep, and perhaps the quality of their lives, dramatically improved by investment in a new bed.

Apart from improving your state of health, a new bed can also provide useful storage. Many designs have drawers built into the bed base, or cupboards and shelving integrated with the headboard. Some modern mattresses offer enough support to be used without a bed base, either placed directly on the floor or on a platform or solid base which could be designed to incorporate a series of drawers. A bed raised high off the floor can be fitted with cupboards acting as low-height wardrobes. These options are well worth considering when you are planning to furnish or reorganize a bedroom; tailormade furniture like this, combining both sleeping platform and storage, may be less expensive than the cost of a conventional bed and individual pieces of storage furniture.

Another good idea is the futon, the Japanese sleeping mat, a firm, thin mattress which is rolled up during the day and spread out only at night. Ideal for back sufferers, this solid mattress made from layers of plump cotton can be left permanently flat, but must rest on a base which allows air to circulate around it. This base could still be used to incorporate neat, concealed storage.

We spend an incredible third of our lives in bed. This includes time spent not actually sleeping but reading, eating or merely relaxing. Space is needed to cater for these additional comforts. Bedside tables are usually ridiculously small and totally inadequate for books, magazines, radio and breakfast tray, and too low for convenient placing of a reading lamp. Shelves above the bed, positioned so you don't bang your head when sitting up, make an ideal support for an anglepoise reading light. They can also house speakers, if you like bedtime music, and you can easily reach for books and magazines without getting out of bed. A mobile storage unit at the end of the bed makes a convenient space for television and video; wheel it round the bed to make a table.

Hanging space is not the only requirement for bedroom storage. Many people use the room for relaxing, reading, watching television, besides the more expected activities of sleeping and dressing. These alcoves have been well planned to cope with a multitude of requirements: drawers below hold small items of clothing (wardrobes often lack this), wider shelves hold ornaments and adjustable reading lights, while higher shelves of usefully varied sizes hold books. Both cupboards can be screened by pulling down blinds that match those at the window and the colour of the bedcover.

Organizing the space

If floor space is tight, don't be tempted to skimp and make do with a smaller bed in order to make room for other items; too much furniture in a small room will make it appear claustrophobic and cluttered. A bedroom is experienced in both darkness and light; masses of furniture towering around the bed can form an uncomfortable presence not conducive to easy, restful sleep. Before choosing other furniture, consider the outlook from the bed position and make sure there will be enough space to get in and out with ease. If the room is really tiny, rather than filling it up so it looks smaller still, consider installing cupboards outside or turning another room close by into a dressing room.

Freestanding furniture does provide flexibility in a bed-room, which can be advantageous if you like reorganizing the room to suit the time of year. A bed positioned beneath an open window may be delightful in summer, but in winter it will be cosier pushed up against an internal wall. Many ranges of freestanding bedroom furniture are designed to seem built-in and storage intended for other parts of the house often looks equally at home in the bedroom.

If you have certain pieces of furniture – antiques or senti-mental heirlooms perhaps – that feel right in the bedroom but cannot be matched with a wardrobe of suitable size, improvise with a simple screen around a dress-shop clothes rail. This offers a temporary and sympathetic stop-gap while you continue the search for just the right item.

Neat built-in storage takes up less floor space than free-

Left: A bed positioned by a window in summer is delightful, and, as all the furniture in this room is freestanding, it could fairly easily be re-arranged for winter.

Below: Two rolls of wallpaper make a heavenly feature of the doors, which conceal a wardrobe, wash basin and lavatory. Pretty paper-covered boxes store small items.

sensitive to architectural features, particularly as this furniture becomes a permanent fixture. Build wardrobes to the height of a picture rail and add the same detail to the top edge, or fix a sympathetic moulding around cupboard doors to make new additions blend with the room's more original features.

Floor-to-ceiling wardrobes built across an entire wall, with the interior carefully organized, can easily provide all the storage needed for clothes. Work out the best combination of hanging space and shelves to accommodate the range of your possessions. Integral drawers are really an unnecessary expense; wire trays on runners are a practical alternative, giving easy visual access to smaller items such as socks, tights and underwear. Don't skimp on hanging space; clothes packed closely together are difficult to see, take out and put away. Shirts and blouses on hangers, rather than folded in drawers, are readily accessible and need no extra pressing to remove fold creases.

Clothes, accessories and cosmetics

Hanging rails should be positioned according to the length and number of the different items of clothing. You need a section for full-height clothes, dresses, long skirts and coats, or you can fit one section with two rails, one at full height, the other mid-way for shorter items. Sufficient hangers make it easier to keep a wardrobe organized – inexpensive wire hangers take up little space but leave unsightly creases; this is resolved by covering the horizontal wires with thick cardboard, folded and stapled in place.

Shoes are logically placed at the bottom of the wardrobe. Leather soles kept off the floor stay in better condition; a wire-frame wine rack is a convenient solution. Alternatively, insist on taking the box when you buy shoes and stack the boxes, the retailer's own method of keeping shoes clean and undamaged. The shoes you wear regularly are unlikely to be returned to their box unless you are incredibly tidy, but occasional shoes kept boxed pile easily at the back of the wardrobe, leaving more space in front for those worn everyday. Use the empty boxes to hold polishes and brushes.

Thick woolly sweaters take up least room when folded on

standing but can't be taken with you should you decide to move. A cheap and simple wardrobe, however, can consist only of a sturdy shelf, built across an alcove or the span between two walls, forming the support for a hanging rail. Clothes can be concealed and protected from dust by curtains or blinds chosen to coordinate with the colour scheme of the room. Wall-to-wall storage can also be devised by fitting sliding doors on floor and ceiling tracks. These doors can be painted or papered to match the walls or totally faced with mirrors to create a feeling of greater space in the room.

Mirrored wardrobe doors can seem out of character in older homes where bedrooms were built with more generous proportions. Built-in storage here needs to be

Far right: A walk-in cupboard is ideal for anyone with a large wardrobe. Practical overhead lighting avoids fumbling in dark corners. Shelves extend up to the ceiling.

Right: A wall of built-in bedroom storage is concealed with curtains to match the fabric in which both shelves and partitions are covered. Dividing wardrobe storage into small sections keeps a sense of order and clothes can be organized into groups – shirts, sweaters, scarves – and, if space permits, into colours. When you have only limited room in a wardrobe, store out-of-season clothes in bags or cases and swap them over when the weather changes.

shelves or retained within small sections. If you have a huge collection they may be better off in a blanket box. If it has an upholstered top or is covered by a cushion, it doubles up as simple bedroom seating.

Restricted space for clothes can be utilized efficiently by dividing clothes into winter and summer wardrobes. Out-of-season clothes are packed away in suitcases or zipped bags made of tough plastic, kept on the highest wardrobe shelves, under the bed or in a different room altogether.

When clothes are stored in cupboards of any kind, don't overlook the potential of fitting inside surfaces with hooks where you can hang belts and jewellery. Two screw eyes or hooks linked together with a fine rod or thin elastic make a simple tie or scarf rack.

Silver belts and necklaces do not appreciate exposure to the air and will quickly tarnish, so are better kept in boxes with tightly fitting lids. Tiny and precious jewels are safer in boxes, too. Office stationers have all sorts of containers constructed of swivel trays, pots and boxes of various types and in various combinations. Suitable sizes make storage for jewellery and cosmetics.

The dressing table is the traditional home for smaller and more personal things, but a similar arrangement may be easily improvised. A wide shelf fixed at table height with narrower shelves above and on either side of a suitable mirror also forms a neat study area or writing desk. The small shelves can be painted or covered with fabric to match the colour scheme, the large shelf acting as the table top protected by a piece of finished glass made secure with clips at the edges. The shelves show off pretty bottles and jars and provide the location for a light angled to illuminate the mirror.

Another inexpensive idea is a wooden or veneered counter placed between two unfinished whitewood chests of drawers, leaving enough space for a chair or stool so you can sit in front of the mirror. Surfaces can be stained or painted, and finishing details such as knobs and handles, chosen to complement other features in the room, can transform such an arrangement into effective storage that looks just as attractive as a ready-made item.

BATHROOMS

Fitted kitchens are a standard feature in many new homes, yet bathrooms are for the most part minimal; a bath, washbasin, and lavatory. And when you think about it, even these few items are not a very happy combination. A separate lavatory is more hygienic and especially practical if two or more people share the home.

If a bathroom is small, its function is easier to define. A large room logically makes a laundry, too, and since a basic essential of a bathroom is heat, a washing machine can only contribute to keeping the room warm – but check installation complies with safety regulations.

Depending on space and the location of the water tank, an airing cupboard often features in the bathroom. If possible, it is more practical to have this cupboard opening into the room from outside, as the only regularly used items are towels. An electric rail dries towels and keeps them comfortably warm; this is better than draping them over a radiator, which inhibits it from heating the room as efficiently. More economical is a rack which hangs above the radiator, so the towels do not monopolize all the heat. Two curtain-pole brackets and a short length of dowelling make a simple, inexpensive rail that can be designed to the length of the radiator or number of towels.

Hand towels should be within easy reach of the basin. Borrow an idea from the kitchen and fit a paper towel holder to the wall or inside the door of a cupboard, or make your own roller towel.

Concealed storage

Unless you are totally reorganizing a bathroom, storage has to be fitted on either side of and above the bath, basin and lavatory. If it is planned well it also conceals the plumbing. Space is usually wasted around pedestal basins and in any major improvement you should consider a counter-top bowl which allows you to decide the most convenient height, rather than being dictated to by manufacturers. If you have small children they will need a solid block or box to use as a step up to the lavatory or the basin. A counter-top basin offers more flexibility in the choice of position, as it is

Safety

DO
- check that all light fittings conform to safety regulations – if in any doubt check with a qualified electrician.
- keep medicines safely locked away in a purpose-built medicine cabinet.

DON'T
- position lights where they can be reached by someone touching a bath, sink or shower tap.
- keep razors, etc. where they can be reached by children.

A perfect balance between style and function has been achieved in this understated bathroom. The top of the basin unit, incorporating a large drawer for cosmetics, extends out further than the cupboards below so you can sit to remove or apply make-up. A narrow slab of marble runs the length of the mirror and displays glass storage and tooth mugs. Beside the bath, a cupboard the size of a small wardrobe is lined with shelves to keep the surfaces uncluttered and easier to clean, while clean towels are stored in two open shelves at the top.

supported by the counter itself and not by the wall, and it can be fitted into a corner with space beneath for a large, wide, L-shaped cupboard. If space around is tight, bi-fold doors overcome the problem.

A mirror for shaving and applying make-up takes up considerable wall space if it is of a size that is easy to use; those combined with cupboards tend to be small and the storage space is insufficient for the cosmetics, perfumes, aftershave and so on that you may want to keep there. A mirror over the basin and one elsewhere for shaving or make-up leaves room for two people to cope with the early morning rush more amicably.

Good lighting is essential here – light should shine directly on to the face to avoid unflattering shadows. Rows of bare bulbs have traditionally framed stage dressing-room mirrors

and for very good reasons. These naked bulbs give the best illumination for applying make-up and shaving. If your bathroom is small, extra mirrors or mirror tiles help create the illusion of space, but ensure the virtually constant view of yourself is seen in the best light, a warm glow from incandescent bulbs rather than the fluorescent type.

Safety is another important consideration. Since the medicine cabinet is conventionally installed here, it should for obvious safety reasons be placed well out of children's reach. Even if you don't have a young family you cannot rule out the possibility of a child using your bathroom; if you do have small children the bathroom can often resemble a field dressing station! Purpose-built medicine cupboards tend to be too small and there is danger if the overspill is stored where small hands can find it or if, when an emergency does occur, the

Left: These unusual triangular shelves combine convenient storage space with accessibility. A mirrored wall not only adds to the dimensions of the room, but emphasizes the shelf shapes.

Below: Double hand basins save frayed tempers in the early morning. The towel rails, well positioned beneath each one, are also the handles of giant drawers for the laundry.

remedy might be found in any number of places.

Though essential, the majority of medicines and first-aid basics are used infrequently and can therefore be considered long-term storage, along with other occasional items such as suntan lotions. Several boxes, with their contents clearly marked, can be stored on the top shelf of a linen cupboard. Items used more frequently such as aspirin, plasters and antiseptic are better kept close to hand. A locking petty-cash box, available at stationers, is a safe and child-proof container.

The gap between door frame and ceiling can provide extra cupboard space for both infrequent essentials and regular supplies of soap, shampoo and toilet paper. Build one yourself or look out for a wall-hung kitchen cabinet. These odd items can be picked up very cheaply in sales. Similarly, a couple of kitchen base units can house a basin sunk into a water-resistant surface, providing space for cosmetics and toiletries on top with generous storage beneath. Again, if there are children in the home, fit safety catches on lower doors if the cupboards are used to store cleaning materials, bleach and disinfectant. Other storage accessories designed for the kitchen work just as well in bathrooms. More efficient use can be made of internal cupboard space with wire drawers fitted on runners under shelves, waste bins and hooks attached to the backs of cupboard doors.

Display storage

A tiered vegetable trolley on castors provides mobile storage for bath oils and salts, soaps, shampoos and bathtime toys. One of the versatile wire-grid systems, hung within easy reach of the bath or shower, can be fitted with hooks for flannels and loofahs, wire baskets for soaps and sponges. Glass shelving makes practical and attractive storage; the shelves are easy to clean and visually do not monopolize space. The transparency makes them suitable carriers for pretty bottles and jars or collections of seashells and plants. Many track shelving systems offer special brackets with upturned lips to hold a sheet of glass securely. Upright supports fixed either side of a window, spanned with several glass shelves, form an ideal showcase for plants.

Most tropical houseplants thrive in the bathroom where the warmth and humid atmosphere comes closest to their natural habitat. In modern bathrooms, waste bins in primary colours make effective containers for large plants. Traditional and period rooms need planters that coordinate with the bathroom's style. Junk china, too unhygienic to use as tableware, can be turned into elegant cachepots. Small flowering plants look attractive in large cups and saucers. Old-fashioned chamber pots are big enough to hold and conceal several small plastic pots, filled with a variety of patterned and textured foliage, typical of the Victorian preference for deliberate clutter. If the plants are standing near the bath or basin, you can use similar containers, plastic or ceramic, to hold sponges, brushes, loose bath crystals and so on. These can stand among the plants on a shelf or counter top.

WINDOW DRESSING

Windows are such a necessary part of any room that, ironically, they are frequently taken for granted, and often even ignored. But as practical and decorative assets, windows are all-important in the scheme of things – light, air, and sunshine are all essential to our mental well-being while windows are our link with the outside world.

All windows are functional, and that can be combined with as little or as much decoration as you like, and since the window is such an integral part of any room it could become a major element in your over-all scheme: a decorative opportunity not to be missed.

So stand back and take a look. What do you want from those particular windows. Should they stand out or blend in? Some windows look best left alone, others need curtains and blinds to emphasize their shape, while some – great view, pity about the shape, and vice versa – cry out for disguise.

Today there is more fabric choice than ever before. From rough wools and tweeds through to splashy chintz and see-through voiles. So somewhere there is something that is just right for you and your window.

An essential part of the decorating process, and one not to be rushed, is choosing which sort of treatment is best for your windows. Warmth, privacy and light are all practical considerations which should be taken into account. Remember, also, that windows and rooms look different in different lights. So notice the way the light falls, both morning and evening, in sunshine and cloud, before taking a final decision about fabric.

When working with fabric always remember that the important areas in which not to skimp are those which are most precious – time and thought. Small details count; in fact detail is really what it is all about.

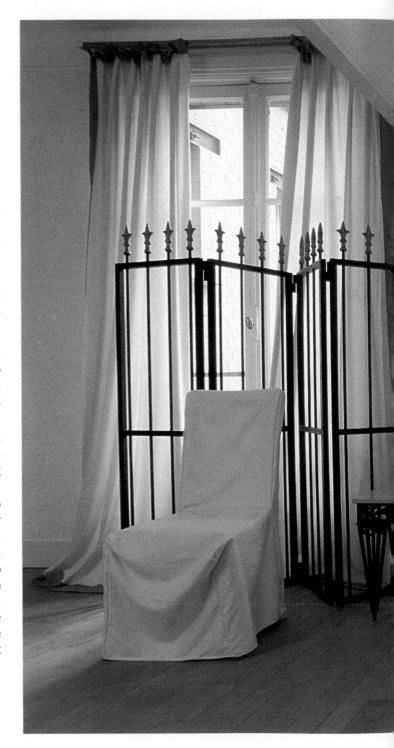

Striking but simple, these diaphanous cream curtains fall elegantly to the floor to create the perfect backdrop.

DECORATIVE USES

The decorative elements of curtains and blinds go a long way beyond merely matching other pieces in the room. Over coordination, in any case, is a plague to be avoided. It is important to incorporate the window into the overall decorative scheme, but remember that the way a window is treated can affect the proportions, the style and the very atmosphere of a room.

Style

Curtains and blinds play an important role in pulling a look together. The wrong type of curtain heading or a glaringly modern blind, for example, can strike a note of discord in the most carefully reconstructed period interior. A fussy festoon blind or formal dress curtains would be just as out of place in a contemporary setting. But between these extremes there are nuances which you must be aware of when planning a decorative scheme.

Atmosphere

The mood of an interior is highly influenced by the quality and amount of natural light. Unfortunately, few rooms can boast an even, gentle diffusion of light; awkwardly placed windows or a poor aspect can create conditions ranging from harsh glare to permanent semi-gloom. Carefully chosen fabrics and window treatments will go a long way towards improving such a dismal prospect.

Cold, harsh light can be filtered with Venetian blinds or other slatted blinds made of wood, cane or bamboo. Sheers, the traditional remedy for softening glaring light, can be made in white, or a pale shade for a warmer look.

Where there is too little light in a room, make the most of what you do get by using pale-coloured fabrics with smooth or shiny surfaces that will reflect light, and take the curtains beyond the window on an extended track, holding them away from the frame with tie-backs.

Making the most of views

Where there is something worth looking at, the window treatment should be kept plain and simple, the window acting

Bring down the window width by hanging the curtains so they permanently meet in the centre. Hold them back with tie-backs.

On tall, narrow windows hang full-length curtains on a track or pole extended out well beyond the sides of the windows.

On short windows, add height by fixing the pole or track high above the window and adding floor-length curtains.

Adding a deep decorative-edge pelmet over the top of long curtains will help to reduce the height of a tall window.

These plain half curtains have been pushed to the sides of the windows to let in the maximum amount of daylight and give an unobstructed view of the garden beyond. When closed, they give privacy to the room without the loss of natural light.

as an extended frame around a picture. A pretty valance, for example, could be used above an arched window with a secluded outlook, or an asymmetric swag draped to balance a tall tree or building.

An ugly view presents a different problem. While it is important to distract from the scene outside, you can rarely block out all the window light. Exclude the view but keep the light by choosing one of the many colourful slatted blinds available (including louvred panels and plywood screens with designs of punched holes). Or choose one of the new, highly individual patterned nets which can be bought in a variety of depths and hues.

Café curtains hung with brightly coloured poles and rings will also distract the eye from the view.

Visual tricks

Curtains and blinds can be used in several ways to correct certain architectural faults. Carefully dressed windows, doors and alcoves can give an impression of increased or reduced height or width.

The height of a window can be reduced with a café curtain, a deep pelmet, valance or draped swags and tails, while alcoves and openings can be made to seem less high with an asymmetric curtain draped permanently across. Windows can be made to look wider by extending the length of the curtain track or width of the blind beyond the actual opening. Striped floor-length curtains will suggest greater height in a low-ceilinged room; and sill-length curtains patterned in a horizontal design will make a high ceiling seem lower.

CURTAINS

Right: Consider the quality of light and the style of furnishing you have when choosing curtains. A bright corridor with lovely antiques is best served by muslin tied loosely on rods.

In every home there are some rooms and some windows where only curtains will do – you may love blinds to distraction, but there are times when they are just not the right treatment for the situation.

Curtains have a multiplicity of uses, both practical and decorative, and it is important that yours fill as many of those uses as possible. They should, for example, keep out cold, keep in heat, and shut out light when necessary. They should also set the scene for the room and your possessions.

Curtains not only affect the appearance of the windows they cover but also alter our perception of the room as a whole. Floor-length curtains with a pelmet and valance will stress the vertical, sill-length ones – extended beyond the window – will emphasize the horizontal. Softly draped curtains, swagged and swept back with ties, will disguise hard angles, while narrow plain curtains used with a roller blind will give the window a clean, sharp look. Bright colours will draw attention to themselves, while pale shades and simple designs will turn the eye away.

Curtains can be bought, ready made, in many standard sizes and designs from most large department stores. They pick their best-selling fabric designs, and a few perennial favourites such as velvet, and have them made up into curtains of widths and lengths which will fit most average-size windows. So if your windows are relatively normal, these curtains could well be a good idea.

Curtains can also be made by professional curtain-makers. At curtain-making's simplest level, there are shops and individuals who will simply follow your measurements and place your chosen material back-to-back with its lining, seam them both, turn them right way around, sew on a heading tape and then hem them. A process which is known, not surprisingly, as bagging.

And then there are the true professional curtain-makers who come to you, and stand by your window, taking measurement after measurement. To use these craftsmen is a course of action that may seem expensive, not to say extravagant, but which for many people is justified by the high standard of expertise and the time saved. The best curtain-makers make all the headings by hand. The curtains are fully lined and interlined, and weighted to hang properly, and then finished off by hand. They are then hung and adjusted until absolutely perfect. If you are thinking of using a very expensive fabric, it is often worth finding out how much a professional would charge you – they usually charge by the drop (or length). It is then fairly easy to calculate and compare the prices based on the number of drops you expect your curtains to have. As with all craftsmen the best way to choose a professional curtain-maker is to see examples of their work, ideally in situ.

Then, of course, you can make the curtains yourself. This is really not a difficult task, provided you take time to measure accurately at the beginning, and take care with each step. The job itself has been made much easier and more enjoyable nowadays thanks to the ready availability of various heading tapes and the wide range of tracks and decorative poles, plus every refinement a curtain-maker could want. The money to be saved by making them yourself is enormous, and you will have the endless satisfaction of knowing that it was all your own work. If you do decide to make them yourself, don't be daunted by all those metres of uncut material lying on the floor – they will soon be tamed into stylish window dressings. Also, when making them yourself it is worth spending just that little bit more time and energy on lining and interlining them whenever necessary. A well-made pair of curtains should last a lifetime, fabric willing, and it doesn't take much more time to make them well than to make them badly.

If you are making them for the first time, go for simplicity, either a plain fabric or a small print or stripe which can be matched easily. Remember, curtains don't have to be elaborate. A simple, clear colour, unadorned by tie-backs or pelmets, etc., can look just as good, if well made, as the most elaborately embellished scene stealer.

Not all windows come undressed, however; many windows come along with inherited curtains that could most kindly be described as adequate. Cheer them up by adding a few touches here or there: decorative tie-backs, borders, a pelmet or valance, or braids.

CALCULATING FABRIC AMOUNT

When cutting out the fabric, spread the fabric out on a large flat surface and cut straight across the width using large, sharp shears. On fabrics with all-over patterns straighten the edge, then measure and cut each length. With large print fabrics, follow the design lines when cutting out each piece. To find the straight edge on even-weave fabrics, pull out a thread and cut along the gap.

When buying curtain fabric, it is important to have calculated exactly how much you will need in advance. Apart from other considerations, bolts of the same fabric may have slight variations of pattern or colour and, if it were necessary to buy more fabric, there could well be a distinct difference in the finished curtains which is often only noticeable when they are being hung.

The length and fullness of a curtain are the first things to be taken into account. As a rule, the length should fall either to the sill, radiator or to the floor. If you choose floor length, decide whether the curtains are to sit just above the floor, touch it, or overflow on to it.

The next step is to choose the style of heading, and this, with your chosen length, will determine the total amount of fabric needed. Some headings require a large amount of fabric while others use much less. A pencil-pleated heading, for example, needs two and a half times the length of the curtain track, while a gathered heading needs only one and a half to two times the track length (see page 167).

Before measuring the window area, either mark the position or put up the pole or track from which the curtains will hang, as this will obviously affect their finished length. Work out whether your track or pole is to be fixed inside or outside the window frame, or extended beyond the frame on both sides. A curtain pole with decorative finials is always supported on brackets outside the window frame.

Although most curtain fabrics are a fairly standard width of 120cm (48in), there are variations, particularly with imported fabrics, so in calculating the amounts needed, always double check the width of the fabric you plan to use.

Once you have established the track, or pole, and chosen the style of heading, measure the length from the correct position at the top edge to the bottom and add 20cm (8in) for hem and heading. For the width, multiply the length of the track by the required fullness for the style of heading plus 10-15cm (4-6in) for the side turnings, then divide by the width of your chosen fabric – usually 120cm (48in) – and round up this figure to the nearest full number to give the number of standard fabric widths needed. Half fabric widths

1. Fold under seam allowance and pin over seam allowance of adjoining piece.

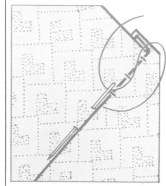

2. Stitch across the join between the two fabrics and run through the flat fabric.

3. Take the needle back across join and through folded fabric. Continue.

Measuring for curtains

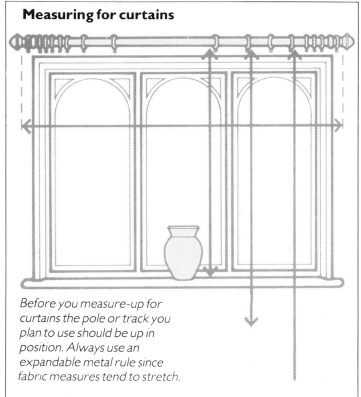

Before you measure-up for curtains the pole or track you plan to use should be up in position. Always use an expandable metal rule since fabric measures tend to stretch.

- Measure the length from the track or pole to the desired height: to the sill, to the top of a radiator below the sill or to the floor. Then add allowances for hem and heading.

- For the width, multiply the track or pole length by the required fullness of the desired heading tape.

- Divide this measurement by the fabric width, rounding up the figure to the nearest full number for the number of fabric widths per curtain.

- Multiply the curtain length by the number of fabric widths for the amount of fabric needed.

- The amount of lining required will be the same as the amount of curtain fabric – but remember to deduct any extra that might have been required to match up patterns.

can be used in curtain making when the amount of fabric needed is slightly over a full number. Position half widths on the outside edge of the curtain. Multiply the curtain length by the total number of fabric widths to get the actual amount of fabric needed.

It is sometimes tempting to try and save on fabric, especially when you see how many widths you will need, but this is always a false economy. The difference between good- and mean-looking curtains has a lot to do with the fullness of fabric. If in doubt, it is always better to err on the side of having too much rather than too little.

Unless a washable fabric has been fully pre-shrunk it is always necessary to allow for shrinkage. This is usually 3-4 percent on a curtain which is less than 2 m (2 yd) long, and the normal hem allowance will accommodate this.

If you are using fabrics with a distinct pattern, it is essential, if you plan on joining together more than one width of fabric in a curtain, to make sure that the patterns match horizontally at the seams. This is done by allowing extra fabric so that the pattern repeats can be adjusted to match. Most assistants at curtain fabric counters are adept at calculating the quantity required (if they have the basic window measurement), but, as a rough guide, measure the height of the pattern repeat and add that measurement to the length of each width after the first one, so that the pattern can be matched exactly to the adjacent width.

This is done by first ladder-stitching the lengths together from the right side with the pattern matching exactly – see steps left; then fold the fabric lengths with right sides together and machine-stitch together on the wrong side and complete with the appropriate seam.

For the amount of lining fabric needed, calculate as for the main fabric even though the lining hem is slightly higher than that of the curtain fabrics. If extra curtain fabric is needed for matching patterns, remember to deduct this from the amount of lining fabric required. Generally, lining fabrics are also 120cm (48in) wide, but they are sometimes available in a limited range of wider widths and using these can, in some cases, be cheaper.

HEADINGS

If you plan to have curtains without elaborate valances or pelmets, then the curtain heading itself will become an important feature. The choice of heading has as much to do with the length and proportion of the curtain as it does with personal taste.

Cased headings

Curtains such as café curtains, short nets and sheers and some long curtains – provided they are lightweight and unlined – can be attached with a simple sewn channel, made by turning over the top of the curtain and machine-sewing two rows of stitching to form a channel, through which a rod or expanding wire can be slotted. The gathered fabric makes a small frill, or heading, at the top.

For the amount of fullness, allow about one and a half times the length of the rod. For the depth, measure from the top of the rod to the required curtain length plus 10cm (4in) for the hem and the correct heading allowance. The heading is usually 1.3 to 2cm (½-¾in) and the casing 1.3cm (½in), which may have to be adjusted to fit your method of fixing so decide on the method and then add the correct allowance, remembering to allow for a double width casing.

Heading tapes

These are narrow strips of strong fabric that can be bought by the metre (yard) in a variety of types and sizes. They are available in white and natural in both cotton and synthetic fibres. For example, lightweight synthetic tapes should be used for synthetic fabrics, sheers and nets. The tapes usually have two or more cords running through the middle and when they are pulled up together form a gathered or pleated heading, depending on the style used. They also have slots for

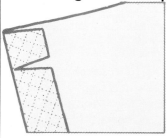
Cased heading

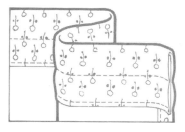

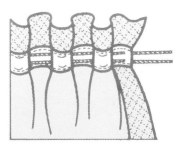
Standard heading tape

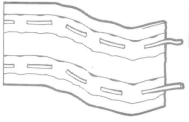
Pencil pleat tape

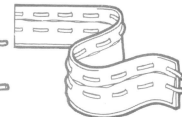
Detachable lining tape

Attaching standard tape

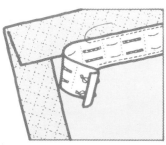
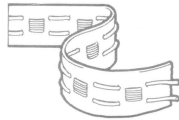
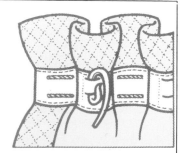

I. Snip into hem along fold line, to within 5mm (¼in) of outer edge. Match edges; fold over.

2. At one end of tape, knot cords on wrong side. Turn under tape end and machine.

3. At opposite end of tape, pull out cords from the front, and gather up curtain.

4. Then thread the hooks through the tape, evenly spaced across the curtain.

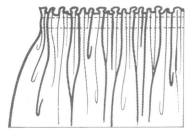

Standard *One and a half to two times track length of fabric is needed.*

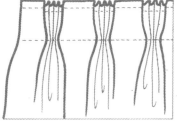

Cluster *required fullness is two times the track length of fabric.*

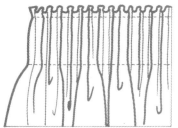

Pencil *Fullness required is two and a quarter to two and a half times.*

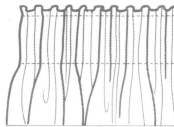

Spaced pencil pleats *Two and a quarter times the track length in fabric is required.*

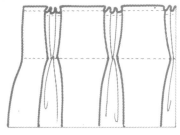

Triple pleats *are either straight or fanned. Two times the track length is needed.*

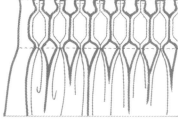

Decorative, *for example smocking. Two times the track length is needed.*

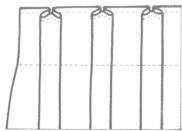

Box *Semi-formal in appearance these pleats are evenly spaced. Two and a half times the track length of fabric is needed.*

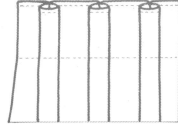

Cartridge *Softly rounded pleats. Two to two and a half times the track length of fabric is needed.*

the hooks, which attach the tape to the curtain runners on the track. The deeper tapes have more than one row of slots so that the height of the curtain above the track can be adjusted by inserting the hooks in either row of slots. Special tapes are also available for detachable linings to be used with any curtain heading tape.

With pairs of curtains, it is important that the style of heading should match in the middle where they butt together – particularly on triple and cartridge-pleat tapes where there is a wide space between each group of pleats. This does not apply if you have an overlap arm on the track. To match the heading, always begin by placing the tape to the curtain edge that will fall in the middle of the track, starting in the centre of a pleat group.

STANDARD PLEATS The tapes for standard pleats form a simple gathered heading suitable for all weights of fabric. Its plain, shallow heading is usually covered by a pelmet or valance. It is particularly useful for small unlined curtains.

CLUSTER PLEATS This gives a fairly shallow heading of evenly spaced pleats suitable for all fabric weights.

PENCIL PLEATS This tape makes a deeper, more formal heading suitable for all types of unlined curtains, lined cotton and sheers, and some medium-weight fabrics for use with a track or pole. Spaced pencil-pleat tape is ideal for heavier fabrics. Make sure the gathers are evenly distributed.

TRIPLE PLEATS Either straight or fanned, these form a deep, stiffened heading suitable for formal lined curtains of all lengths for use on a track or pole. They are ideal for all types of cottons, and medium- to heavy-weight fabrics.

CARTRIDGE PLEATS These softly rounded and distinctly formal pleats are suitable for all types of curtain – especially for heavier, lined floor-length curtains.

DECORATIVE HEADINGS These tapes give a crisp decorative appearance and can be used on short or long curtains – lined or unlined – using cotton, medium-weight or sheer fabrics.

BOX PLEATS These give a semi-formal appearance and can be used for all types of curtains and sheers hung from a track or pole. They are especially good for thicker, lined curtains.

MAKING CURTAINS

Making unlined curtains

Apart from those curtains made from self-edged nets and sheer fabrics, the technique for making an unlined curtain is basic to making any other type.

Begin by joining the fabric widths together using 1.5cm (5/8in) flat fell seams, having first removed or snipped into the selvedges. Turn over 2.5cm (1in) double turnings on the side edges and an 8cm (3in) double hem on the bottom edge, and press to the wrong side.

Mitre the bottom corners. After basting and slip-stitching the mitre, continue to slip-stitch around the sides and hem using a matching-coloured sewing thread, picking up only one or two threads of flat fabric with each stitch. Enclose weights in the hem, if needed (see page 171), and finish the top edge with your chosen heading (see page 166).

MITRING A CORNER With the curtain wrong side up, and the side and bottom turnings pressed in place, mark the turnings at the outer edge with pins. Unfold the corner to leave single turnings and then fold the fabric diagonally from pin to pin. Refold the side turning and the hem, baste and slip-stitch the mitre together working from the outer corner to the inside edge.

Unlined curtains

1. To join widths place fabric right sides together; machine. Trim one allowance in half.

2. Fold wider seam allowance over narrower seam allowance; press against fabric.

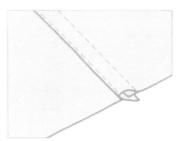

3. To enclose and neaten the raw edges stitch down seam again, close to fold edge.

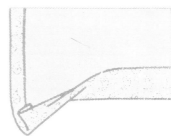

4. Turn in 2.5cm (1in) double turnings on side edges and a double 8cm (3in) hem.

Loose-lined curtains

1. After stitching widths together snip into the seam allowance and press open.

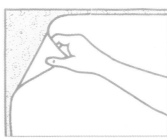

2. Place lining and fabric with right sides together, matching side edges.

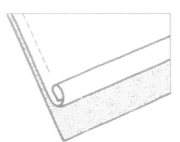

3. Stitch down sides to within 15cm (6in) of hem. Turn up a double 2.5cm (1in) lining hem.

4. Matching centres press curtain, so side seams lie 1cm (3/4in) in from outer edges.

Making lined curtains

Unless the curtains are semi-sheer and intended to filter light, use a lining. It will protect the curtain fabric from sunlight – giving it extra life – and reduce heat loss and noise.

Loose-lining The side edges are stitched together, the top edges treated as one, and the bottom hems stitched separately. First, calculate the amount of fabric needed; it should be 4cm (1¾in) narrower than the finished curtain.

Join the main fabric and lining widths, using 1.5cm (⅝in) flat seams. Clip into the selvedges, and raw edges, every 10-15cm (4-6in), and press them open. With right sides together, place the lining to the main fabric and, taking 1.5cm (⅝in) seams, machine-stitch the sides to within 15cm (6in) of lining edge. Clip the seams. Turn up a double 2.5cm (1in) hem on the lining, mitre the corners and slip-stitch to close. Machine-stitch the hem. Turn the curtain right side out, match the centres of both fabrics and press the side edges. Turn up a double 5cm (2in) hem on main fabric; mitre and finish as for unlined curtains. Slip-stitch the rest of the lining to side edges.

Turn down top edge, cutting and turning in the corners at a slight angle. Add your chosen heading tape.

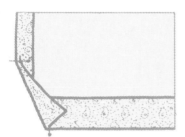

5. Mark turnings with pins. Unfold corner then fold corner diagonally through both pins.

6. Refold in side and hem edges, so mitre is formed across the corner; slipstitch.

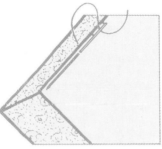

7. Slip-stitch down side edges, just picking up one or two stitches of flat fabric.

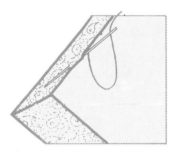

8. Slide the needle through the folded hem edge and bring out ready for the next stitch.

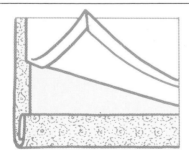

5. Turn up a double 5cm (2in) hem on the bottom edge of the main fabric.

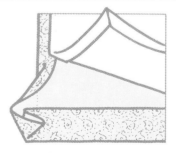

6. Mitre the corner of the main fabric in the same way as for unlined curtains.

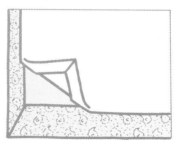

7. Slip-stitch the remainder of the side seam down to the lining hem edge.

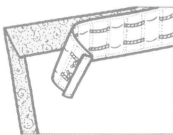

8. Turn down the top edges at an angle (if necessary). Attach heading tape.

Right: Curtains made using professional techniques are both long-lasting and opulent looking: two headings, pencil and pinch, are used here, with elaborate plaited tie-backs.

Lock-stitched lining The technique of lock-stitching the lining and main fabric together is used by professional curtain makers and gives a better finish to the hang of the curtain. It is worked in vertical rows across the curtain width and involves lightly catching the lining to the curtain fabric with large loose stitches.

First, estimate the amount of curtain fabric needed, and allow the same amount of lining minus allowances all round. With the main fabric right side down, press in 5cm (2in) single turnings on the side edges, and a 15cm (6in) single turning on the hem. Mitre the corners as for unlined curtains, using single turnings only. Slip-stitch the mitre together. Herringbone-stitch down both side edges and across the hem, picking up only one or two threads of the main fabric. Turn in and press 2cm (¾in) on side edges and a 5cm (2in) hem on the lining mitring and stitch the corners in the same way.

Place the curtain fabric right side down on a flat surface, and then the lining on top, right side up. Smooth flat and pin down the centre. Fold half the curtain fabric back and lock-stitch the lining to the main fabric from the top edge to just above hem edge and taking long, loose stitches. Work more rows of lock-stitch about 40cm (16in) apart across the curtain width working from the centre outward both ways, with rows of stitching beginning at the top and working towards the hem.

Smooth the lining in place and slip-stitch to the side edges and hem, covering the raw edges of the main fabric. Fold over the top edge of the curtain fabric and lining. On heavy fabrics mitre and slip-stitch the corners. Baste the turning and apply your chosen heading.

Interlining will undoubtedly add a professional quality to your curtains. A soft layer of fabric stitched between the curtain fabric and lining will make them hang in beautiful rounded folds as well as provide an effective insulation against cold draughts, and protect expensive curtain fabric from dust and strong sunlight. With interlined curtains, it is usual to lock-stitch the interlining to the fabric, then add the lining in the same way as for lock-stitch linings.

Lock-stitch lining

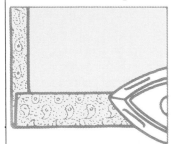
1. Turn in 5cm (2in) single side turnings and 15cm (6in) hem at the base edge and press.

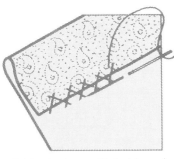
2. Herringbone stitch side and hem edges, only taking one or two threads of fabric.

3. Place lining over curtain fabric, wrong sides facing, and pin together down the centre.

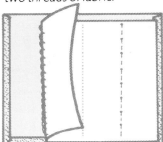
4. Work rows of vertical lock-stitching from the centre outwards across the curtain.

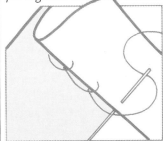
5. Make long loose lock-stitches in a thread that matches the fabric, picking up only one or two threads.

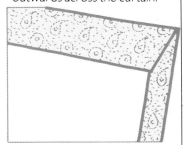
6. On heavier fabrics, mitre the top corners of the curtain before adding the heading tape to the top folded edge.

Interlining

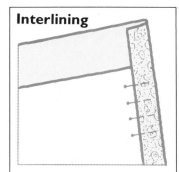

1. Overlap the edges of the interlining by 1cm (⅜in) and herringbone stitch.

2. Fold back the curtain fabric and lock-stitch to the interlining down the centre.

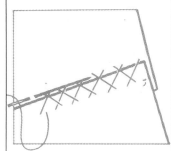

3. Turn in side edges, and complete in the same way as for lock-stitched lining.

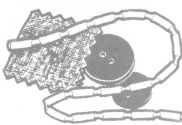

Two types of curtain weight: discs with two central holes are stitched in place like a button, or enclosed inside a fabric bag. Alternatively, fabric-covered weights, they come in a continuous length which is stitched down at intervals along the hemline.

Calculate the amount of curtain fabric and lining needed as for lock-stitched lining. You will need the same amount of interlining as the finished flat curtain. Widths of interlining should be overlapped by about 1cm (⅜in) and then herring-bone-stitched together.

It should then be spread on a flat surface (floor if needed) and the curtain fabric placed on top, right side up, smoothed flat, and pinned down the centre. Half the curtain fabric is folded back and lock-stitched as for lock-stitched lining. This is repeated every 40cm (16in) across the curtain width. Baste around the outside edges through both layers.

Turn the fabrics over and, with the interlining on top, make single turnings on the side edges and hem, and stitch as for lock-stitched lining. Apply the lining and heading in the same way. When lock-stitching the lining, avoid stitching over the same rows made when lock-stitching the interlining.

HANGING CURTAINS

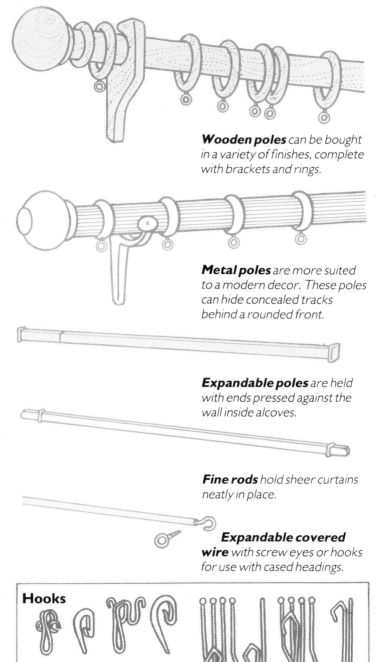

The unseen parts of curtain hanging are the most important of all – no matter how well a curtain is made, the effect will be ruined if it is hanging like a drunken sailor from the track.

Tracks

It is essential to decide at the beginning exactly how you want your curtains to be attached. Tracks can be fixed either to the ceiling or to the window frame – to the width of the frame, or extended beyond and attached to the wall. You should also decide whether or not to have a pelmet or valance to cover the track. If so, the track itself need not be elaborate. A soft valance usually needs a second track which is either clipped to the curtain track or fixed on extended brackets outside it.

If you decide to have a track without a pelmet or valance, then the track should be as unobtrusive as possible. There are several types available in plain and coloured plastic – produced in a fairly limited range of colours.

Metal tracks are on the whole sturdier – and more expensive. They are recommended for heavier curtains, which need a lot of support.

Tracks for bow and bay windows should be sufficiently pliable for them to be bent accurately to shape. As with other windows, you may prefer your curtains to overlap in the middle of the window. In that case, the extended track should also be cut and bent to fit. Both tracks should overlap each other by up to 15cm (6in).

Poles

These are available in several different styles and decorative finishes made from wood, brass and other metals. Wooden poles can be mitred to fit around bay windows and some metal poles are adjustable. Many of them are accurate reproductions of antique poles – often with beautiful decorative finials. They can be bought in standard and made-to-measure lengths, complete with the appropriate rings and brackets, with or without cords, and in various colours.

Where uncorded poles are used, especially with heavier fabrics, it is best to buy draw rods. These hang from behind, attached to the runners close to the heading edges.

Wooden poles can be bought in a variety of finishes, complete with brackets and rings.

Metal poles are more suited to a modern decor. These poles can hide concealed tracks behind a rounded front.

Expandable poles are held with ends pressed against the wall inside alcoves.

Fine rods hold sheer curtains neatly in place.

Expandable covered wire with screw eyes or hooks for use with cased headings.

Hooks

Above: Metal and plastic hooks for standard tapes. Right: Metal hooks for decorative tapes.

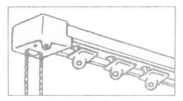

Ceiling-mounted *tracks are a useful alternative system.*

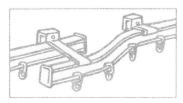

Wall-mounted *track with an overlap arm.*

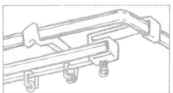

Valance rail *clips on to the front of the main track.*

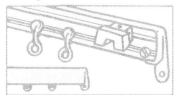

Concealed *standard track in white plastic.*

Rods

For lightweight curtains such as nets, sheers and café curtains, you can buy thin metal rods and expanding wires – for slotting through a cased heading – which are supported by small hooks and screw eyes. These metal rods come either in chrome, brass or with a white plastic finish.

Adjustable rods are also available in either a plastic or brass finish. The plastic type has a spring mechanism which allows it to fit a variable space, and is fitted inside the window reveal. The other kind works like a telescope at one end and is fixed either inside or outside the window with brackets.

Hooks

These come in many different shapes and sizes, in both plastic and metal finishes. Plastic hooks are usually sold in conjunction with plastic runners specifically designed for plastic tracks. For best results, a hook should be inserted at each end of the curtain and about every 8cm (3in) in between.

Metal hooks made from brass or aluminium are much stronger and should always be used on heavier fabrics. They include the standard curtain hook and hooks for the draw-string heading tapes, as well as pronged hooks for slotted curtain tapes. These hooks are sold separately and in two sizes – for hanging higher or lower on the track or pole – so make sure you have the right hooks.

New curtain poles are sold with fittings attached into which a standard hook is fitted. Metal hooks are used on hand-stitched headings, where they are stitched behind the pleats.

Runners

Runners are designed to glide easily along the pole or track and have loops at the bottom for holding the hooks attached to the curtain. They are usually made to suit a particular track and include the traditional rings in brass, wood or plastic for rods and poles, and plastic- or brass-finished runners that hang from specially shaped tracks either from the lower edge or slot into the back of the track. Most runners have the hook suspended in such a way that, when the curtains are hung, both the track and runners are hidden. One type of runner combines a second loop to hold the hooks on the lining at the same time. Nowadays, combined hooks and runners are sold with some tracks.

The runner on the outer end of the track – usually called an end-stop – is anchored to the track and stops the curtain from sliding off, and the outer hook is slotted into the end-stop on the outer edge of the track.

Cord pulls

Whether you have plastic or metal tracks, pelmets, or valances, if your track does not have integral cord pulls, it is worth thinking of adding a cording set. These are specially fitted so that the curtains can be opened and closed simply by pulling an extension of the cord fitted to one side of the window, thus preventing wear to the curtain edge by constant pulling. One set of cords, for example, can also be arranged to operate sets of curtains on double windows, if they have a combined track.

Dressing the curtains

After hanging curtains – especially the heavier floor-length ones – the folds and pleats need to be 'set' so that they hang evenly from heading to floor.

Open the curtains to the draw-back position and straighten each fold and pleat. On cartridge-pleated curtains, each of the pleats can be lightly stuffed to hold their rounded shape – use tissue paper, or a soft tissue. When all the folds are even, tie soft ribbon or cord around the curtain at the top and bottom. Leave for about three days for the folds to set.

PELMETS AND VALANCES

Pelmets and valances give a decorative and formal finish to the tops of curtains and at the same time hide the curtain heading and track from view. They can be used to create a dramatic effect and to alter the proportion of a window. The pelmet or valance, for example, can be fixed higher than usual to make the window appear taller, or extended at the sides to make it appear wider. Although they are often made from the same fabric as the curtains, they need not match.

Pelmets

Pelmets can be plain wooden boards with either an upholstered, stained or painted finish, or they can be made from stiffened fabric and attached to a pelmet board in the traditional way. The lower edge in each case can be straight or decoratively cut to suit the style of the curtains and general decor of the room.

Before calculating the amount of fabric needed for a pelmet, make sure that the curtain track and pelmet board are fixed in the correct place. The pelmet board should be attached to the wall – usually about 5-8cm (2-3in) above the frame, but this can be varied to suit individual needs.

THE PELMET BOARD should be cut from plywood about 100mm (4in) deep by 12mm (½in), and project at least 5-8cm (2-3in) at each end of the track, so that the pelmet does not interfere either with the curtain track or the smooth running of the curtains. Screw a 100mm (4in) rectangular piece of plywood at right-angles to each end of the board. Attach the board to the wall with small brackets.

Flat pelmets can have a variety of differently shaped edges. Match the decorative edge to the decor and the curtains.

Making a pelmet

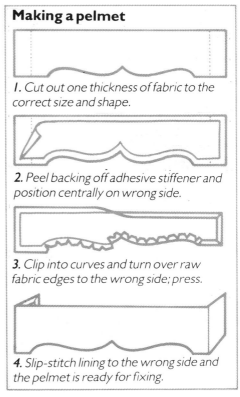

1. Cut out one thickness of fabric to the correct size and shape.

2. Peel backing off adhesive stiffener and position centrally on wrong side.

3. Clip into curves and turn over raw fabric edges to the wrong side; press.

4. Slip-stitch lining to the wrong side and the pelmet is ready for fixing.

Soft, fabric valances should enhance and tone with the curtains hanging beneath them. Use a matching or contrasting fabric.

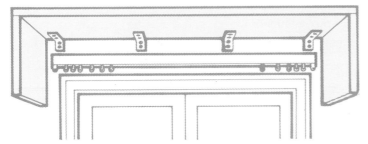

Position pelmet board 5-8cm (2-3in) above and beyond frame.

THE PELMET For the length of fabric needed, measure around the track from wall to wall, and then make a paper pattern of the pelmet shape. Measure the depth – this can vary between one-sixth and one-tenth of a floor-length curtain – and add 3cm (1¼in) all round for turnings. Cut the pelmet stiffener to the finished size, and the lining 1.5cm (⅝in) larger all round than the stiffener.

Cut out the main fabric across the fabric width so that the weave matches that of the curtains. Join any fabric widths to either side of a central fabric width. Peel backing from one side of stiffener and place centrally on the wrong side of the main fabric; press in place. Clip into the curves and mitre the corners on the main fabric before folding the turnings to the wrong side. Peel backing from upper side of stiffener; press fabric turnings on to upper side. Fold in and press 1.5cm (⅝in) turnings to the wrong side of the lining, and mitre the corners. With the lining right side up, press in place to upper side of stiffener, pin and slip-stitch it to the main fabric round the outer edge. If preferred, a decorative trim can be applied to the edge of the pelmet using clear fabric adhesive folding the trim into neat mitres at each corner. Hide the join under the mitre on one side section.

Stick touch-and-close spots to wrong side of pelmet, along both edges, 7cm (3in) apart. Stick the opposite halves of spots to the pelmet board to correspond. Press pelmet to board.

Valances

Valances give a softer, more informal look than pelmets. They are usually made from unstiffened fabric and sewn in soft gathers, ruffles or pleats, using handmade or commercial heading tapes. The bottom edge may be plain or ruched – made by gathering or pulling up standard heading tape stitched in vertical rows across the valance. The shape of the valance may follow the original line of the window, or it can

be curved to fall down either side of the window, in which case, make sure that the depth of the curve is in proportion to the height of the window. Most valances are attached either to a pelmet board with tacks or drawing pins, or a valance track with curtain hooks. They can also have cased headings which would be slotted on to a narrow rod which gathers up the fabric at the same time as holding the valance in position.

For a simple valance using a heading tape, first fix the pelmet board or track in place, and then calculate the amount of fabric needed as for curtains – repeating the same heading on the valance as on the curtain. Estimate the depth in the same proportion as for pelmets. It is usual to line simple gathered valances and interline the other pleated varieties. Cut out the fabric and make up the valance like the curtain.

A professional-looking fabric-covered board pelmet.

ACCESSORIES

Cords and ropes

For a period, classic look, use cords or ropes. These can be bought already knotted, with or without tassels. They come in different thicknesses and fibres, including metallic threads, and in a full range of colours and they can occasionally be dyed to order.

Borders and trims

Some manufacturers of cords also make matching coloured borders and trims – in furnishing weights – in a wide variety of designs. They are used often for edging plain or patterned floor-length curtains, pelmets and valances, and can also be applied to other soft furnishings, such as sofas and chairs.

Tie-backs

Adding a touch of prettiness or formality to many curtain types, tie-backs are essentially a useful way of keeping the curtain clear of the window in order to let in as much light as possible. Choose them with care. Before deciding, it is a good plan to spend time experimenting with different ideas. First, draw the curtains away from the window and tie them loosely with a length of string. Move the string into different positions to see which is best. Stand back so that you can see how well the curtains fall.

Tie-backs can be plain or decorative bands of fabric which are held in place by small rings attached to the ends and a hook fixed to the window frame. Shaped tie-backs are usually stiffened with interfacing or buckram and look parti-

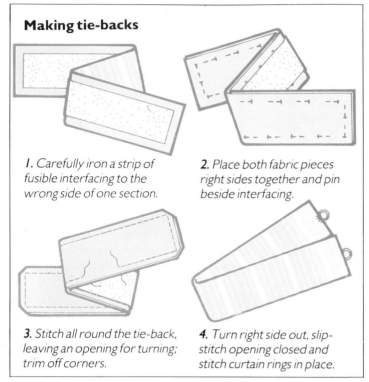

Making tie-backs

1. Carefully iron a strip of fusible interfacing to the wrong side of one section.

2. Place both fabric pieces right sides together and pin beside interfacing.

3. Stitch all round the tie-back, leaving an opening for turning; trim off corners.

4. Turn right side out, slip-stitch opening closed and stitch curtain rings in place.

cularly good with an elaborate pelmet. They are quite easy to make provided you use a paper pattern. Tie-backs can be made from matching or contrasting coloured fabrics or different-patterned fabrics. The edges can be piped, bound or trimmed with braid.

Some of the most successful and original tie-backs may be nothing more than a length of self fabric tied in a simple bow, or pieces of fabric that would be hard to display elsewhere. A pretty silk scarf tie-back, for example, made by tying the fabric in a loose bow or knot, or a false bow tie, made by using

Tie-backs look good with shaped edges, frills and bows.

Twisted cords with tasselled ends are quick and easy to use.

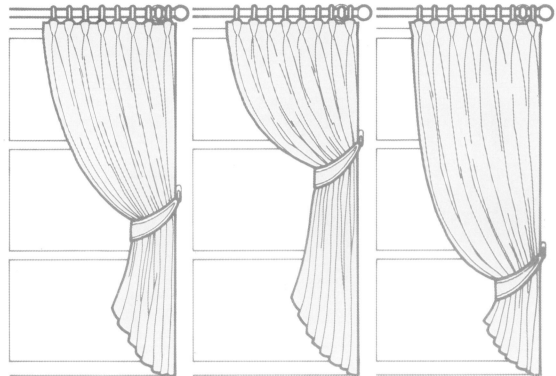

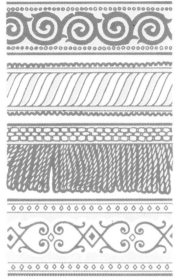

Left: Altering the position of the tie-back round the curtain will dramatically change the look of the curtain and the window. Below: You can add braids and fringes to plain tie-backs.

the standard tie-back shape with a ready-made bow attached to it, could look good. Plaited tie-backs can look effective, especially in colours picked up from the curtain fabric.

To make a simple tie-back, first measure the required curtain fullness. For each tie-back, cut out two pieces of fabric to this measurement by 10cm (4in) deep (this average depth can be adjusted to curtain proportion) plus an extra 1.5cm (⅝in) all round, and one piece of iron-on interfacing cut to the finished measurement. Press the interfacing to the wrong side of one section. Baste both sections right sides together

and machine stitch around leaving a 10cm (4in) opening in one side. Trim corners, turn through to right side, press and slip-stitch opening. Attach a curtain ring to each end; just overlap the outer edge and blanket stitch in place.

For formal window dressing when a pelmet, valance or swags and tails are used, coordinating tie-backs are traditionally used; match up decorative braids.

Reproduction brass rosettes and round-end tie-backs can be bought in several different shapes and sizes, and suit a severe curtain.

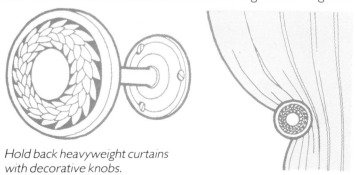

Hold back heavyweight curtains with decorative knobs.

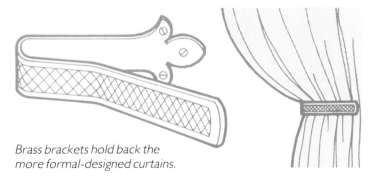

Brass brackets hold back the more formal-designed curtains.

IMAGINATIVE IDEAS

Left: A carefully planned interior uses a striking fabric to cover the wooden shutters and small scatter cushions. Drapes hung from a ceiling-mounted track create an alcove for a mattress, which acts as a sofa by day and a bed by night.

Above: A very simple pine bed has been transformed into a luxurious four-poster using masses of inexpensive cotton, tied to the bars with tapes. Confident use of the fabric for generous folds is the key to the idea's success.

Right: Brass eyelet kits are easy to use to make these attractive flat-hung blinds which are also reversible, with two layers of fabric stitched together. Dowels are driven into drilled holes in the window frame and painted in contrast for the pegs.

BLINDS

Blinds are a relatively inexpensive and practical solution to covering windows – either large, small or problematical. They help keep out noise and, to some extent, draughts, and also control light, although they are not as efficient as curtains at providing insulation and warmth.

Blinds work very well on small windows and in small rooms, where the amount of fabric in a curtain would otherwise be overpowering. They make ideal coverings for alcoves, shelves or cupboards where there is limited space for outward-opening doors. A series of narrow blinds can also work equally well on large expanses of glass or on awkward sloping windows.

Most blinds are operated either by a spring mechanism and roller, or by a linked cording system and pulleys. They can be ceiling, wall or window mounted.

Ready-made

There are many excellent ready-made blinds available in very wide ranges of size, colour and finish, including roller blinds in stiffened spongable fabrics, pleated paper blinds, wooden slatted blinds, vertical louvres, and Venetian blinds in plastic, wood or metal.

Made-to-measure

Many large department stores offer a made-to-measure service for fabric blinds – normally roller, but sometimes Roman, festoon and Austrian as well. Some will make up from the fabric you supply, but there is usually a wide range of fabric from which to choose, including special blind fabric with, for example, a plain body and a simple pattern across the bottom. Alternatively, there are also studios that will screen-print or hand-paint blinds exclusively for you – this could be the opportunity to improve an uninteresting view or to personalize your blinds in an original way.

Roman blinds are an elegant treatment in keeping with the stark formality of this room. A door leading to the balcony is separately covered, to match.

Measuring for blinds

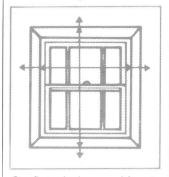

On flat windows, without a recess, measure across the window from one side of the frame to the other. Alternatively the brackets which hold the blind can be positioned on the wall to either side.

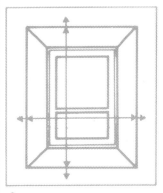

On recessed windows, measure either the width across the inside of the recess or measure across the window outside the recess, then the depth.

Do-it-yourself

Fabric blinds can be quick and easy to make at home. The equipment needed is fairly minimal. Complete roller-blind kits, and the tapes, cords and accessories for Roman, festoon and Austrian blinds, can be bought from most department stores; wooden laths, battens, screws and brackets are available from do-it-yourself suppliers. You will also need standard sewing equipment and a few handyman's tools.

CHOOSING FABRIC Select fabric for blinds with care, avoiding the type of thin, lightweight material that would stretch and sag in the middle, or make untidy edges when rolled up. Equally, heavy fabrics may roll unevenly and bunch up around the roller, or they may put too great a strain on the roller mountings.

Generally, roller blinds work best with a firm, closely woven fabric such as cotton or cotton/polyester mixes – and these are best in keeping out the light, too. PVC and specially stiffened blind fabric can be bought in wide widths and an excellent choice of fade-resistant colours and patterns, also with spongable finishes and non-fraying edges. These pre-stiffened fabrics do not usually need side hems, but if the blind is to have a lot of use, it is worth turning in a 1cm (⅜in) side hem.

An alternative is to use spray-on stiffening on other fabrics – even lace can be used as a blind if treated this way. Fabric-stiffening sprays are available in aerosol or spray form and can be used safely in the home. You will find that most fabrics will shrink slightly when sprayed so allow for this in your basic calculations. To find out how much stiffening a particular fabric will need, test-spray a small piece first in a well-ventilated room and leave to dry. Always follow the manufacturer's instructions as the procedure for different products may vary slightly. Also, spray-stiffened fabrics always need side hems to prevent fraying.

Blinds are hung either flat against the glass inside the window recess or outside the window frame. They can be fixed to the outer moulding on a separate batten, or directly to the wall. For accurate results, take all measurements using a retractable metal rule.

ROLLER BLINDS

Roller blinds are as popular today as they were in Georgian and Victorian times. Their simple, unobtrusive lines are easily adaptable to both modern and traditional interiors, but they are particularly suitable for kitchens and bathrooms, where curtains are not always a practical solution.

The blind consists of flat, stiffened fabric secured to a wooden roller and hung from special brackets at each side of the window frame. A spring mechanism at one end of the roller allows the blind to be pulled up and down.

Although a roller blind works well on its own, it can look equally good with curtains, which need not function as such but merely consist of lengths of fabric caught back at the sides. Blinds are also good teamed with sheers for a more delicate effect. A shallow fabric pelmet can be fitted to hide a blind when it is not in use. For greater emphasis or to provide a border for a plain blind, accentuate the window frame with colour or decorative stencilling.

Blind kits

Very easy to use, these come in two weights – standard, and heavy-duty for large windows. The basic kit consists of a wooden roller with a detachable cap and pin at one end, and a spring-winding mechanism at the other. The roller is available in various standard lengths, but can easily be sawn

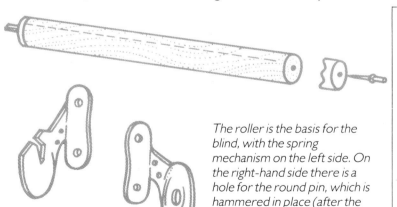

The roller is the basis for the blind, with the spring mechanism on the left side. On the right-hand side there is a hole for the round pin, which is hammered in place (after the roller has been cut to size) through a metal end cap.

Making a roller blind

1. Hammer the pin through hole in the cap. Do not rest the roller on the spring mechanism while hammering.

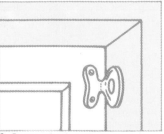

2. Screw the brackets in place at the window: the square-shaped bracket on the left and pin-hole bracket on the right.

Left: Simple roller blinds are often ideal for a room where the focus is elsewhere – dining for example. Their neutrality blends well with traditional or modern furniture.

down to give the precise length you need. Most rollers also have a guideline already marked along the length for attaching the fabric, but if not, then draw a line with a ruler before you begin to make the blind.

Also in the kit are brackets, which fit into a recessed window or at each side of a window, and a narrow lath, which is slotted through the base of the blind to add weight and to help it hang well. The final component is a small pull cord attachment, which fits behind the lath.

Making a roller blind

Before taking any measurements, decide whether the blind is to hang inside or outside a recess and then establish the roller size. For a recessed window, measure the width of the recess exactly and deduct 1.5cm (⅝in) at each side to allow for the roller fittings. For a window without a recess, where the blind is mounted on a window frame or wall, it is better to extend the measurements by about 4 to 5cm (1½ to 2in) at the top and sides to prevent light showing around the edges. Trim roller to size, if needed; cover cut end with cap, and hammer pin in to secure it in position.

Before calculating the amount of fabric needed, the roller should be fixed in place. For fixing into a recess, screw the brackets 3cm (1¼in) below the top of the recess, to allow for

the rolled-up blind (use rawlplugs for fixing brackets to a wall), and slot in the correct size of roller.

For width of fabric needed, measure the length of the wooden roller (add 2cm [¾in] for side hems for spray-stiffened fabric). For the length, measure from the top of the roller to the sill (or length needed) and add 30cm (12in) to allow for the bottom hem casing and to make sure the roller is still covered when fully extended. Cut out making sure the edges are square and pattern repeats centred.

If using spray-stiffened fabric, turn a 1cm (⅜in) hem down side edges. Zigzag stitch, centring stitching over raw edges.

For a plain bottom edge, make the casing for the lath by folding over 4 to 5cm (1½ to 2in) double turning to the wrong side. Press and stitch across the casing. Press the fabric well and stiffen if needed. Slot the lath through the casing and stitch to close. Screw down the cord pull to the centre of the lath, on the wrong side. With the fabric right side up, fold over and press a 2cm (¾in) turning on the top edge. Place the roller on top with the spring mechanism to the left, and then tack the fabric edge to the guideline at 2cm (¾in) intervals.

To make sure the winding mechanism is at the right tension, carefully roll up the blind by hand and insert it into the brackets. Pull the blind down as far as it will go. Check to see if it springs back to the top. If not, remove the blind and repeat.

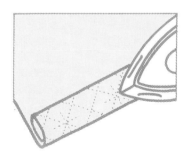

3. *Fold over double hem along the bottom edge of the blind to provide a casing in which to slot the wooden lath.*

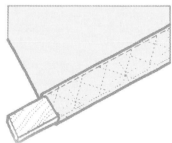

4. *Slot the lath into the casing to stiffen the base of the blind. Slip-stitch each end of casing to hold lath.*

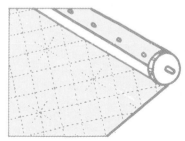

5. *Tack the top folded edge to the roller along marked line. Place the tacks at 2cm (¾in) intervals with one at each end.*

6. *Thread cord through cord pull and screw to the centre back of the lath. Then thread through an 'acorn'.*

Decorative edges

The hem or base of a roller blind need not be left plain. If the wooden lath is inserted slightly higher up the blind, the fabric below can be shaped into scallops, curves, zigzags, or a castellated edge where a decorative rod is slotted through loops in the bottom edge. You will need extra blind fabric for the facing. This should measure the width of the blind by about 13cm (5in) wide.

For a shaped edge, you should use a stiffened fabric. First make the casing about 13cm (5in) away from the bottom edge: simply stitch a 4cm (1 ½in) tuck in the fabric, press it flat towards the top and stitch along both edges. Apply the facing wrong sides together using fabric adhesive or double-sided iron-on bonding. Then make a paper pattern as wide as the blind and 13cm (5in) deep. Fold it concertina-wise into equal sections. Draw the required shape on the paper and cut out through all layers. Position pattern on the wrong side of blind and with a pencil lightly draw around. Carefully cut out. Stick trim over outer edge. Alternatively, you may prefer to close zigzag stitch around the edge before cutting out.

Scalloped edge

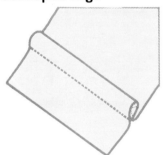

1. Stitch a 4cm (1 ½in) tuck near to the base of the blind to form the casing for the lath.

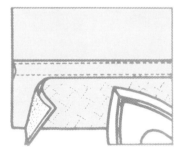

2. Fix facing in place to base of blind using double-sided iron-on bonding.

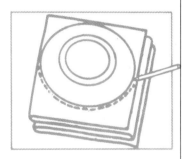

3. Fold up the paper concertina-wise and use a plate as a template.

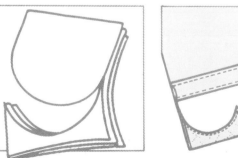

4. Keeping the paper folded, carefully cut round the shaped edge, to form the pattern. Unfold paper pattern.

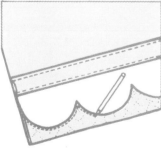

5. Place the pattern to wrong side of blind below the lath casing and mark round; cut out round the shaped edge.

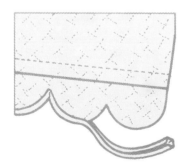

6. Fold trim evenly in half over the raw fabric edges and stick or stitch in place, to neaten and finish the lower edge.

Castellated edge

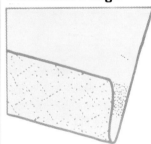

1. Fold back the facing to the wrong side of blind and stick, leaving a channel for the rod.

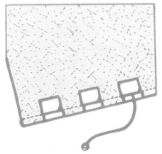

2. After completing the edge insert the rod and tie the cord and ring pull to the rod in the centre of the blind.

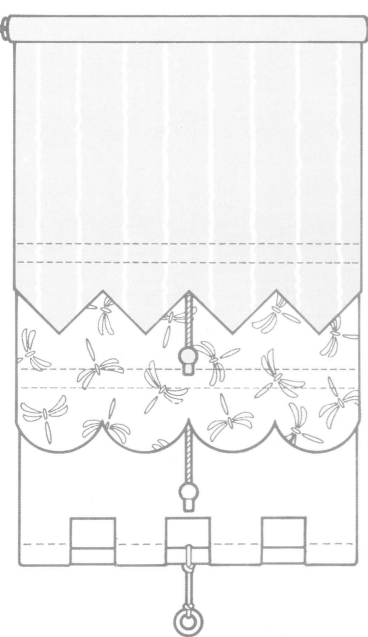

For a castellated edge, a casing has to be made at the bottom for the rod. For the length of fabric needed, measure from the top of the roller to the sill and add 33cm (13in) to include a 13cm (5in) facing. Fold back the facing to the wrong side. Make and trace around the pattern and cut out, as before. Stick together, leaving a 4 to 5cm (1½ to 2in) casing for the rod. Slot the rod through the casing and knot the pull cord to the rod.

Twisted cord, braid or fringing can all be applied around the lower edge of the blind using clear fabric adhesive.

Above: Three popular roller blind finishes: zigzag, scallop and castellated edge. Try to match the mood of the blind edge to the fabric. Divide up the edge so the shapes are evenly spaced across the blind.

Right: Blinds can be given a decorative edge to soften their somewhat utilitarian look. Here a shallow scalloped edging trimmed with white braid adds interest to a brightly coloured, plain fabric roller blind.

ROMAN BLINDS

Roman blinds use less fabric than curtains and combine the softness of fabric with the neutral elegance of a flat surface. Small patterns stripes or plains are best for their deep folds.

Roman blinds look newer and smarter than a roller blind. Requiring only a small amount of fabric, they pull up into softly folded pleats that look neat without being stark. Like roller blinds, they work well on their own or with draw curtains. Choice of fabric is important – many designs, particularly large round motifs, do not look good with the geometrical effect of the pleats. Both vertical and diagonal stripes, on the other hand, can look extremely smart – even quite dramatic, as can plain fabrics, or fabrics that have a definite texture.

Roman blinds are usually made from lined curtain fabric. This helps to keep out light and improves the shaping of the pleats. The blind is attached to a length of wooden battening, which is fixed into the recess of a window or above the window frame. Like roller blinds, Roman blinds are hung flat to the window with a wooden lath slotted through a casing in the lower hem, but pull up in the same way as festoon blinds. Cords are passed vertically through a series of rings attached to the back of the blind, and are knotted and held firmly on a cleat at the side of the window. Choose from either a narrow heading tape and slot through with split curtain rings, or use a special ringed tape which either combines tape and evenly spaced plastic rings or tape which contains cord rings, again spaced at regular intervals along the tape.

Making a Roman blind

Decide first whether your blind is to fit inside the window recess or outside the window frame; this will determine the length of the batten. If outside, the batten should be supported by brackets rawlplugged into the wall.

To work out the width of fabric needed, measure the length of the batten and add 9cm (3½in) for side turnings and seams. For the length, measure from the top of the batten to the sill and add 13cm (5in) for hem casing and fixing to the batten. For the lining width, measure the length of the batten and deduct 3cm (1¼in). For the lining length, measure as for the main fabric.

You will also need a number of ringed tapes, depending on the width of the blind – tapes are spaced between 25 to 30cm (10 to 12in) apart – each as long as the blind. For each tape,

Making a Roman blind

1. Join any fabric widths. Stitch fabric and lining together at side edges. Press seams.

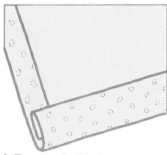

2. Turn up double hem at bottom edge and stitch across the blind twice to form a casing.

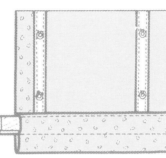

3. Slot a lath into the casing and slip-stitch up both sides to hold firmly in place.

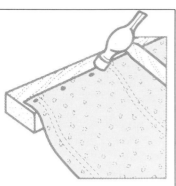

4. Fold both top edges of blind over the upper edge of the battening and fix in place.

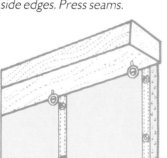

5. Fix a screw eye into the underside of the battening at the top of each row of tape.

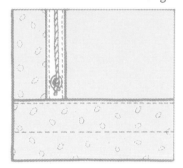

6. Tie cord to the bottom ring and thread up through all the rings above on each tape.

7. With all the cords threaded to one side, pull up together to raise or lower the blind.

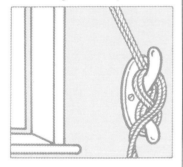

8. Tie cords together and wind them round the cleat in a figure of eight to hold the blind.

you need a screw eye and cord. The amount of cord needed will be double the length of the finished blind plus the width measurement multiplied by the number of tapes used.

Trim or snip into the selvedges of the fabric and lining before cutting out the correct size and mark both centres at top and bottom with pins. With right sides facing, baste and machine-stitch 1.5cm (⅝in) side seams. Press the seams open. Turn the blind to the right side. Match the centre pins together at top and bottom of blind and press sides so seamlines will be 3cm (1¼in) in from edges. On the bottom edge, with lining and fabric together, turn over 1cm (⅜in), then 10cm (4in) to the wrong side, forming a casing, and pin.

Pin lengths of ringed or heading tape to the wrong side, beginning by covering the two seamlines and making sure the rings will align horizontally. Tuck the ends of the tape into the hem. Add more rows between, spacing them about 25-30cm (10-12in) apart. Using a zipper foot, stitch the rows of tape down each side, through both layers of fabric. Stitch across the hem, catching in the ends of the tape, and stitch a second row about 4cm (1½in) below, for the casing. Insert the lath to fit just inside the edges and slipstitch both side edges to hold lath in position.

On the top edge, zigzag both fabrics together. Place 2cm (¾in) over top edge of batten and tack or staple at 10cm (4in) intervals. At the top of each tape, fix a screw eye into the underside of the batten.

THE CORDS Cut the cord into equal lengths and, beginning at the right-hand side, knot the cord to the first ring and thread up through the rings above. Continue to thread the cords through the screw eyes towards the left until all the cords are hanging together. Fix the blind to the window. Attach a cleat to the window frame about one-third up from the sill. Knot the cords together level with the sill, pull up the blind and wind the cords around the cleat to hold.

GATHERED BLINDS

Both festoon and Austrian blinds gather vertically into soft, luxurious folds and ruffles. These blinds could be lined and operate in a similar way to the Roman blind, with cords running through ringed or looped tapes stitched to the back. The Austrian blind is fuller than the festoon and constructed like a curtain with a heading tape and track. For either type of blind choose between narrow heading tape and split curtain rings or looped tape.

Festoon blinds
These are attached to the window in the same way as a Roman blind. For the length of fabric needed, measure from the batten to the sill and add one-third extra. For the width, measure the length of the batten plus 6cm (2½in) for side turnings. Calculate the amount of tape, cord and screw eyes as for Roman blinds.

MAKING A FESTOON BLIND Make single 3cm (1¼in) turnings on the side edges of the fabric, cover with tape and add more rows of tape in between, as for the Roman blind, making sure the rings or loops align horizontally. Stitch a double 2cm (¾in) turning on the bottom of the blind, covering the tape ends. Fold over a 2cm (¾in) turning on the top edge, and press. Loosen the cords just below the turning and pull up each tape until the blind fits the window. Even the gathers. Wind the excess cords into small bows and knot securely. Fix to the batten and finish as for Roman blind.

Austrian blinds
Flounced and frilly, Austrian blinds pull up into softly ruched swags, and usually hang fairly low in the window from a gathered heading.

The blind is either gathered on to a pole or fixed to the window on a batten, with a standard curtain track and runners fitted to the front edge. Calculate the amount of fabric needed in the same way as you would for a festoon blind but allow twice the width. If using a frill allow twice the fabric width by 14cm (5½in) deep. Calculate the amount of narrow heading, or looped tape, cord, and screw eyes as for the Roman blind.

Austrian and festoon blinds work well in a wide range of fabrics and prints. Here, a plain creamy-white Austrian blind has been chosen as a discreet but stylish window treatment.

Making an Austrian blind

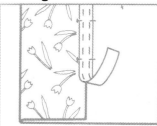

I. Turn in 3cm (1¼in) down each side. Stitch heading tape over raw edges. Stitch extra tapes across the blind.

2. Turn over a 3cm (1¼in) hem at the base of the blind and tuck under 1cm (⅜in). Stitch, catching down tape.

3. At the top, turn over 12.5cm (5in), tuck under 1cm (⅜in). Stitch along fold and again 7.5cm (3in) above for casing.

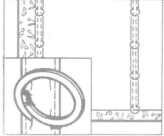

4. Slip split rings through tape pockets, with first row 2cm (¾in) from hem edge. Pull up each tape, if desired.

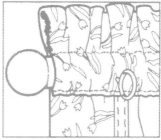

5. Thread pole through top casing, adding end finials. Fix screw eyes into base of pole at the top of each tape row.

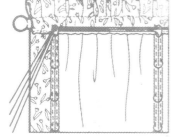

6. Knot first length of cord to first ring then up through all the rings above and screw eyes to one side. Repeat.

MAKING AN AUSTRIAN BLIND Make a single 3cm (1¼in) turning on the side edges of the blind fabric and around the frill, leaving the top edge free. Pin the tape over the raw edges and then pin the remaining tapes at equal intervals across the blind, as for the Roman blind. If using a frill, run gathering threads through top of frill, match to bottom edge of blind and stitch right sides together. Turn over raw edge to neaten. Alternatively, turn up 1.5cm (⅝in) then 2.5cm (1in) to make a hem. If using a pole, follow instructions above. Or apply heading tape and thread on hooks, as for unlined curtain. Complete by slotting the hooks into the runners.

CUSHIONS AND COVERS

One of the earliest forms of furnishing employed by man, cushions were for centuries the only thing coming between him and the stone or wooden seats that provided him with something to sit on. Even now, a pile of downy cushions improves even the most highly padded piece of furniture and gives a welcoming, friendly look to any room.

If you are short on cash or sewing skills, two pieces of fabric simply stitched together will make a perfectly serviceable cover, but for the slightly more ambitious, there is no end to the styles and effects that can be created: square, round or fancy designs; flat shapes, those with generous welts, or fat, cylindrical bolsters; trimming of every description — piping, borders, frills or pleats.

Use bright cushions to relieve large areas of neutral colour, or layer softly-hued ones to build up a subtle pattern-on-pattern effect. Choose fabrics that match your other furnishings if you like a controlled, co-ordinated look, or search out pretty, single specimens if yours is a more relaxed style.

Make cushions work for you by adding them to chests, trunks, window ledges and blanket boxes to make extra seating. Pile them on a divan to disguise the sleeping area in a bedsitter, but be careful to choose pads of an appropriate size, and be generous with them, since a few tiny cushions strung along the back of a bed will only look untidy.

Invest in two or three huge floor cushions to expand the entertaining facilities in a teenager's bedroom or to supplement the existing seating when the whole family comes to call. Try to avoid choosing floor cushions as your only seating however; undeniably economical, this arrangement is almost always uncomfortable for elderly people or those with any physical disability, so unless you are very sure that everyone you entertain is young and spry enough to enjoy this very casual style, make some effort to adapt your floor cushions for wider use. You could do this by adding back cushions and putting them both on a raised plinth.

A perfect setting for sun-drenched breakfasts. The severe lines of this slatted wood bench (and its hard surface) have been relieved by a cheerful bank of stripey cushions in a variety of bold colours and patterns.

Above: Use cushions to gain extra seating when you entertain a crowd. There are so many piled on this trunk that several could be pressed into service as floor cushions, perhaps for children.

Right: Built-in benches often make the best use of dining space, but usually at the expense of comfort. Few would complain about this arrangement, however, made luxurious by adding cushions.

Left: The occupant of this small but well-planned flat has catered for all social eventualities: one or two guests are accommodated on the sofa and chair, while larger numbers spill over on to the cushion-covered mattresses, which also provide a bed for overnight visitors.

Below: The rough, natural surfaces and long, low, simple lines of this striking modern house make a perfect background against which to display the rich colours and intricate patterns of primitive textiles – on the walls, on the divan and, most dramatically, on the huge cushions.

CUSHION CONSTRUCTION

Fillings, clockwise from left: foam, in chips and as solid block; synthetic wadding; kapok; Polyester filling; curled feathers; polystyrene granules.

To be (and to remain) practical as well as pretty, your cushions should have a soft, resilient filling, a casing to prevent this filling from escaping and to provide a smooth surface, and an outer cover that has been neatly and accurately sewn using techniques appropriate to the type of cushion you want.

Fillings
Most cushion pads contain one of the following types of filling:
FEATHERS One of the most traditional and widely-used fillings – and certainly the most expensive – feathers (or more luxurious still, feathers and down) will repay their initial cost by providing soft and inviting cushions that need only a gentle shake to regain their original shape after use.

Many department stores carry a large range of feather pads in the most commonly required sizes and shapes (square, rectangular, round) so for simple cushions without welts you should have no trouble finding one to suit your purpose. If you want to make your own, you can use the feathers from old cushions (or pillows) in shapes that are no longer wanted (transfer the filling into its new case out of doors on a still day). but remember that feathers have a finite existence, so you'll be disappointed if you try to recycle very old, droopy cushions that have lost all their resilience. When choosing the new casing, it's particularly important that you look for special, closely woven material – downproof cambric or ticking – that will not allow the feathers to leak out.
KAPOK Another old-fashioned stuffing material, kapok is a vegetable fibre (it looks much like raw cotton) that surrounds the seeds of a tropical tree. Kapok pads have a similar look and feel to feather ones, but they cannot be washed and they will become thin and lumpy much more quickly. Although it is still available, this filling has largely been replaced by longer-lasting man-made materials.
POLYESTER FILLING is a very efficient man-made alternative to kapok. It has the advantages of being completely washable and also hypo-allergenic.
FOAM is used in two forms for filling cushions: solid blocks, or shredded into tiny chips. Cushions made from both types are completely washable, and therefore particularly suitable for

use outside on garden furniture or in children's rooms.

Use foam blocks cut to size for awkwardly-shaped squab cushions, or for inexpensive large cushions shaped to fit the seat of a sofa or chair (pages 216-17). Solid foam is sold in several densities to suit different purposes, so tell the assistant what you want it for and ask for advice.

Foam chips are widely available and constitute one of the cheapest fillings possible, making them the most common choice for floor cushions. The main disadvantage of this material is its bumpy uneven texture that shows through all but the thickest fabric.

You may feel tempted to omit the inner casing of a foam cushion, especially when you're using a solid block filling, but foam tends to crumble into small particles in use, and the casing is particularly important because it contains these bits.
SYNTHETIC WADDING is made from man-made fibres like Polyester, bonded together to make a useful soft-furnishing material that is extremely light, completely washable and available in several weights (thicknesses): ask for it under the trade names of Polyester, Courtelle or Dacron.
POLYSTYRENE GRANULES are most commonly used to stuff large floor cushions and 'bean bags'. They move around within the cushion so that it moulds itself to the shape of the sitter, provided the cushion is not over-stuffed.

Cutting the cover
First, think about the size of your finished cushion and choose an appropriate fabric. Floor cushions, for example, may be subject to heavy wear, so cover them in a fabric that will be suitable. Fabric widths can range from 90cm (36in.) to 150cm (60in.), depending on whether it is intended for dressmaking or furnishing, so remember to take width into account when estimating the amount you need. Plain or small-patterned fabrics can generally be used most economically, because the cover pieces can be cut out side by side. Large patterns will require more fabric, since you should centre the main motif on each cushion.

Square and rectangular cushion covers should be cut on the straight grain of the fabric. To do this, either cut into the

fabric (through the selvedge if necessary) and tear it across the width; or pull one weft thread and cut along the gap.

If you find that your fabric is printed inaccurately – with the design running at an angle to, rather than along, the straight of grain – follow the pattern rather than the weave: on a small area like a cushion irregularities would be very obvious.

Generally speaking, cut your two cover pieces to the same size as your pad: by the time you have sewn the cover up, deducting a seam allowance of 1.5cm (⅝in.) all round, you will have a cover slightly smaller than the pad and therefore a firm, plump cushion. If your pad is firmly stuffed already, or if you are making cushions with welts, allow extra fabric for the seam allowances before you cut the cover pieces out. Unless otherwise stated, the seam allowance on all the projects in this chapter is the standard 1.5cm (⅝in.).

Hints on making up

Unless you are very experienced in sewing, you will get the best results if you pin each seam, then tack it in place temporarily before stitching it neatly with a sewing-machine or by hand. Remove all tacking stitches when the cushion is finished. When you are more confident you will find pinning is sufficient in most cases to hold the fabric before sewing it.

To neaten seams, trim the seam allowances to 1cm (⅜in), then overstitch all the edges together by hand or machine, using a zigzag stitch if your machine has a swing needle. Frilled or piped cushions (pages 198-9 and 200-3), or any with several layers of fabric caught into one seam, may need neatening in this way. If you want a seam to lie flat, for example when making a bolster cushion (pages 210-11), zigzag each raw edge separately, then press the seam open.

Make French seams where extra strength is required – for example on floor cushions, where the seams are put under strain – or when raw edges would look better enclosed, as on a single frill (page 198). With wrong sides facing and raw edges matching, stitch a 6mm (¼in) seam. Turn the seam back on itself so the right sides of fabric are facing. Stitch another seam 1cm (⅜in) from the seamed edge.

You will get a neater finish on all your work if you press it carefully at each stage.

FASTENINGS

The simplest fastening method, and one that will ensure a neat finish, is a line of slipstitching along the cushion's edge. Pin, tack and stitch your two pieces of fabric with right sides facing along three sides and round all four corners; stitch in for about 5cm (2in.) on the fourth side, leaving a central opening. Turn the cover to the right side, push out the corners and press, turning in the edges of the opening in line with the remainder of the seam. Insert your cushion pad or stuffing and slipstitch closed.

Zip fasteners

The most common type of fastening is a zip. Choose a light- to medium-weight zip in a colour that co-ordinates with your fabric, 8cm (3in.) shorter than the side into which it will be inserted. Stitch it into place using the zipper foot on your machine, or by hand using small even backstitches. For a zip across the back of a cushion, remember to cut the back cover piece larger than the front by 3cm (1¼in.), then cut it in half. Insert the zip centrally or low down near an edge.

Touch-and-close spots

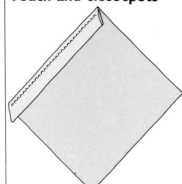 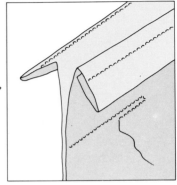

1. Pin and stitch a 1.5cm (⅝in.) hem along matching edges of both pieces of fabric. Fold hem over again for 1.5cm (⅝in.) and press.

2. With right sides facing, stitch pieces together alongside hem for 4cm (1½in.) in from both sides, leaving a central opening for fastenings.

Slipstitching

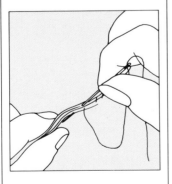

1. Fasten thread inside one folded edge. Take needle through opposite fold for 3mm (⅛in.). Take the needle across opening and repeat.

Non-fastening vent

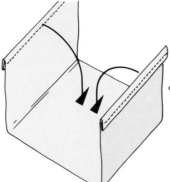 

1. Cut fabric twice as long as the cover, plus 8cm (3in.). Add 3cm (1¼in.) to width for seams. Stitch a 1cm (⅜in.) double hem on short edges.

2. Right sides together, fold the hemmed ends of the fabric so they overlap in the middle by 4cm (1½in.). Stitch side seams. Turn to right side.

Inserting zip in seam

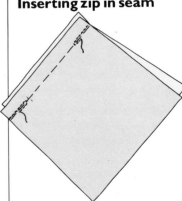

1. Right sides facing, pin and tack the two pieces of fabric together along one edge only. Stitch in from both ends for 4cm (1½in.) leaving opening.

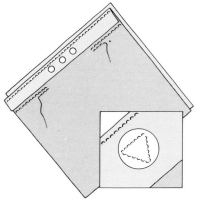

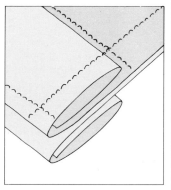

3. Using a triangular pattern of stitching, anchor touch-and-close spots through single hem; or handstitch press fasteners in position.

4. With right sides facing, stitch remaining three sides of cover together, catching down the pressed double hems with the stitching at each side.

Press or touch-and-close fasteners

For press fasteners or light-weight touch-and-close spots or strips, add an extra 3cm (1¼in.) seam allowance to one dimension when you cut out the fabric. This allows for a double hem on to which the fasteners can be stitched.

Positioning your fastening

If your cushion has a large motif on it, or if the pattern runs in one direction only, the fastening should be inserted in the side that runs along the base of the design.

Pretty alternatives

For a very pretty effect, leave one side of the cushion open, slipstitch a hem along each edge, then attach lengths of ribbon at corresponding positions and tie your cover closed. You could even do this all round the cushion, without stitching any of the seams at all. For a laced effect, make two rows of reinforced holes using an eyelet kit (page 218), then thread cord or ribbon through and tie.

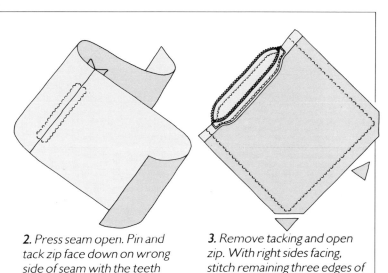

2. Press seam open. Pin and tack zip face down on wrong side of seam with the teeth over the tacked section of seam. Stitch from right side.

3. Remove tacking and open zip. With right sides facing, stitch remaining three edges of cushion cover. Turn cover to right side through zip.

Inserting zip across back

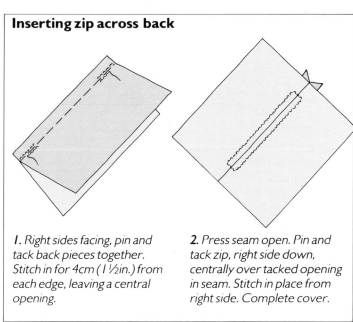

1. Right sides facing, pin and tack back pieces together. Stitch in for 4cm (1½in.) from each edge, leaving a central opening.

2. Press seam open. Pin and tack zip, right side down, centrally over tacked opening in seam. Stitch in place from right side. Complete cover.

FRILLS

One of the quickest and easiest ways to trim any type of cushion is with a frill, plain or pleated, in a fabric that matches or contrasts with the cover. Try gathering your frill at the corners only, or layer several frills of different widths and fabrics into one seam; you could also pipe the front cover piece as well (pages 200-3). Frills create an instant impression of extravagance, and you could exploit this by stitching several of them on to a cover piece in concentric circles, working from the outer edge inwards.

Depending on the degree of fullness you want, cut the fabric for the frill 1½-2 times the perimeter of the cushion. With a pleated frill, the width of each pleat should divide equally into the sides of the cushion, with one extra pleat at each corner. Multiply the width of the pleat by three, then multiply by the number of pleats: cut a strip of fabric to this length, on the straight of grain.

To make inverted pleats, as shown in our picture, make sure you have an even number of pleats down each side, then fold alternate pleats towards the previous one.

Cushions with frills

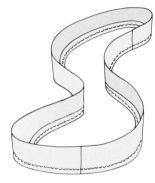

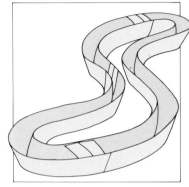

1. *For single frill, cut fabric on straight of grain and join strips with French seams. Stitch a 1 cm (⅜ in.) double hem along one edge.*

2. *For double frill, join bias fabric strips, right sides facing, using plain seams. Press seams open. Fold lengthwise, wrong sides together.*

Pleated frills

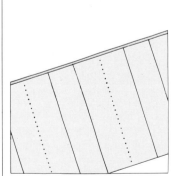

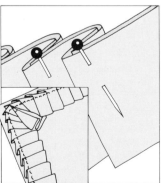

1. *Make up frill (double or single) as before. Mark knife pleats indicating placement and fold lines. (Broken lines are inner fold lines.)*

2. *Fold fabric to form pleats. Pin, tack along both edges, and press. Attach to cover piece: there will be two pleats at each corner. Stitch and complete.*

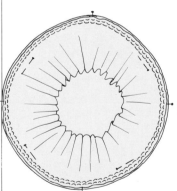

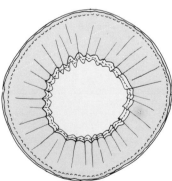

4. *Match sections of frill with markings on cover piece, right sides together (5. shows single frill). Ease gathers to fit, and pin in position.*

5. *Stitch frill to cover piece, anchoring the gathers in place. Right sides facing, stitch on remaining piece and complete the cover.*

Use decorative borders to give your cushions a distinctive style – soft frills for a purely feminine effect (right) or neat pleats for a crisp, country feeling (below right).

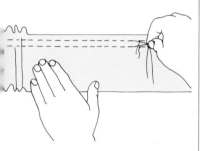

3. *Mark the edge of one cover piece and the frill into sections. Run two rows of gathering stitches along each section of the frill. Pull up gathers.*

6. *On a square cushion, divide frill into four sections. Pull up gathers and match sections to sides. Allow extra gathers at corners. Stitch and complete.*

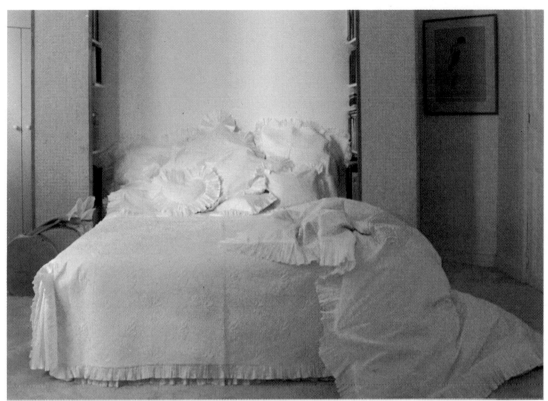

PIPING

Piped cushions are popular, simple and endlessly variable. Piping can be fat, thin or even flat (join strips as below, press in half lengthwise, and attach to your cover piece without any cord); it can be gathered or plain. You can even layer rows of piping one on top of another, using different colours. If you want the effect of piping without the effort, stitch a length of braid or twisted cord around the edges of your finished cushion cover.

Covered piping cord not only gives a professional finish to cushion seams, it also makes them stronger – an important factor on seat and floor cushions. The cord itself is available in a wide range of sizes from 00 to 6, so choose the one most suitable for the weight and content of your fabric: for most cottons nos. 3 or 4 would work well, but if you are unsure take along a piece of your fabric when you buy your cord, and ask for advice. Most piping cord is pre-shrunk, and this is important since cord that shrinks more than its covering fabric will cause your piping to pucker the seams. Unless you are certain this pre-shrinking has been done, simmer the cord

Corded cushions

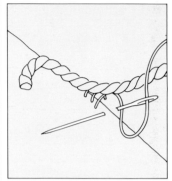 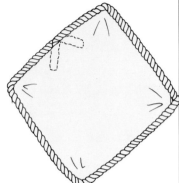

1. Leave a small opening centrally in cover seam. Stitch cord along seam line, picking up a few threads across seam and through base of cord.

2. At the opening, tuck the cord ends into the seam so they overlap inside the cover. Stitch cords together, then the opening round them.

Simple piping

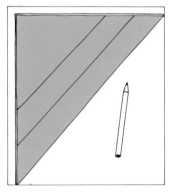 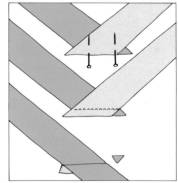 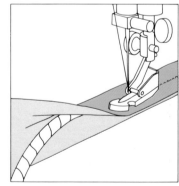 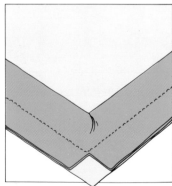

1. Fold fabric diagonally so selvedge lies parallel with weft threads. Working from fold, mark strips of required width. Cut out strips.

2. Right sides facing, stitch strips together along straight grain taking 6mm (¼in.) seam allowance. Trim ends. Press seams open.

3. With wrong sides facing, fold finished strip in half lengthwise around piping cord. Stitch alongside cord, using piping foot attachment.

4. On square cover, stitch piping to right side of one piece, raw edges together. At corners, snip into piping fabric up to stitching.

Those not particularly adept at needlework can add an attractive trim to their cushions by stitching on a length of ready-made cord, which is available in plain colours or with several different colours twisted together.

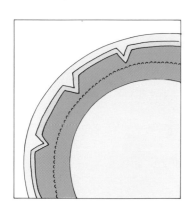

5. On round cover, snip into piping fabric at 2.5cm (1 in.) intervals before placing round cover piece. With raw edges matching, pin, tack and stitch.

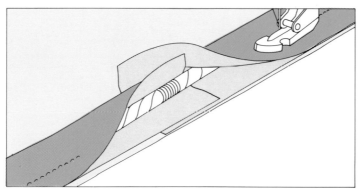

6. To join the cord, trim both cord ends and butt them firmly together. Bind over the join several times with strong sewing thread.

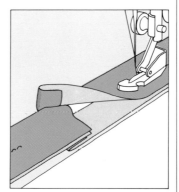

7. To join fabric, trim so one edge overlaps the other by 2cm (¾in.). Turn under 1cm (⅜in.) and place over raw edge. Complete stitching.

for three minutes, then dry flat before you start to assemble your piping.

Fabric for piping is always cut on the bias so it has enough 'give' to go round the cushion. Cut strips wide enough to cover the cord, adding 3cm (1¼in.) for seam allowances. Always join the strips together on the straight of grain to prevent the seams from stretching out of shape. Stitch the fabric round the cord using the piping or zipper foot on your machine, and stitch very close to the cord. For gathered piping, your strip of fabric will need to be 1½-2 times the length of the cord, and in this case do not stitch too close to the cord – the fabric will not pull up easily to form the gathers.

If you want a much plumper border round your cushion, use rolled up synthetic wadding instead of piping cord. Cut your fabric strips on the bias as before, but wider.

For a fastening, either insert a zip across one cover piece before you attach the piping; or stitch the piping to one cover piece first, then insert a zip or other fastening into a seam before joining the cover pieces together.

Gathered piping cord

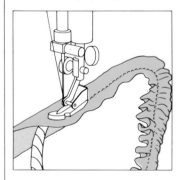 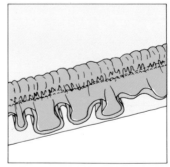

1. Place cord inside fabric. Stitch for 20cm (8in.). Raise foot leaving needle in fabric. Gently pull cord through fabric to gather; repeat.

2. Position the gathered cord round the cover – whether square or round – making sure gathers look even. Join ends of cord and fabric as on page 201.

Fat piping

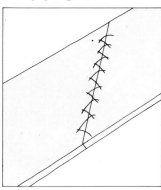

I. Cut several lengths of medium-weight wadding 7cm (3in.) wide. Cut ends diagonally; butt ends and join with herringbone stitch.

2. Join ends as before to form a circle. Roll up the wadding to make a sausage-shaped ring, and hold in place temporarily with pins.

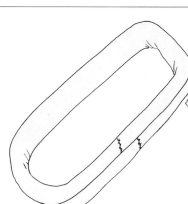

3. Wrong sides together, fold fabric in half round wadding. Stitch, removing pins as you go. Position and stitch piping to cover as on pages 200-1.

How to make continuous piping fabric

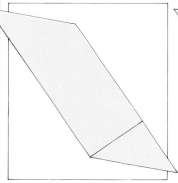

I. Cut a rectangle of fabric 25 × 50cm (10 × 20in.). Fold down one corner at right angles. Cut off triangle and stitch to opposite end.

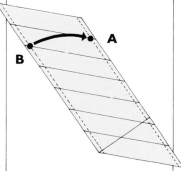

2. On right side and using tailor's chalk, mark out strips parallel to bias edge. Mark A and B as shown, 1cm (⅜in.) from outer edges.

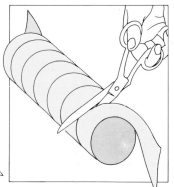

3. Right sides facing, place A to B. Stitch edges together to make a tube. Turn to right side. Cut out one long piping strip following marked lines.

SIMPLE BORDERS

These cushions have the plainest, perhaps the most elegant border of all, a simple 'flange' of about 6cm (2½in.) wide. In our picture we show cushions with single and double borders, with colours mixed and matched, but you could be more inventive in your combinations: for a bold, graphic look, cut each cover piece in four sections, two in each of two colours, and stitch together in a chequerboard pattern before you assemble the cover. You could line the borders of a double-bordered cushion with contrasting or co-ordinating fabric; or use a border print – a scarf or handkerchief.

To make a single border, add twice the width of your border plus seam allowances to each dimension of your cushion pad, and cut your cover pieces to this size. For a double flange you will need to add four times the width of the border, plus seam allowance.

A single bordered cushion can simply be slipstitched closed. Zips or press fasteners should be inserted across one cover piece before you make the cushion up: add extra seam allowances to one dimension of one cover piece.

Cushions with double borders

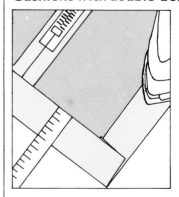

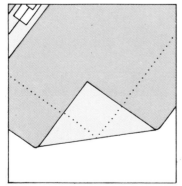

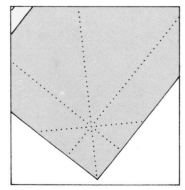

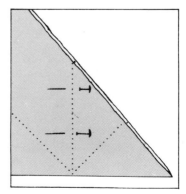

1. Lay back section flat, wrong side up. Fold in a border of the required width plus seam allowance all round and press. Repeat for other piece.

2. Open out. Fold in each corner point until pressed lines on corner align with those along edges of cover. Press this diagonal fold.

3. Open out corner again. Then, with wrong sides facing, fold cover in half diagonally through corner, matching fabric edges carefully. Press.

4. Right sides facing, fold in half along bias and stitch across corner along fold line now at right angles. Trim seam to 6mm (¼in.) and press open.

Single borders

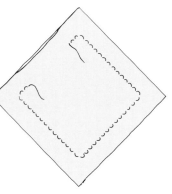

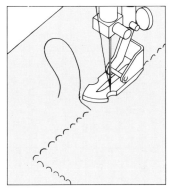

1. Right sides facing, stitch squares together, leaving gap for filling. Turn to right side. Stitch round cover at chosen width leaving same opening.

2. Insert filling through both openings. Stitch across inner opening, matching up with previous stitching using piping foot attachment.

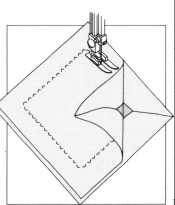

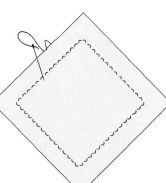

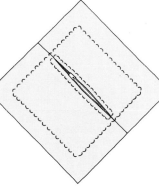

5. Turn corner through to right side and press resulting mitre. Repeat these steps on remaining corners of both top and bottom cover pieces.

6. Wrong sides facing, and matching mitred corners together, stitch cover pieces together at required border distance from outer edge.

3. Turn in open edges in line with the remainder of the outer seamed edge. Slipstitch the two folded edges together to close.

4. Insert any fastening across one cover piece before you begin. Open zip, if using. Stitch cover together, turn to right side and stitch round pad.

CUSHIONS WITH WELTS

Cushions with narrow welts come into their own when a geometric, box-like shape is required, or when you want some degree of additional thickness in a throw cushion. (More substantial, welted seat cushions are described on pages 216-17.) You could use a contrasting colour or pattern for the welts, or gather the top and bottom cover pieces of a round cushion as if it were the end of a bolster (page 210): give it a plain, not gathered, welt. Welted throw cushions are usually filled with pads of the same shape, or you could use slabs of foam.

Cut the welt pieces on the straight of grain, adding seam allowances. For a square or rectangular shape, or any cushions with corners, cut the welt in as many sections as sides and match the seams to the corners. Once you have attached your welt to one cover piece, insert a zip or press fasteners before attaching the other cover piece; or insert a fastening across the latter.

For a gathered welt, cut your strip of fabric 1½-2 times longer than the cushion's perimeter.

Welts for square cushions

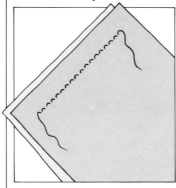 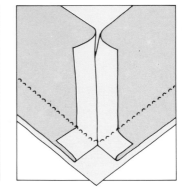

1. Right sides facing, stitch welt pieces into a ring, leaving 1.5cm (⅝in.) unstitched at either end of each seam. Press open.

2. Right sides facing, stitch welt to one cover piece. At corners seams will split open: stitch across top to provide sharp corners. Complete cover.

Welts for round cushions

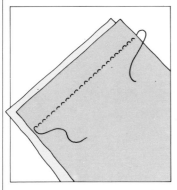
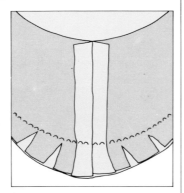

1. Right sides facing, join welt pieces together across their full width. Stitch into a ring long enough to go round cushion. Press seams open.

2. Snip into seam allowance of both edges of welt at 2.5cm (1 in.) intervals. Right sides facing, stitch welt to one cover piece, then the other.

Gathered welt for a square cushion

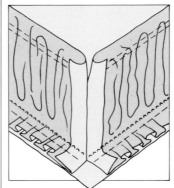

1. Join and gather welt as described opposite and below. Stitch to cover pieces, splitting open seams at corners. Leave an opening.

2. Turn cover to right side. Insert cushion pad. Turn in edges of opening in line with seam and slipstitch together to close.

Gathered welt for a round cushion

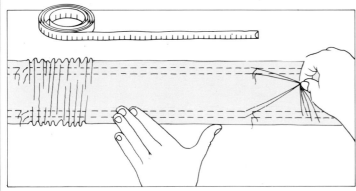
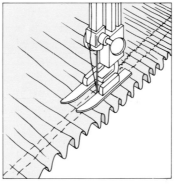
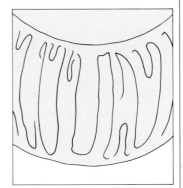

1. Stitch welt strips together as above. Divide both welt and cover pieces into sections, as for frills (page 198). On each section, work two rows of gathering stitches along each edge of welt. Pull up equally, and match to sections on cover piece. Adjust gathers, distributing evenly along welt.

2. Stitch over gathers along both edges to anchor fullness in place before attaching welt to cover: follow inner rows of gathering stitches.

3. Right sides facing, stitch gathered welt to round cover pieces, leaving an opening. Turn to right side. Insert pad; slipstitch opening.

QUILTED COVERS

The technique of quilting, originally developed to anchor layers of fabric and padding together to provide thickness and warmth, can also be used to give an interesting surface texture to cushions. Since a light-weight fabric will be easiest to work with, you might like to use dressmaking fabric, which gives you a much wider range of plain and printed designs to choose from. Either quilt both the front and back of the cushion cover, or leave one side plain.

To make one quilted piece, first cut out a piece of your covering fabric slightly larger than required, then cut out a piece of backing fabric to the same size. Use an oddment of similar weight for this purpose, or buy a small amount of cotton lining. Finally, cut a piece of medium-weight synthetic wadding, again to the same size.

Decide how far apart you want the lines of quilting to fall, keeping in mind the size of the pattern repeat, and measure in this distance from the edge to arrive at the first quilting line. Stitch along this line, then continue across the fabric using the quilting bar on your machine to get the rows of stitching consistently spaced.

Once the quilting is finished, treat the fabric as you would a single covering piece. You could make it up with a frill, with piping or with both; make a quilted bolster; or quilt a piece of fabric larger than your pad and make a cushion with a border (pages 198-9 and 204-5). Don't always quilt on the straight of grain: quilt diagonally across the cushion, quilt a spiral from the centre out, on a geometric pattern quilt with it or against it, or quilt squares one inside the other (start from a small square in the centre and use a quilting bar to stitch squares moving progressively outwards). You can also use quilting techniques on novelty cushions (pages 212-13). A pile of cushions made from the same fabric would look particularly striking if they were all quilted in different patterns.

When you have mastered the simple grid technique, you might like to attempt more complex patterns, or try quilting around the motif on a patterned fabric.

Simple quilting

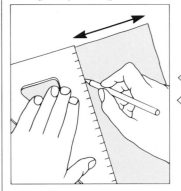

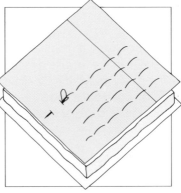

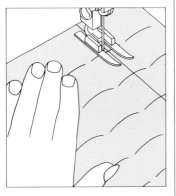

1. With a set square and a piece of tailors' chalk or a soft pencil, mark the first quilting line on the right side of one piece of fabric.

2. Place fabric to backing fabric with wrong sides facing, sandwiching a layer of wadding in between. Tack together in rows, matching raw edges.

3. Stitch through all three layers along the first quilting line already marked. Add the quilting bar to the sewing-machine.

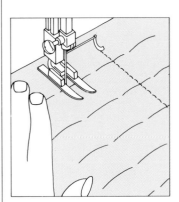

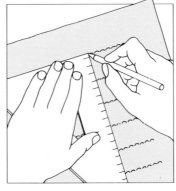

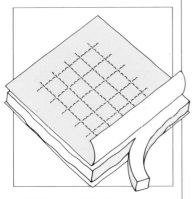

4. Set quilting bar guide to required spacing and position bar on first row of stitching. Stitch remaining rows across the fabric in the same way.

5. With set square against first row of stitching, mark first quilting line at right angles to the first set. Stitch this and remaining lines as before.

6. Trim wadding between fabric layers to 1.5cm (⅝in.) from outside stitching lines. Complete cushion cover in the usual way.

BOLSTERS

Cylindrical cushions traditionally found along the backs of beds, couches and *chaise-longues*, bolsters are still in common use in some countries like France, and, as in our picture, are often used to support a row of throw cushions of all shapes and sizes. They are commonly of a length to fit across a bed, either double or single, and can be invaluable for increasing the seating flexibility of a divan; but their uses can be much more varied than that. Small ones make good neck pillows, whether for watching television or for making a long car journey a little more comfortable; bolsters in a slightly larger size might also be useful in the back seat of a car, particularly if you have disabled or elderly passengers. In the house, children or teenagers who are really comfortable only when they are sprawled on the floor might appreciate a large bolster, particularly if it was so long it could be curled round itself, tied in a knot, or coiled into a bucket seat. Such a bolster could be as long as 10 metres (11 yards), with a diameter of 20-25cm (8-10in.), depending on the width of your fabric. Use heavy cotton, perhaps ticking, and cut it in half length-

A bolster cushion

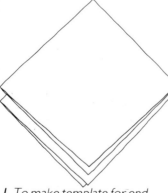

1. To make template for end circles, cut a square of paper slightly larger than required circle. Fold paper accurately into quarters.

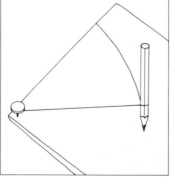

2. Fasten a piece of string into folded corner with a drawing pin. Tie to a pencil so its length is the radius of required circle. Draw an arc and cut out.

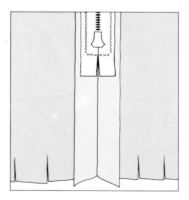

3. Right sides facing, stitch main fabric into a cylinder, leaving central tacked section. Insert zip. Cut notches in both ends 2.5cm (1 in.) apart.

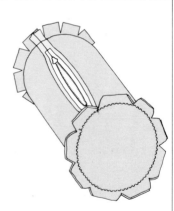

4. Adding seam allowance to template, cut two end circles. Notch as before. Open zip. Right sides facing, stitch to cover. Turn to right side.

The two full-sized divans in this pretty bedsitter are transformed into attractive and comfortable sofas by the clever use of fat bolsters, padded backs and elegant flanged cushions (pages 204-5). This arrangement would be useful in any room where self-containment is an advantage – a guest room or a bedroom for a teenager or an elderly relative.

wise. Sew the two strips together, then sew into a tube and add circular ends. Fill it with polystyrene granules. More traditional bolsters are usually filled with a firm pad.

To make the cover, cut a piece of fabric the width of the circumference of the pad by the pad's length, plus seam allowances. Your cover can have a plain, flat end, perhaps piped or with a frill set into the seam. For a gathered end, the simplest method is described below, but you can also gather by cutting a strip of fabric the length of the circumference of the pad by its radius, plus seam allowances. Join into a ring, then stitch one edge to the bolster tube. Sew gathering stiches along the other edge, pull up, and attach a covered button. This type of finish will benefit from piping sewn round the tube before attaching the ungathered end: you will get a much neater finish. Buttons covered in matching fabric can look very neat, but for a really dramatic effect use a silky tassle instead. Another variation might be to make your cylinder of fabric much longer than your pad so you can tie the ends close to the pad with ribbon or cord, Christmas cracker-like.

Gathered bolster ends

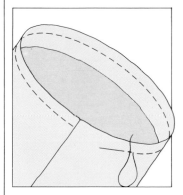

1. Right sides facing, stitch fabric into a cylinder. Fold in a 1.5cm (⅝in.) single hem at each end. Work gathering stitches by hand near edge.

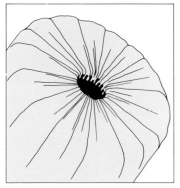

2. Insert cushion pad, centring it inside cover. At each end, pull up gathers tightly and evenly and fasten off gathering thread.

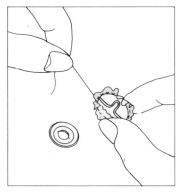

3. Cover two buttons by cutting circles of fabric and gathering round button shapes according to manufacturer's instructions.

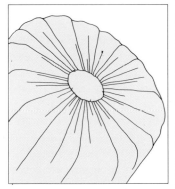

4. Using double thread, stitch buttons in place through their shanks over the central openings at each end of the bolster cover.

CUSHIONS WITH A DIFFERENCE

If you want your cushions to have a stronger impact than those made in simple shapes with ordinary fabric, search shops and markets for unusual coverings or use your imagination to create a collection of whimsical shapes.

Don't limit yourself to new fabrics for your covers – discarded curtains, tablecloths or articles of clothing can all be re-used. Old fabrics often have a softness and a lovely faded quality that you won't find in newer materials, and any stained or worn sections can be avoided (**1**). Market stalls specializing in old floor or table carpets will occasionally sell off damaged ones very cheaply, so consider transforming a plain sofa with a pile of exotic cushions made from sound portions of these.

If you can find a pretty, fold-over night-dress case, you'll have a ready-made cushion cover: just insert a pad of the right size and slipstitch round the edge (**2** and **3**). Look for lacy or embroidered tray cloths, antimacassars or table mats, and stitch them on to a plain backing. Sew two large handkerchiefs or printed scarves together (**4**); two square shawls would make a beautiful cover for a floor cushion.

Look at the objects around you to get ideas for novelty cushions. Children will love them and they make ideal presents, particularly when the cushion can be linked to a special interest or hobby.

For a complex shape like a shell (**5**), make a tracing paper template by copying an original. Quilt wadding on to the cover pieces before you sew them together.

The spherical shape needed for cherries (**6**), footballs etc., can be achieved by cutting the fabric in segments like an orange, or by taking large darts into the long sides of a rectangle of fabric. Cover rolled-up wadding for the 'twigs'.

A basic bolster construction forms the body of the pencil (**7**). To enable you to achieve the zigzagged join between body and shaped point, assemble all the sections flat and appliqué the decorative details before you stitch the cylinder closed. Stuff, then add the flat end with appliquéd 'lead'.

Make a child's seat in the shape of a house (**8**). A cube of foam forms the house, and a shaped piece the roof. Make covers for each section separately, and decorate with fabric paints before stitching together. Glue roof to house.

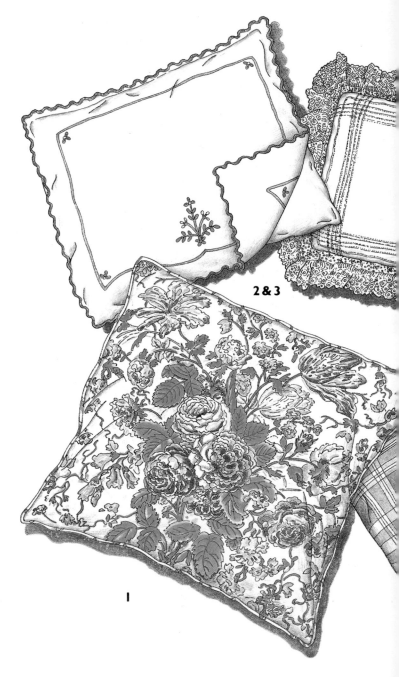

2 & 3

1

SHAPED SEAT PADS

The easiest way to make your dining chairs more comfortable is to add simple, tie-on pads, shaped to fit their seats. These cushions can serve as a pretty furnishing accessory if you choose a covering fabric that co-ordinates with the curtains or blinds, or one that picks up one of the main colours in the room. Unlike throw cushions, seat pads like these usually get plenty of wear, so make sure your fabric is strong and closely-woven, or be prepared to renew the covers frequently.

When making shaped pads and covers, a paper template will ensure an accurate fit. Tracing paper is best as you can see through it, but newspaper or brown wrapping paper can be used too.

Your cushion will be anchored to the back struts with ties, and the number you need depends on the chair. The one in our picture needs four, but where your cushion is not shaped around the back strut you may be able to use just one, rather longer: fold it in half, then place the fold parallel with the raw edge of the cover piece and sew into the seam. Be bold and adventurous with the ties: for example, long, wide ones could be tied in enormous floppy bows; you could use ribbons instead of fabric; or make the ties and the piping in a different coloured fabric to the rest of the cover. It might be fun to make all the cushions for a set of chairs in the same fabric but with a different type – or colour – of tie on each one.

Add your fastening in the seam in the usual way, before you stitch the two cover pieces together. Slipstitching the opening closed is of course easier, but for these cushions it's worth taking the extra trouble to fit a fastening since you will want to remove the covers frequently for washing, especially if there are young children in the household.

Below are instructions for making the simplest of pads, but you could also make a shallow welted version following the instructions on pages 206-7. Pipe both cover pieces before you add the welt, and if possible set the ties into the welt seams at the back of the cushion: they will then be set in vertically. Set a zip into the seam joining welt to bottom cover piece, and position it at the back of the cushion.

A shaped seat pad

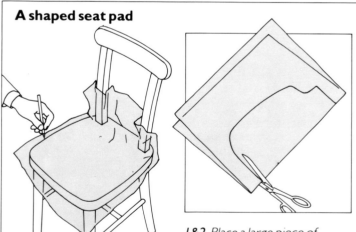

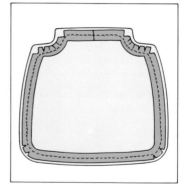

1&2. Place a large piece of tracing paper on seat and mark round the edges. Cut out template, replacing to mark position of back struts.

3. Using template, but adding 1.5cm (⅝in.) seam allowance all round, cut out two cover pieces. Reinforce back corners with a row of stitching.

4. Make up enough piping in matching or contrasting fabric to go round cover. Attach to one cover piece in the usual way, notching at corners.

The addition of simple, shaped, tie-on cushions to your dining chairs will soften their appearance and encourage family and friends to linger and chat long after the last scraps of food have disappeared.

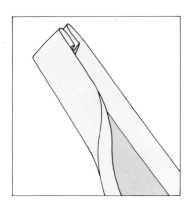

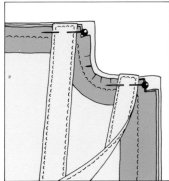

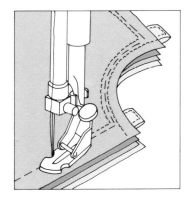

5. For each tie, cut a piece of fabric 30cm × 5cm (12in. × 2in.) and turn in 1cm (⅜in.) all round. Fold strip in half lengthwise and stitch all round.

6. Pin two completed ties over piping on right side of each back corner over previous stitching line, as shown in diagram.

7&8. Right sides facing, stitch two halves of cover together, catching in ties. Turn to right side. Insert pad, complete cover and tie on to seat.

DEEP SEAT CUSHIONS

Cushions to sit on or against, such as the seat and back cushions on a sofa, need to be substantially firmer than throw cushions, and are usually stuffed with very luxurious feather pads or, more cheaply, with suitably dense foam. The former will very probably have to be custom-made, while foam is quite awkward to cut at home, and you will be well advised to ask your dealer to shape it for you from a template. Either pad will be dense and substantial and will require a long zip in the cushion cover to accommodate it: this is inserted into the centre of the back welt and, on a square cushion, extends round each back corner for about 8cm (3in.). Seat cushions will sustain heavy wear, so strengthen the seams by adding piping to the covers.

Follow the instructions below for seat cushions on cane chairs, for deep cushions on a sofa with loose covers, and for substantial cushions to pad a windowseat or bench. You can, of course, stitch the zip into the seam between the welt and bottom cover piece, positioning it centrally at the back of the cushion: pipe the bottom cover piece first.

Deep seat cushions

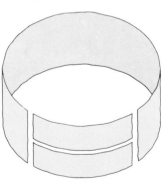

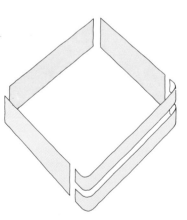

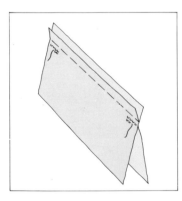

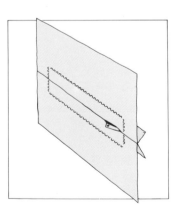

1. For round cover, cut welt in three sections as shown, with the strips on either side of the zip at least 8cm (3in.) longer than the zip.

2. For square cover, cut five sections extending back welt strips for 8cm (3in.) along the adjoining sides to allow large opening.

3. Right sides facing, tack two zip sections together. Stitch in for 4cm (1½in.) from each end, and fasten off, leaving central tacked section.

4. Centre zip behind tacked section, then pin and tack in place. Stitch from right side of fabric in usual way. Leave zip closed.

The technique of adding a gusset or welt to your cushion cover to accommodate its depth works equally well for both modern and traditional styles.

Far left: The neat, welted construction of these custom-made seat and back cushions helps them achieve their cool geometric shapes as well as their upholstery-like softness.

Left: Thinner pads add colour and comfort to a set of cane dining chairs. These cushions are piped and shaped to fit the chair seats, but the method of construction is exactly the same.

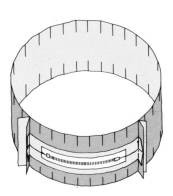

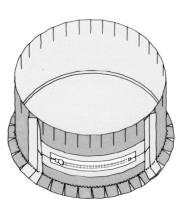

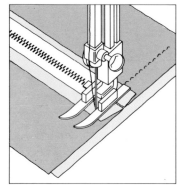

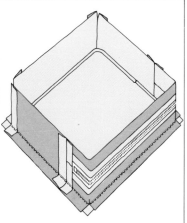

5. For a round cover, pin and stitch welt pieces into a ring. Snip notches into seam allowance on both edges spaced 2.5cm (1 in.) apart.

6. Open zip. Right sides facing, pin welt to cover piece, which you have already piped. Stitch, then stitch welt to other, piped, cover piece.

7. For a square cover, stitch welt sections together, right sides facing, leaving 1.5cm (⅝in.) open at each end of front seams.

8. Snip into seam allowances at back corners of welt. Open zip and pin welt to piped cover piece. Stitch welt to each cover piece in turn.

DECK AND DIRECTOR'S CHAIRS

For value, good looks and practicality, few items of seating score higher than those classic folding chairs in canvas and wood, the deck chair and the director's chair. Many well-loved examples have sound frames even if their covers are torn, dirty or faded. Remove the old cover by easing out the original tacks with a mallet and small chisel. Then measure the frame and cut out your fabric, hemming it down the sides if you are not using deck chair canvas, which comes in a specially narrow width. For a director's chair you will also need an eyelet kit: cut holes in the correct position in the fabric, insert the eyelet and bang down hard with a hammer or other tool. The screw and butterfly nut will fit through these holes.

If you have been put off using deck or director's chairs indoors by the limited designs of deck chair canvas, look for interesting alternatives. You might quilt a fabric you like on to canvas, with wadding in between: follow the instructions on pages 208-9. Or look for an old oriental carpet that is worn or damaged in places: you might be able to salvage a piece large enough to make an unusual cover.

Above: Stripes are the order of the day in this sunny, nautical bathroom. The boldest of all are reserved for a smart director's chair that provides comfortable seating in a tight corner, and is a catch-all for clothes.

Cover for a director's chair

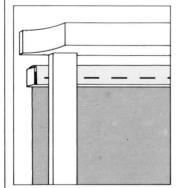 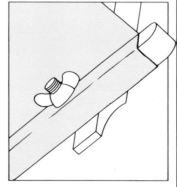

1. Position seat canvas on frame so raw edges are at sides. Turn these under and staple canvas around side rails at 3cm (1 ¼in.) intervals.

2. For back, wind canvas around struts and staple in place as before. Hold strut and canvas to frame with screw and wing nut.

Below: Some of the nicest deck chairs are covered with crisp white canvas to set off the golden glow of the wood, a combination echoed throughout this country dining room.

Above: Almost everything in this ad hoc dining room can be folded away to clear a path for traffic. The ever-practical deck chair waits patiently until it is needed, taking up virtually no room at all.

Cover for a deck chair

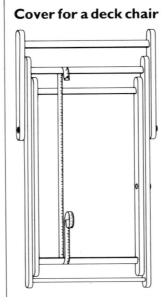

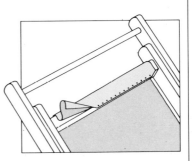

To estimate canvas, lie the frame flat. Measure between end rails, allowing 2cm (¾in.) at each end for fixing. Turn under raw edges and anchor canvas with tacks 5cm (2in.) apart, beginning in the middle and working outwards.

THROW-OVER COVERS

Whether you choose this casually-draped style because you like its soft, informal look, or to compensate for a lack of sewing skills, you'll find it suits many decorating tastes.

Begin with a chair or sofa that has a sound frame and padding – sturdy old pieces can often be culled from relations or bought cheaply at secondhand shops. Many new ranges come covered only in calico, and an item from one of these makes a good basis for a no-sew cover.

The easiest covering to buy is fabric by the metre – plain or quilted – which is available in a huge choice of colours and textures. The only stitching involved is a simple hem along each edge or perhaps a seam joining two widths.

Look too at flat double sheets, which come in an array of colours and patterns, or try a soft blanket for a warm, cosy effect. A pretty rug could camouflage a tatty armchair, while a huge tablecloth might suit a two- or three-seater sofa. Look out for beautiful bedspreads as well.

The soft, resilient layers of padding in a quilt make it an ideal throw-over cover.

Right: A huge bedspread tucks neatly around the chunky form of a modern sofa in this restrained interior. The simple square pattern of the quilting echoes the geometric shapes in the Kelim rug that features so largely in the room's design.

Below: On a smaller scale, this daintily sprigged cot coverlet has been draped simply, but to great effect, over a delightful wooden loveseat.

INDEX

Acknowledgments

Illustrators: Linda Broad; Gerrard Brown; Graham Corbet; Terry Evans; Hayward & Martin; Coral Mula; Mulkern Rutherford Studio; Richard Phipps; Rob Shone; Ed Stewart; Diane Tippell; Elsa Wilson.

The publisher thanks the following photographers and organizations for their permission to reproduce the photographs in this book:
6-7 Elizabeth Whiting & Associates/Tim Street-Porter; 9 Elizabeth Whiting & Associates/Pam Elson-Murray; 12-13 Elizabeth Whiting & Associates/Spike Powell; 16-17 Jessica Strang (Henrietta Green); 19 Habitat; 20-1 Jessica Strang (stencils from Lyn le Grice, Bread Street, Penzance); 23 Syndication International/Options; 28 La Maison de Marie Claire/Eriaud/Comte; 32 above Davies, Keeling & Trowbridge; 36 Jonathan Bartlett (by courtesy Timothy Wright, paint finish by Jonathan Bartlett); 37 Arcaid/Lucinda Lambton (stencils from Lyn le Grice, Bread Street, Penzance); 44-5 Simon Brown/Conran Octopus (Jenny Taylor); 47 IPC Magazines/World Press Network; 49 La Maison de Marie Claire/Pierre Hussenot; 51 Maison Française/Christian Gervais; 57 Habitat; 58-9 Camera Press; 59 Elizabeth Whiting & Associates/Neil Lorimer; 60-1 La Maison de Marie Claire/Yves Duronsoy; 61 La Maison de Marie Claire/Pierre Hussenot; 62 World of Interiors/Michael Boys; 63 Ken Kirkwood (designer George Powers); 64 World of Interiors/Michael Boys; 64-5 World of Interiors/Michael Boys; 67 Conran's; 68 Camera Press; 69 Habitat; 70-1 Camera Press; 72 La Maison de Marie Claire/Serge Korniloff; 74 left World of Interiors/Fritz von der Schulenburg; 74 right Camera Press; 75 Habitat; 76 Elizabeth Whiting & Associates; 77 right Susan Griggs Agency/Michael Boys; 78 Habitat; 79 Camera Press; 80 above Camera Press; 80 below Habitat; 81 La Maison de Marie Claire/Gilles de Chabaneix; 82-3 Ken Kirkwood; 83 Habitat; 84-5 Camera Press; 89 Bill McLaughlin; 92 below Pat Hunt; 93 Houses & Interiors; 94-5 Camera Press; 96-7 Camera Press; 99 La Maison de Marie Claire/Antoine Rozès; 102 Ken Kirkwood/Conran Octopus; 103 Good Housekeeping (Jan Baldwin); 104 Habitat; 105 Transworld Features (Casa Brava); 106 Habitat; 107 left Sheppard Day; 107 right Arcaid/Julie Phipps; 111 Habitat; 112-13 Elizabeth Whiting & Associates/Tim Street-Porter; 114-15 World of Interiors/Bernard Naudin; 115 Guy Bouchet; 116 Elizabeth Whiting & Associates/Spike Powell; 116-17 above Abitare/Gabriele Basilico; 117 below Syndication International/Options; 117 right La Maison de Marie Claire/Eriaud; 118-19 Gilles de Chabaneix; 120-1 Elizabeth Whiting & Associates/Friedhelm Thomas; 121 Bill McLaughlin; 123 Habitat; 124-5 Habitat; 126 left La Maison de Marie Claire/Pierre Hussenot; 126 right Elizabeth Whiting & Associates/Julian Nieman; 127 Good Housekeeping (Jan Baldwin); 128-9 Camera Press; 130-1 Paul Ryan; 132 Syndication International/Options; 133 Bill McLaughlin; 134-5 Camera Press; 136 Stafford Cliff/Ken Kirkwood; 137 World Press Network; 138-9 Good Housekeeping (Jan Baldwin); 141 left Good Housekeeping (Jan Baldwin); 141 right Camera Press; 142 Habitat; 143 La Maison de Marie Claire/Claude Pataut; 145 right Poggenpohl; 146 Elizabeth Whiting & Associates/Michael Dunne; 147 La Maison de Marie Claire/Serge Korniloff; 148-50 Habitat; 151 Abitare/Silvio Wolf; 152 World of Interiors/Michael Boys; 153 Elizabeth Whiting & Associates/Michael Dunne; 154-5 Sunday Express Magazine/Simon Brown; 156-7 Camera Press; 158-9 Photograph by Jacques Dirand, from 'French Style' by Susanne Slesin and Stafford Cliff (Thames & Hudson); 161 Gilles de Chabaneix; 163 World of Interiors/James Mortimer; 171 Good Housekeeping (Jan Baldwin); 175 Camera Press; 178 World of Interiors/James Wedge; 178-9 Habitat; 180-1 World of Interiors/Clive Frost; 182 Maison Française/Christian Gervais; 185 Sunway Blinds; 186 Camera Press; 188-9 Bill McLaughlin; 190-1 La Maison de Marie Claire/McLean/Berthier; 192 La Maison de Marie Claire/Nico Dhar/M. P. Pellé; 192-3 Camera Press; 193 above La Maison de Marie Claire/Hussenot/Charras; 193 below Camera Press; 199 above Gilles de Chabaneix (Agnès Colmar); 199 below Fritz von der Schulenburg; 201 Camera Press; 208-11 Bill McLaughlin; 215 Elizabeth Whiting & Associates/Neil Lorimer; 216 Elizabeth Whiting & Associates/Tim Street-Porter; 217 Elizabeth Whiting & Associates/Gary Chowanetz; 218 Good Housekeeping (David Brittain); 219 left La Maison de Marie Claire/Pateaut/Puech; 219 right La Maison de Marie Claire/Eriaud/Comte; 220 La Maison de Marie Claire/Chabaneix/Bayle; 220-1 Abitare/Gabriele Basilico.

Special photography for Conran Octopus
Simon Brown: 15 (Jennifer Taylor); 29 (architect Ian Hutchinson); 31 (Paul Hodgkinson); 32 below (Roger Britnell, paint by John Ebdon); 33 (architects de Blacam & Meagher); 40-1 (Graham Carr); 48-9 (architect Shay Cleary); 66 (architect Shay Cleary); 72-3 (architect Shay Cleary); 91 (architect Shay Cleary); 144-5 (architect Shay Cleary).
John Heseltine: 92 above; 93 above; 98-9 below; 195; 202-3; 206.
Peter Mackertich: 77 left; 110.
Shona Wood: 14 (fashion designer Stephen King, paint finishes by Jonathan Bartlett); 17 above (Robert & Colleen Berry); 17 below (Holland/Hyatt); 21 (Penelope Beech); 24 (Anthony Paine); 25 (Penelope Beech); 27 (Michael Snyder, carpentry by Christopher Penfold); 34 (Penelope Beech); 38 (Holland/Hyatt); 39 (Robert & Colleen Berry); 204-5.